THE
AGENTS
DIRECTORY

THE ESSENTIAL WRITER'S REFERENCE

THE
AGENTS
DIRECTORY

emmis

books

EVERYTHING YOU NEED TO KNOW
TO SELL YOUR BOOK OR SCRIPT

Rachel Vater

For further information, contact the publisher, Emmis Books, at: 1700 Madison Road, Cincinnati, Ohio 45206.

COVER DESIGN: Steve Sullivan

ISBN 1578601444

Library of Congress Control Number: 2004106425

CONTENTS

WELCOME LETTER

When I speak at writer's conferences, the question I hear most often is, "How do I get a good agent?"

Most writers who are ready to sell their work understand that an agent is an essential asset. An agent's job is to send out your work, advise you on offers, negotiate the contract for you, and give you career advice and editing tips. Many writers find out the hard way that without an agent, they can't even get their writing in the door of the major publishing houses. If they do manage to get their work into an editor's office, it often goes into a pile of other manuscripts where it sits for months until the editor or editor's assistant gets a chance to glance at it and send a form rejection letter in reply.

However, when an agent submits your work, it gets a warmer welcome. Editors give it much higher consideration and a faster response with more feedback. And when editors do offer a contract, an agent can usually get a better price for your work and can protect your interests. An agent will keep track of your royalty payments and make sure you get paid in a timely manner.

While the benefits of having an agent may be obvious to you, if you're like most writers, actually submitting your work to agents is daunting. Where do you begin? How do you avoid scams? How do you present your work professionally? Who do you have to know to get your manuscript taken seriously?

This book was designed to take the fear out of finding an agent. Remember, agents need new clients with books to sell or they go out of business. Nearly every literary agent in this directory is actively looking for new clients—writers like you! But the work must be submitted professionally to an agent who is interested in handling the type of work you've written.

As a former editor at Writer's Digest Books and now the Rights Director and Assistant Agent at the Donald Maass Literary Agency in New York, I'll tell you exactly how to approach an agent by mail, at a writer's conference, or by networking. Examples of query letters and straightforward checklists on how to format your work will help you make a great impression on an agent without any gimmicks.

Also included in this directory is a list of fifty-five conferences across the country and tips on how to pitch your work to the agents who will be there. There's also a great resource list of writer's organizations to help you network with other writers in your field who can give you feedback and support your commitment to writing.

There's no better way to begin your quest for an agent!

ALL ABOUT AGENTS

WANTED: AN AGENT

So you know you want an agent, but let's first talk about
what an agent actually does. A literary agent is a publishing
industry professional who represents a writer to editors.
A dramatic agent represents scriptwriters to producers.
In fact, editors at most of the larger publishing houses
and the big producers won't accept unagented work.

So why are the biggest places closed to submissions
directly from writers? Well, now that everyone and their
cat has access to a computer, there are thousands upon
thousands of manuscripts making the rounds. As you can
well imagine, most of these manuscripts are not ready for
publication or production. Since agents are very selective
about the work they represent, anyone they submit it to
can expect better quality writing than 99% of the other
manuscripts coming into the office on a daily basis.

Not only is it personally validating to find an agent
who's willing to represent you, it's also a professional
asset. Agents often suggest ways you can enhance your
work or tailor your proposal for a specific publisher
before they begin to submit it. That extra edge can be
just enough to get your work accepted rather than sent
back to you with a rejection letter.

Once you get an offer for a contract, an agent will
help you evaluate it, negotiate the deal, and get paid
fairly for each of your rights. Because an agent only
makes a 15% commission, he'll work to get the highest
advance and royalty payment for your work, so having
an agent usually pays for itself. An agent will also keep
as many rights for you as possible and then sell them for
you to the best or highest bidder. Some of these rights
include film rights, foreign rights, and subsidiary rights.

There are times when you may not want an agent for
your work. If you're looking for a place to publish your

poem, short story, or other short piece, you're better off marketing these projects yourself. Your pay is likely to be too low for an agent to consider handling, since he would only make a tiny commission for handling something this small. Likewise, if your work targets a specific, small audience, you should consider marketing it yourself to small presses or university publishers. (For instance, a book addressing an academic niche or an obscure hobby won't require, and probably won't interest, an agent.)

Now that we know all the responsibilities of an agent, let's take a closer look. What's the difference between a good agent and a bad one?

PROFILE OF A GOOD AGENT

A GOOD AGENT WILL NEVER ASK YOU FOR MONEY IN ORDER TO REPRESENT YOU. A legitimate agent will charge you only a 15% commission for domestic sales and a 20% commission on foreign sales, which usually is split with the co-agent who specializes in this type of sale. Any reimbursements for photocopying, long-distance phone calls, and postage expenses made on your behalf should be discussed with you before you agree to an agent's representation. These expenses should not exceed an amount you feel comfortable with, and they should be itemized. Some agents charge for these expenses only if they sell your work. Others do not charge at all.

A GOOD AGENT IS SELECTIVE. He knows how to spot good work. Literary agents are drawn to their profession because they love books. Dramatic agents love movies. Because of this feeling, they know how to recognize work that's ready for publication or production. Many agents were editors or other insider industry professionals before they became agents. They're selective about who they take on as a client. They have to love the work and believe they can sell it.

A GOOD AGENT HAS CONNECTIONS. Agents are people who do lunch, attend conferences, and do a fair share of schmoozing. They're network kings and queens. Literary agents know which editors are looking for murder mysteries and which are hoping for nonfiction books about cats. Dramatic agents know which producers are looking for romantic comedies and which are looking for suspense thrillers. They keep up regularly with who's looking for what, playing the matchmaker between the writer and the buyer.

Well-connected literary agents often live in New York, but if they don't, they travel there frequently to meet with editors face-to-face. Literary agents who agree to a code of ethics and make enough sales in a year are eligible to join the Association of Author's Representatives (AAR); a list of members can be found at www.aar-online.org. Not all eligible agents choose to join. Dramatic agents most often live in California, and similarly, many dramatic agents choose to join the Writer's Guild of America (WGA). A list of members can be found at www.wga.org.

A GOOD AGENT HAS A STRONG SALES RECORD. Legitimate agents make a lot of sales every year. How many? Well, literary agents should have at least eight. Every sale should be to a reputable publisher that offers a paying contract. Dramatic agents spend a lot of time helping their clients with development and packaging and may make only a few sales.

A GOOD AGENT RETURNS PHONE CALLS. An agent should always be willing to answer your questions or give you updates on submissions or offers. Discuss with him or her how often you should check in and what type of feedback you can expect in return.

A GOOD AGENT IS EXCITED ABOUT YOU AND YOUR WORK. It isn't every day that an agent finds a new client, and he should certainly be willing to discuss your work and remember your book's subject and characters.

PROFILE OF A SCAM ARTIST

A BAD AGENT CHARGES FEES TO STAY IN BUSINESS. Whether he calls it a reading fee, critique fee, editing or proofreading fee, or a marketing fee, a bad agent tries to make money from his clients rather than his commission from sales. You should always be suspicious of an agent who offers to edit your manuscript himself or refers you to specific, fee-charging editors or book doctors. If your work is rejected, you should revise it on your own or with the help of someone you trust who doesn't have any affiliation with an agent. It's a conflict of interest for agents to charge for editing and also represent a writer.

A BAD AGENT ACCEPTS TOO MANY CLIENTS. Because a bad agent is trying to make his money from his clients rather than from his sales, he'll try to take on as many clients as possible. Often he'll send a form letter to offer representation rather than contact you by phone. You may even notice typos in the letter and generic praise for your work, such as, "I loved the wonderful characters, beautiful setting, and exciting plot." Don't be fooled.

A BAD AGENT DOESN'T KNOW ANYONE IN THE BUSINESS. I know of one particularly bad agent in Illinois who operates more like an expensive mailing service. She makes ten photocopies of a manuscript, stuffs them into envelopes, addresses them to big publishers, and writes ATTENTION: EDITOR on them rather than any real editor's name. She doesn't know anyone who works at the publishing house, and so her work goes into the slush pile with all the other unsolicited manuscripts that come in directly from authors. I asked an editor about her, and he said anything he got from her he sent back without even opening the envelope. She's notorious for submitting sloppy work and clearly has no idea how to negotiate a contract. Editors would rather work directly with an author than with a bad agent.

A BAD AGENT MAKES FEW OR NO SALES OR SELLS TO VANITY PRESSES. Because a bad agent quickly gets a bad reputation, he will find it very difficult to make any sales. It's a small world in publishing, and editors won't respect a submission just because it comes from someone who calls himself an agent. Reputation is everything, and poor agents will make few or no sales. Often these agents will start submitting work to vanity presses, publishers that charge the writer money rather than pay an advance. If you find an agent online, make sure you confirm that he or she has made sales to reputable publishers before you submit your work to him or her.

A BAD AGENT WILL IGNORE YOUR CALLS AND E-MAILS. A bad agent has signed on so many clients that he has a hard time keeping up with who's who. When you do get in touch with a bad agent, he's often rude and evasive. He'll often say he doesn't want to disclose information about his other clients and sales to protect their privacy. He'll also say he's been submitting your work to major publishers. He'll say he talked to an editor the other day who was very interested in the concept of your book, but he will refuse to disclose the editor's name or the name of the publishing house.

A BAD AGENT WILL BE INDIFFERENT TO YOUR WORK. If you ask him a question about your book or script, he'll have to scramble to find out who you are and what your plot is about. Sometimes you'll get some generic praise, but don't allow your excitement at getting an offer from an "agent" cloud your intuition. Remember, a bad agent is worse than no agent at all.

With so many scam artists out there, how can you look for an agent with confidence? Start with the agents in this directory—all of the agents have been pre-screened. However, if you find an agent who meets any of the above criteria for a bad agent, please report him or her to Emmis Books immediately. If you're unsure about an agent who has offered you representation, please feel free to contact me at rvater@maassagency.com; I will be happy to address your concerns.

AGENCIES: DOES SIZE MATTER?

Some of the biggest agencies out there have a reputation for being powerful, but are they necessarily the best places to submit your manuscript? The top five agencies in the business not only represent writers for books, television, motion pictures, and theater, but they also represent actors. These may seem like attractive places to submit your work, but in reality, unless you're already an established author or screenwriter, your chances of getting an agent at one of these agencies are slim to none. If you do land representation from an agency this size, you may find yourself lost in the shuffle or put on the back burner in favor of the more well-known clients the agent represents. Also, the agent may be willing to represent one project for you, but if it doesn't quickly generate much interest, he can become disinterested and begin to focus on other clients.

However, many agents get their start at big agencies, and then leave to form their own agencies. For instance, the William Morris Agency has a renowned training program for agents, starting recruits in the mailroom, and slowly moving them up through the ranks as they learn the business.

Boutique agencies usually offer clients more one-on-one attention and are often more open to taking on new clients than are the bigger agencies. A boutique agency may have three or four agents who work together closely.

Stephanie Lee, from Manus & Associates, says, "Though a client will work with one agent in particular, we are all very team-oriented and collaborative, so each client essentially receives the benefit of all our knowledge put together."

Some agencies are even smaller, with only one or two agents. The Richard Henshaw Group is comprised of agent Richard Henshaw and associate agent Susannah Taylor. They feel their size is a benefit to clients. "We are a deliberately small agency. We enjoy working closely with our clients to build their careers."

Whether you end up working with a small agency or a large one, you should feel that your agent is approachable and willing to work with you for the life of your career, not just on your current project.

WHERE DO AGENTS COME FROM?

You'll notice in the listings that agents come from a remarkable range of backgrounds. Many of them have had extensive prior experience in the publishing industry before making the leap to a career as an agent. Others worked with a larger agency until they had a client list and enough experience to strike out on their own.

Probably the most common background for agents is an editing background. They've worked at publishing companies and are familiar with the business. A lot of agents have claimed they couldn't give writers the one-on-one support as editors that they can now provide as agents. These agents tend to put more emphasis on helping authors polish their manuscripts before they even begin sending the work out to publishers. Stephanie Lee says of her colleagues at Manus & Associates, "We are all extremely editorial agents with writing backgrounds. These days, agents have to be good editors!"

Not all agents started out working in the publishing industry. Agent Jodie Rhodes worked in the advertising business, and she's also a published novelist. She explains how her marketing and writing background helped her start as an agent and why it continues to help her clients get published.

"The two greatest assets I have to offer writers are my marketing and editing abilities," she says. "When I started my agency, I lived 3,000 miles from the center of the publishing world, I didn't know a single editor, and I didn't have a single writer! I got my name out there by writing columns for local and regional writers' magazines, interviewing New York editors for these columns. That began bringing me some talented writers and put me on a first-name basis with all kinds of editors who remembered me when I started sending them manuscripts."

Rhodes says that being a published novelist gives her empathy with her clients, but her writing skills are even more useful to them when she markets their work. "I know how to write appealing marketing letters," she says. "I know how to zero in on the essence of a writer's book and present it to editors." This approach gets her clients instant attention, but Rhodes cautions, "The marketing only opens the door for writers. The editing I did for my writers, endless, exhausting hours all done for free, that's what turned them into published authors. So you could say that my marketing abilities connected me to editors, and that was vital, but my editing created salable books. It took both to make me successful."

Although most agents are willing to help their clients polish their work, writers have to already have a manuscript that's close to publishable before an agent will agree to represent them. Rhodes agrees. "Although I

?Where else can you find an agent?

- The Acknowledgments page in the front of your favorite book. Published authors will often thank their agents in the front pages of their books. Once you find the name of the agent, you can search online for his or her contact information.
- The Web site of the Association of Author's Representatives (AAR), which can be found at www.aar-online.org. None of these literary agents charges fees, but many of them have full client lists and are not currently accepting submissions. Also, the list doesn't specify what type of work the agents handle.
- The Web site of the Writer's Guild of America (WGA), which can be found at www.wga.org. Some of these agents may charge fees. Many of them have full client lists and will not respond to query letters.
- The Literary Marketplace (LMP). An expensive directory that lists more agents than any other guide. However, it doesn't specify what type of work the agent handles and includes some agents who charge fees.
- Other book directories. Be aware that many other directories include agents who charge fees.
- Advertisements in writer's magazines. I strongly advise writers against responding to any ads for agents in magazines, since all of them charge fees (even the ones that say they don't) and most have never made any sales (even the ones that claim sales to major publishers). I have never seen a legitimate agent advertise.
- Preditors & Editors, an online list of agents found at www.anotherealm.com/ prededitors. This directory simply alphabetizes agents and agencies by their first name and has warnings about some agents with bad reputations.

still give editing direction, I no longer do that intensive cover-to-cover editing I once undertook as a new agent."

As you look through the listings, you'll notice other occupations agents have held, including lawyers, speakers, authors, teachers, and promoters. Regardless of an agent's background, he or she should be enthusiastic about your work and have the connections to sell it. If you're lucky enough to get offers from more than one agent at a time, relax and trust your intuition.

While some agents take a lighter or heavier approach to editing their clients' work, in the end, all agents submit work to the same top publishing houses and will negotiate your contract to protect you in similar ways.

ENTHUSIASM IS KEY

Once you've found a legitimate agent with a good reputation, the size of the agency and the background of the agent matter far less than the passion the agent has for your writing and for representing you. Agent Jodie Rhodes explains how her enthusiasm for the work she represents fuels her to help an author revise.

"The most exciting story is that of author Kavita Daswani," she says. "Last year around this time she sent me ninety-nine single-spaced pages in which she destroyed her character on page sixteen." To make matters worse, it was a first-person narrative, but it jumped around among many points of view. "An absolute no-no," Rhodes explains. "But despite these negatives, there was a wonderful voice here and my instinct said this was a potential winner. She was a brand new writer and this was her first book."

But Rhodes received another shock after she offered representation to Daswani. "I found to my horror that the ninety-nine pages were all she'd written. She begged me to market them, but I firmly told her I couldn't until she finished the book." Not only did Daswani have to finish the book, she had to rewrite the first pages following Rhodes' editing. But Daswani wasn't deterred, and she revised as Rhodes had instructed.

Rhodes agreed to market the book if Daswani could finish it by the time editors had read the opening pages. "That's usually six weeks," Rhodes explains. "But Lord help us, editors jumped on those opening pages like they were the second coming and asked for the complete manuscript immediately. Somehow, Daswani managed to write the entire rest of the book in two weeks … except she clearly ran out of steam because the ending was a mess."

Because Daswani is an Indian author, Rhodes's instincts told her it would have strong international appeal and she simultaneously marketed it in New York and London. "But not only did it have a terrible ending," Rhodes says, "I didn't know whether to market it as a memoir or a novel. So I hedged my bets, explaining upfront we knew the ending needed to be rewritten and that they had their choice of publishing it as either a memoir or a novel."

Rhodes's dedication to the book paid off quickly. "A feeding frenzy exploded world wide with this book," Rhodes says. "For two weeks I was bombarded with 300 e-mails a day, 200 phone calls starting at five a.m. because of the time difference in Europe. Last September I held simultaneous auctions in London and New York with Putnam paying $250,000 for North American rights and HarperCollins paying $230,000 for UK/Commonwealth rights. It's also been sold to eight other countries."

Kavita Daswani's book, *For Matrimonial Purposes,* was published in June 2003 with great reviews, and Rhodes reports that Daswani is well into her second book.

Rhodes's passion for the work she represents is also necessary to keep her submitting a work rather than giving up after a host of rejections. "I received an incredibly brilliant historical novel called *The Dwarf in Louis XIV's Court.* I totally fell in love with it and found it the most exciting book I'd ever received. Sheer genius by Paul Weidner, a critically acclaimed stage director. It was his first book as well."

Despite her enthusiasm for the book, Rhodes found to her surprise that she couldn't sell it. "I could get editors interested because I write very compelling marketing pitches," she says. "Almost all of them admitted the writing was superior, but no offers."

After a year of effort and a staggering eighty-seven rejections, Rhodes finally made her sale to the University of Wisconsin Press and to a publishing company in Israel. Even now, she remains a determined advocate for the book. "We're now trying to sell world rights to other countries and currently have interest in Germany and Poland," she says.

It may seem like a crusade that even an author would have given up on, but Rhodes's tireless support sprang from her connection to the work. "It was a book that I felt was so good it deserved to be published," Rhodes explains. "I refused to give up."

GENRE: CAN YOU HANDLE IT?

No matter how engaging your work is or how well written, there are some agents out there who will not want to represent it. No, I'm not talking about agents who have a full client list. I'm talking about agents who simply don't handle your type of writing.

I've heard agents explain how exasperating it is to receive inappropriate submissions; it's a waste of their time and the writer's postage and efforts. Sometimes it's simply preference. An agent often represents the type of work he enjoys reading. By avidly reading books in that genre, he knows what's out there, what's already been written, and what's fresh.

Other times agents won't represent something because it conflicts with their morals. One agent explained that she's a vegetarian, so a cookbook with the best meat dishes in the world won't compel her to offer representation. Another agent passed up a book on how to successfully cheat on your spouse. She knew the book would have been a commercial success, but she didn't want to propagate the message it was sending.

There are some agents who handle only nonfiction books and others who represent only novels, so check each listing carefully to make sure you're submitting your work to agents who handle your particular type of writing.

There are a few even more specialized agents who have learned one market very, very well, and that's all they represent, whether it's children's literature, science fiction, cookbooks, or medical books. Therefore, it's crucial that you do your research before you begin submitting.

APPROACHING AGENTS

Now that you've evaluated what an agent can offer and which agents handle your type of work, how do you get an agent's attention? You've probably read that agents are most eager to consider writers who come to them by way of referral. Of course, most writers don't live next door to a famous author or have a best friend who's an editor to refer them. What other options are there?

CONFERENCES

There are many writer's conferences held across the country each year. Some of them are small workshops with few or no industry professionals available to meet with you one-on-one, but they can be useful for meeting other writers and creating a support group who will read your work and give you feedback. Other conferences have agents and editors who speak and are available for short, individual meetings with attendees. These meetings give writers a chance to pitch the idea of their book or script and ask the agent, editor, or producer for feedback.

All the conferences listed in this directory have agents in attendance. If you find a conference you're interested in attending, check the conference's Web site or send them an SASE for a brochure to find out more information about specific speakers and workshops. Remember to register for conferences early to get the best rates. Some conferences have a limited number of attendees, so the sooner you register, the better. Check the conference section in this directory to find upcoming events in your area or to plan your next vacation around a specific conference.

WRITER'S ORGANIZATIONS

What about those agents who accept manuscripts by referral only? Even if you don't know anyone in the publishing business yet, there are ways other than conferences for networking with authors, agents, and editors.

Especially useful for new writers are writer's organizations, such as the Romance Writers of America. These groups offer support to new writers and usually have an abundance of useful information for writers on their Web sites. For writers who don't have any connections yet, this is a great way to meet other writers in your community or online. The value of finding readers for your work and getting the opportunity to read the work of other aspiring writers can't be overstated.

The feedback you receive can help you polish your work to professional levels, and reading another writer's manuscripts can be just as eye-opening. You'll begin to see what not to do from the mistakes they make, and you'll learn from their strengths as well. Some groups offer insurance for their members at a discounted price, which can be useful for freelancers who don't have insurance available through a nine-to-five job.

These organizations usually have published authors who are members, and you may have a chance to meet them at a local event such as a book signing or a workshop. Many writers are delighted to talk about how they found their agent, and if you become friends, it isn't out of line to ask them for a referral.

If your organization has local monthly meetings, you may get to know a whole community of supportive non-published writers who are at your level. I've heard of groups like this making a pact with each other that the first one to get an agent or get published will offer referrals to the rest of the group.

Joining an organization can also look impressive on your list of credentials. For instance, if you contact an agent regarding your romance novel, you can mention that you're a member of the Romance Writers of America. You'll get bonus points from the agent for taking the extra step of getting involved in a writer's organization, especially if you win one of their contests or have an endorsement from a published writer who is also a member. A list of writer's organizations and their contact information can be found in a later section of this book.

THE QUERY LETTER

The most common method to contact an agent is, of course, the query letter. All of the agents in this directory accept query letter submissions, whether by mail or e-mail. There are a few who require a referral, but most agents are willing to consider work by new writers if the query letter is compelling.

COMPOSING THE QUERY LETTER

A query letter is, quite simply, a one-page letter that introduces your book and yourself to the agent.

It's amazing how nervous writers get over a one-page letter, but then again, it's an agent's first—and sometimes only—impression of you and your writing. Some writers resort to what they hope are attention-grabbing gimmicks, but such approaches usually backfire. Others try to play on an agent's sympathies with self-deprecating tactics. Strangely, some writers even try bribery with Godiva chocolates or imported coffee. Even more tragically, there are writers who are so nervous about query letters that they fail to submit their work at all.

But it doesn't have to be such a painful process! In fact, there's a very easy and professional format for query letters that you can use to present your work clearly and list your credentials concisely. It can all be done in three paragraphs that I like to think of as the hook, line, and sinker.

THE HOOK

Your first paragraph is the one you'll use to summarize your book. At this point you might be thinking, "How in the world am I supposed to squish my whole book down to one paragraph? Is that even possible?"

Fortunately, that isn't necessary. Just do it the *TV*

Guide way: They tell you just enough information to make you want to watch the movie. A woman is framed for a murder committed by her husband. Or: A daughter realizes her parents kidnapped her from her biological mother.

Of course, these are just one-sentence descriptions, but there's a lot contained in those little sentences! So how do you decide what information to include in your summary? One of my favorite methods is the one I learned in journalism school. The questions to ask are: Who? What? When? Where? and Why?

For fiction, this means character, situation, setting, and era when it takes place. It also includes the motivation or goals of the characters, how they got into their current situation, and the obstacle that will make it difficult for them to better that situation.

For nonfiction, this includes who your audience is, what benefit your book will give readers, under what circumstances they'll need this information, and why.

Let's take a look at some examples of novel summaries.

> Talia Landers, a soft-spoken secretary at a law firm in downtown Chicago, has just lost her job, the lease on her apartment, and her dog. Figuring she's got nothing more to lose, Talia decides it's time to take some risks. First, she's going to get even with the man she hates most in the world, Alan Smothers, her evil, sexually harassing former boss. Next, she's going to confess her crush on her handsome next-door neighbor Jeffrey Matthews—as soon as she can get her mouth to move in his presence. Finally, she's going to take a career risk that's such an outrageous stunt it will either make her famous—or kill her in the process. Not a bad to-do list for a twenty-eight-year-old . . .

After reading this paragraph, we have a sense of the protagonist and a couple of the other characters in the story. We know this is a modern-day story that takes place in Chicago. We see that all the losses in Talia's life are motivating her to suddenly set some big goals, but we also see the element of risk involved that makes us worry about her. We can also tell this is a contemporary romance novel with a comic feel to it.

SYNOPSIS CHECKLIST

☐ Keep your synopsis short. Three to five pages is the recommended length. Some agents want nothing longer than one page.

☐ Introduce all major characters, typing names in all caps the first time you mention each one.

☐ Write your synopsis in narrative, like a mini-novel. Do not break the narrative to insert any commentary, such as, "This scene flashes back and forth between John and Joan."

☐ Include the ending to the story. Don't leave the agent hanging and expect him to request your book so he can find out how it ends.

☐ Get rid of all vague phrases, such as "at some point" or "one night." Be specific with "the next morning" or "the night after his diagnosis," or else delete the phrase entirely.

☐ Delete all unnecessary adjectives and qualifiers, such as "horrible guilt" or "painful empathy."

☐ Keep things in active voice, not passive. All sentences should be written in present tense, even if your novel is written in past tense.

☐ Remember to give the character's motivation for his behavior, not just his actions.

☐ Don't shy away from using contractions like "can't" rather than "cannot." Forget what your English teacher said in high school. The tone of your synopsis should be conversational.

☐ Run a spell check and then have one of your friends read it carefully to catch any mistakes that you or your computer may have missed.

Here's another sample:

Steven Hartz, a postal worker in Miami, has a peculiar talent. He's very good at sketching, but he isn't an artist. In fact, all of the sketches have been drawn in his sleep. More disturbing, all of the sketches are coming true. First, there was the portrait of Maria Seever—two days before he actually met her. And then, more sinister, came the sketches of the crimes, all two days before they occurred. The places in the sketches are his familiar haunts, and Hartz begins to wonder if he's involved in the crimes somehow. Fearful of turning to the police, Hartz determines to solve the mystery himself—with the help of Maria, the psychic from his first sketch, who knows far more about what's going on than she's telling.

Again, we know the protagonist, where he lives, and his main problem—he's involved in a crime and can't go to the police. We know it's a dark novel, a horror or thriller, and that it has some supernatural elements. We also have a hint of some of the plot twists, but some of the strings are left dangling, hooking the reader and making him want to see more.

Notice in these samples how two completely different books both unfold in a unique direction but use the same formula. We have a taste for both books now, and even though they're nothing alike, both show promise.

Also notice that neither description tells the whole story. Each gives the reader, a prospective agent, just enough to spark interest and to request the entire book.

For nonfiction, the method is similar. You'll need to explain what the book is about, who will want to read it, and why the topic is important. For example:

Eighty-five percent of Americans own a diamond or other precious gemstone, but the background of these beautiful pieces of jewelry can be ugly. *The History of Gemstones* will expose the story behind the ornaments, where the supply comes from, who really controls the market, the role of advertisers, and how consumers can put a stop to the unethical gem trade that preys on the poor while funding countries that sponsor terrorism.

Notice that in addition to introducing topics the book will cover, we are given an audience (diamond and gemstone owners) and a reason this book will benefit the reader (offering ways consumers can make a difference).

For a how-to book, you'll use a similar approach:

Your child should be in showbiz! Or maybe you'd like to make some extra money doing commercials, acting in local films, or modeling clothes for department stores. You probably don't think you have the right look or the right connections, and besides, aren't there a lot of scam artists out there? *The Talent Agent Directory* has the answers to your questions. With listings of more than 1,000 legitimate agencies across the United States and Canada, as well as helpful articles to steer you in the right direction, you'll learn everything you need to know about getting started in a coveted modeling, performing, or acting profession.

Again, we see that the audience is adults curious about getting themselves or their children into acting or modeling. We see how the book will benefit readers by offering them advice and steering them in the direction of legitimate talent agencies.

Remember, you don't have to include every character, plot twist, or benefit—just enough to inspire the agent to request your whole manuscript or proposal.

THE LINE

Here's where you give a short introduction of yourself, your line of work (if relevant), and your qualifications. Even if you've never published a book before, dig up some useful facts to support your interest or knowledge in the subject you're writing about. Many new writers worry that they don't have any impressive publishing credentials, but there are other ways to establish credibility.

For the above examples, the query writers could all present different qualifications:

> I'm a member of Romance Writers of America, and I've had my novel critiqued and edited by several writers.

It's easy to join a writer's association such as this one, but it shows the agent that you take your writing career seriously.

> I've been researching psychics who aid police in capturing criminals, and I've extensively interviewed one who works with my local police department to verify some of the facts used in my book.

You'd be surprised how few people take the time to do any research. With the internet, it's easier than ever to find someone who's an expert in the area you're writing about. Most people love to talk about their jobs to someone who's genuinely interested, and if they find out you're a writer, they'll likely be even more flattered and pleased to give you information about what they do for a living or as a hobby.

> As a gemologist, I've been collecting stories on "blood diamonds" and other atrocities related to the gemstone market, and I've carefully researched every fact in this book. In addition, I've interviewed some of the key people who developed a way to microscopically "brand" a gemstone to let consumers know where the gem was mined.

If your job gives you the credentials to write on a topic as an expert, it's essential to emphasize that expertise in your query letter.

> I've been an actress and a model myself, and I've seen first-hand the pitfalls that make people shy away from this fun, lucrative industry. With this book, I've outlined how new-comers to the business can avoid scams, find inexpensive photographers, and build a resume. I've also explained the industry unions, what they offer, and how to join. There are also interviews with successful models, actors, and agents. While there are a few guidebooks on this topic, none includes such detailed listings or how-to articles.

Not only the strength of your own experience, but also the ability to get quotes from other experts, can help sell your book idea to an agent. Another impressive touch is showing that you've researched the other books out there on the shelves and know how your book is different and better.

For nonfiction, it's imperative to show that you're an expert on the topic and have the ability to promote the book once it's published. If you have professional speaking experience on your topic, a Web site that gets a lot of traffic, or a regular column in a newspaper, mention these assets in your query letter. If you don't have this experience, find ways to establish yourself as an authority on the subject.

This process isn't as difficult as it sounds. My father worked with a man in the construction business who volunteered his time whenever disaster struck. Whenever there's a flood, fire, or bomb that requires volunteer hands, he asks off work and goes there immediately, right into the thick of things. He's been featured on national television as a "disaster expert." And he is. He's just a regular guy, a construction worker. But if he can establish credibility by being in the right place at the right time to meet the right people, then so can you.

SAMPLE LETTER

Date

Mr. John Jones
1234 Storybook St.
New York, NY 10025

Dear Mr. Jones: ── For the greeting, always use Mr., Ms., or Dr.

When the protagonist faces this unique, startling conflict, he decides to aim for this goal. Unfortunately, there are specific obstacles in his way. His accomplice helps him overcome them and becomes a love interest, while his antagonist does terrible things to thwart him. ── This is your paragraph to hook the agent and make him want to read more about your book.

In my occupation, I often deal with similar conditions that the protagonist faces. My articles on the subject have appeared in several magazines, including *Magazine Title* and *Another Magazine*. I've also published short stories and interviews. To research my book, I interviewed an expert at what my protagonist does for a living that gets him into the conflict. ── Give your writing credentials here, your line about why you have the ability to write this stellar book.

I noticed that you represented *Book Title* by Author's Name, a book I enjoyed so much I stayed up all night to finish it. The tone of my book is similar in such-and-such a way. If my book interests you, I'd be delighted to send you the full manuscript. You can reach me at (123) 555-4567 or by e-mail at Jill.Writer@aol.com, or you may use the SASE. Thank you for your time. ── Sink the deal with a polite thank you to the agent and the reason you chose to solicit him. Give relevant contact information.

Sincerely,

[Handwritten Signature]

Typed Name

THE SINKER

Finally, you're ready for the closing paragraph. This is where you show you're a gracious person who appreciates the agent taking time out of a busy schedule to read your query letter. Remember, a little flattery never hurts, and if you've done your research on this agent, a few kind words will be easy to sprinkle into the mix. If you've met the agent at a conference or read one of the books he represented, be sure to mention that as well.

For example:

> Thank you for taking the time to consider my book, *Masterful Minds*. I noticed that you represented Jean Rittenberg for her marvelous book *Seer Sights*. Rittenberg is one of my favorite authors—you can tell she researches every detail, but she's amazing at flowing those details seamlessly into the narrative. I think you'll find our styles similar in that way, and I'd be delighted to send you a copy of my entire manuscript for your consideration.

Notice that you aren't comparing your work to John Grisham or Danielle Steele here. Agents have many more authors on their client lists than the best sellers, and they'll be pleased and flattered that you've taken the time to sample other books they've represented—and that you're familiar with the type of work they handle. Taking the time to personalize the letter will also prove to the agent you aren't mass mailing a generic query letter to every agent. It proves to the agent that he has been thoughtfully chosen rather than randomly selected.

Even though you absolutely should include a self-addressed stamped envelope (SASE), make sure you also include your contact information so you can be reached easily just in case your letter gets separated from the envelope by whoever opens the mail.

Sign off respectfully with your typed name and a hand-written signature.

Now that you have a query map, try fitting your own story or book idea into this query letter format. Even without any gimmicks, the originality of your own writing and your unique personality will shine through to the agent. And then you've got 'em: Hook, line, and sinker.

SUBMITTING THE QUERY

Now that you've written your query letter, it's time to submit. First, make sure that you follow the agency's guidelines. Some agents may want to see your first five pages. Some may want to see a synopsis, which we'll discuss later.

QUERY QUIRKS: What not do

- Do not praise your novel with words like "page-turning," "gripping," "heart-wrenching," or "astounding." Don't tell an agent that your family members loved it, that your English teacher gave you an A on it, or that your writing group voted it the "best in class." Let the agents read your work and decide for themselves.
- Do not disparage yourself or your work. There's no need to confess that you're a first-time novelist. The majority of query letters are from first-time novelists. Likewise, there's no need to tell the agent how many rejections you've had.
- Do not send out query letters until your novel is finished. I mean it. No exceptions. For nonfiction, you may submit a proposal without having finished your book, but for a novel, you're wasting your time and the agent's if it's not complete when you query.
- Never say that your work has been "professionally edited." There are a lot of scams out there offering editorial services to first-time writers, and this is no guarantee that the finished work is ready for publication. This will not impress an agent.
- Do not compare yourself to famous authors, saying you're the next Tom Clancy or Anne Rice.
- Do not use colored paper or stationery or unusual fonts.
- Never ever send money to an agent for a reading fee, marketing fee, critique fee, or whatever else he or she may call it. This is the equivalent of pouring your money down the sewer drain.

Because it often takes an agent weeks or months to reply, I recommend sending queries out in batches, but no more than eight to ten. If you get several requests for your manuscript, make sure that the agents accept simultaneous submissions. If they request an exclusive look at your manuscript, you'll have to decide whether to grant that request. If you decide not to grant this request, you should state in your cover letter that a few select agents are simultaneously considering your work. Sometimes this will actually make agents get back to you more quickly.

QUERY BASICS CHECKLIST

- ☐ Create your own letterhead on your computer to give your query letter a professional look. Include your name, address, phone number, e-mail, and fax number, if relevant.

- ☐ Always include a self-addressed stamped envelope (SASE) with your query.

- ☐ Keep your query to one page; three short paragraphs, if possible. It should consist of a greeting, an introductory paragraph to highlight the main idea of the book, a second paragraph to explain why you're qualified to write it, and a third paragraph to thank the agent for his time and give your contact information. Close with "Sincerely" or another polite closing and your name.

- ☐ Watch your spelling and grammar.

- ☐ Be sure to follow an agency's submission guidelines.

- ☐ Remember that praise never hurts. You'll often find that an author thanks his agent on the Acknowledgments page of his novel. Keep a record of agents who represented books you enjoyed and their track record. Then when you query, mention to the agent that you liked other books she represented and why else you might want that agent above any other. An agent, like a writer, enjoys feeling singled out and special.

- ☐ Send out a batch of queries. Construct a wish list of agents you'd especially like to represent you, and then send out about ten query letters at a time. Be sure to personalize each letter in some way.

If you don't hear from an agency where you've submitted a query letter, do not call the agent. Simply scratch that agency off your list and keep submitting.

If you don't hear promptly from an agency that requested your manuscript, wait the amount of time the agent has requested, and then follow up with an e-mail. It may take some agencies longer to get back to you due to the amount of submissions they receive. Patience is difficult when you know your work is out there somewhere, but resist the urge to follow up too quickly or trouble the agent with phone calls. You want agents to know you're an easy author to work with, and that means you're a professional who doesn't fall to pieces under pressure.

Sometimes you will be asked to submit part of your manuscript. Make sure you follow the instructions and submit only what the agent requests. If she asks for three chapters, send only the first three chapters. Agents are not only looking for authors who can write well, they're also looking for clients who are professional, courteous, and willing to follow directions.

SYNOPSES & PROPOSALS

Sometimes agents will ask to see a synopsis or proposal with your query letter. A synopsis is a summary of your novel or script, usually between three and five double-spaced pages. A proposal is for nonfiction books, and it is also a concise summary of what agents can expect your book to cover.

WRITING THE SYNOPSIS

A synopsis is a condensed narrative version of your novel. It should be written in present tense, and the story should unfold as it does in your book. A well-written synopsis proves to an agent that you know how to structure a satisfying plot, so be sure to include all the major plot points as well as the ending. Although you may feel this is a terribly "dry" version of your book, the synopsis will tell the agent some important things:

1. You know how to structure your book effectively and tie up all the loose ends. The best books have many conflicts and unexpected twists and turns. Your synopsis will prove you've included some.

2. You have an original idea rather than a plot that's already been written a thousand times. Some themes have glutted the market and gone out of style, such as repressed childhood memories of abuse. An agent will know immediately that the story isn't marketable if its subject, plot, or devices have been exhausted.

3. You've written a book in a genre that the agent represents. If you've called it a mystery, but it's clearly a supernatural thriller, the agent will realize your error in minutes by reading your synopsis. She may not want to waste time reading a huge portion of the manuscript only to find it fits a genre she doesn't represent.

4. You have strong, proactive characters and the agent can find them sympathetic, admirable, or interesting. I'm surprised by how many times I've read a synopsis where the protagonist gets into a muddle, and someone else rescues her in the end, rather than the protagonist saving the day herself by her own ingenuity.

5. You have a setting that is compelling and integral to the plot. New novelists often have "talking heads" in their novels, where too often their characters are just standing around talking rather than getting out there and doing something.

Make sure your contact information is in the upper left corner of the first page. In the upper right corner, type the novel's genre, the word count, and the word "Synopsis." Skip a couple of lines, and then center your title in all caps. Skip a few more lines, indent, and begin your story. The first time you mention a character, type the name in all caps. Even if your novel is written in first person, your synopsis should be written in third person.

Agents often depend on a synopsis to judge the marketability of your story, so it's essential to include all major characters and plot points. Be careful not to break the narrative with commentary. Keep the action of the plot moving forward and avoid phrases such as "in the final scene," or "then there's an exciting car chase."

Finally, at the end, type THE END in all caps and center it.

SAMPLE SYNOPSIS

Note that your synopsis should be double-spaced

Writer's name	Supernatural Mystery Thriller
Address	80,000 words
Phone number	Synopsis
E-mail	

ASTRAL GHOST

Most people can dismiss their nightmares as nonsense once they wake up, but if JENNA BRINKMAN dreams of a car accident, she'll hear about it on the news the next day!

One night Jenna witnesses a knife attack in her dreams, and she recognizes the victim as KEVIN RICHARDSON, a star basketball player. While his body lies in a coma at the hospital, Kevin realizes he can walk around like a ghost, and he finds that Jenna is the only one who can see him, but only while she's asleep.

Knowing she is his only chance for justice, Kevin heckles Jenna until she agrees to help him track down his attacker. He leads her to a threatening note made from cut-out newspaper letters that he receives the morning of his attack, and Jenna notices the rough edges of the paper.

Once Jenna works her way into Kevin's inner circle of friends, she begins to suspect one of them did it. But which one? MARK DAWSON, Kevin's best friend and teammate? Or maybe STAN WILLIAMS, Kevin's cousin and P.R. manager. She also learns that GREG SCHROEDER, Kevin's wise-cracking friend, is in love with Kevin's girlfriend SHERRY PARKER. Greg's wood-working knives make Jenna nervous. They look familiar. When Greg catches her studying them, he gives her one, and Jenna puts it into her jacket pocket.

Jenna accepts when Stan asks her out, but she realizes she may have feelings for Mark. Jenna notices a cut-up newspaper in the back seat of Stan's car on their way to dinner. She excuses herself to call Mark, and he picks her up. At Mark's house, she notices an old computer printer, the kind that has perforations that tear off and leave a rough edge, and she realizes Mark is the one. He sees she knows and explains he's hated Kevin for always getting the glory and the girls.

Mark knocks Jenna out with chloroform, ties her up, and drives her to the woods. But Kevin has been following them and he tells Jenna to buy some time—he has a plan. Jenna uses the knife Greg gave her to cut her ropes and she fights with Mark until the police arrive. The police tell her someone named Kevin called them.

At the hospital, Kevin is awake from the coma, and he thanks Jenna for bringing his would-be killer to justice. She tells him he owes her, and he gives her a kiss and a promise to make everything up to her. Jenna accepts.

THE END

WRITING THE PROPOSAL

For nonfiction, the book proposal is a marketing tool you'll use to sell the idea of your book. It is not necessary to have the book completed, but it's helpful to include some writing samples, articles, or sample chapters so the agent has an idea of your writing style and the tone of the project. The proposal consists of several parts:

THE OVERVIEW This is a summary of the idea of the book and the audience. You should explain why there is a need for a book like this one, and how your book will cover this topic in a better way than any other book out there. Include your credentials for writing the book and why you're an authority on the topic. If you plan to include photographs or illustrations in your book, you should mention that as well.

AUTHOR This is where experience and credentials are necessary. The author should also have a platform, a means of establishing himself as an authority on the topic and regularly reaching his audience. Whether this is writing a syndicated newspaper column, or conducting workshops across the country, or having a business that's a household name, an author needs to present himself as someone readers will trust as an expert.

OUTLINE This is a layout of the book, chapter by chapter, as you plan to write it. Be prepared to work with an agent or editor to make changes to your plan, but write it with as much detail as possible, including all the areas you plan to cover in your book.

MARKET Who will be interested in your topic? Think as broadly as possible. Include how you plan to reach each segment of your audience. Do you conduct seminars? Do you regularly write for a magazine or newspaper? Are there any organizations or societies that would be especially receptive to your book? Do you have a Web site that gets a lot of traffic? What kind of publicity can an agent expect from you?

COMPETITIVE TITLES This section requires some bookstore research. Find out what's already out there on your topic. List the book title, author, publisher, copyright date, number of pages, and retail price. Write a brief summary of each book and in what way your book is different.

EVIDENCE OF NEED There are other ways to prove you have an audience, and you may be one of the first authors to write a book on a particular topic. If there is a built-in audience and you can prove it exists and would be willing and eager to buy your book, show that here. You can include statistics or surveys to prove the audience already exists or to show the growing popularity of a topic that hasn't been covered before.

SAMPLE CHAPTER(S) These pages demonstrate your writing ability for the agent. Through them you can show that you know how to effectively organize your thoughts and convey information to the reader. The chapters give the agent a sense of your style and tone and provide evidence that you have the writing skills to pull off a project of this scope without working with a ghostwriter.

POLISH UNTIL IT SHINES

Now that you know what goes into a submission package, you might be tempted to get your work into the mail as soon as possible. But stop and ask yourself if your work is as ready as you can make it. Remember that if you submit your work prematurely, you can't call and tell an agent that you want to revise part of your submission. It's too late.

You only get one chance to make a professional submission with your book, so before you submit, make sure you're putting your best work out there by asking yourself the following questions:

IS IT COMPLETE? If you were selling a car, you'd want to make sure you had all the parts. You wouldn't want to lose a sale just because a hubcap was missing or the rear-view mirror fell off. Yet a lot of authors will begin querying agents before they've completed their manuscripts. They don't have a whole book to sell yet, but they hope someone will take a chance on them anyway—before they finish it. Nobody wants to buy part of a car, and no agent wants to risk representing part of a manuscript. So remember, novels must be completed before you try to find representation. Nonfiction books must have a complete proposal and outline and at least one sample chapter.

IS IT POLISHED? You've seen the diamond necklaces on the home shopping channel. They sparkle and glitter as if they've never seen a speck of dust in their lives. They have to. Because even if they're the clearest diamonds in the world, if they weren't polished, no one would want to buy them. A dull necklace wouldn't make anyone grab a phone off the hook, and your writing is the same way. Don't send out your manuscript without polishing it until it glows. A good idea is not enough to sell a manuscript— the writing has to be polished. Most authors do several drafts, and some of them can do ten, twenty, or even thirty drafts before they get every word just right. If this sounds like a lot of work, it is. If you get tired of your story and think you can't possibly look at it one more time, set it aside for a few weeks while you work on another project, and then you can look at it with renewed enthusiasm later.

HAVE YOU GOTTEN A SECOND OPINION? After you've polished your manuscript as much as you possibly can, it helps to have a friend or two look it over for you. We tend not to notice flaws that we've seen over and over again, but a friend can look at your materials with fresh eyes. He'll have the ability to notice if you have a pet catch phrase that shows up in your book over and over again. One of the writers I edited had her heroine rolling her eyes so often I thought they were surely going to pop out of her head. Once I pointed this out to her, she was surprised she hadn't noticed it herself, and she was able to take the phrase out. This made her work much more readable without that distracting phrase popping up and ruining the flow.

Getting someone else to read your work will also help you catch any stray misspellings you may have overlooked. It's surprising how many you can miss even after a solid proofread, so be sure to ask your friendly readers to circle any they see.

Finally, readers can help point out where something just isn't working in your text. Sometimes a character will behave in a way that isn't believable, and you'll have to delve further into your character's psyche and let readers know it's possible for that behavior to occur. If you've changed your story line at all, you may have continuity problems if you've left any pieces in your book that no longer make sense to the overall plot. Your readers will spot this readily. ("How did your character end up with the knife when she left it sticking out of the table?")

These readers can be your friends, but it's even better if they're fellow writers or editors. This is where those contacts that you made at writer's conferences or through writer's organizations come in handy. You may also contact a bookstore in your area or check your local paper to see if you can find any writer's groups where you can "workshop" your book.

DO YOU HAVE A STRONG PITCH? Once your book is finished, you'll need to craft the perfect pitch to sell it. This will be your opening paragraph in your query letter, or the verbal pitch you give to an agent at a conference. It's the hook for your book. You can start with a catchy question or provocative phrase, but you'll need to spend some time getting it just right. The pitch is what will get an agent's attention, and if your opening isn't interesting, the agent won't read any further.

HAVE YOU GOT THE FACTS? Once you've grabbed their attention, you have to back it up with facts. Take the time to do some research for your book. If it's nonfiction, find other books on a similar topic to yours and figure out why yours is better, more complete, or special. Find out who your market is and offer statistics. If your book is the first of its kind, find facts to prove that there's an audience out there who wants the information you can offer.

If you're writing a novel, make sure you haven't glossed over any places that need true-to-life details. If your book has characters who are nurses, talk to some real nurses to make sure you have your facts right. People love to talk about their work, and even if the only nurse friends you have are merely acquaintances, they'll likely be glad to answer your questions if you ask. Make sure you've also gotten your facts correct with setting and objects in your book. The details are what makes your book feel authentic to readers, so don't cheat them out of that experience.

DO YOU HAVE THE CREDENTIALS? While I was an editor, a writer told me he had figured out patterns in men's and women's behavior based on ten different parenting styles he had observed while growing up. He was eager to sell a book on this topic, but when I asked him about his qualifications, I knew he shouldn't even bother typing a query letter. The man didn't have a degree in psychology, and he had never been a formal counselor. His book idea may have been original, and his theories might have been true, but he didn't have the qualifications to write on the topic with any authority. These days, not only is an advanced degree or experience in your field necessary, you also need to have a platform—a way of reaching your audience.

For nonfiction books, it's imperative to establish yourself as an expert. Write a weekly column for a local paper, set up some radio interviews, or do some public speaking at seminars, conferences, or conventions to establish your credibility on the topic.

ARE YOU PLUGGED IN? Writing to publish isn't a hobby. It's an occupation that requires a huge amount of time and dedication. And it doesn't just involve sitting at your computer and typing. Writers today need to educate themselves about the publishing business as much as possible. Read *Publishers Weekly,* check out some books on the subject, and dig up as much information about publishing on the internet as you can. Find out what publishers are doing. Read articles about new agents. Find out what kinds of books have sold for huge advances. Once you start educating yourself about the business, you'll feel a greater sense of being a professional writer.

When I was a new editor attending my first writer's conference, I was worried that I wouldn't know the answers to all the questions people asked me. I was surprised when I realized how easy the questions were to answer. And I hadn't learned the answers by working as an editor. I'd learned most of them by reading books and magazines about writing and publishing. You can do the same. Learn to think like a publishing insider, and you'll know what agents and editors want and how to make your work stand out by coming across as a professional.

HAVE YOU BROWSED THE SHELVES? Where would your book be if it were published and sitting on the shelf in your local bookstore? That's the section you should be visiting frequently. Find out about existing titles and how your work compares. Read books that are in your genre or on your topic. Find out what you like about these books and ask yourself if your book has those qualities. If you love the case studies in a nonfiction book, gather some of your own to include in your book. If you love the fiery heroine in the romance novel you just read, steal some of her attributes for your own characters. Good writers are almost always good readers.

By reading good books on your book's future shelf, you'll learn tricks to pacing, plot, structure, and characterization that would take you a lifetime to learn on your own by the trial-and-error method.

HAVE YOU LOCATED A BUYER? As you're browsing through the books on that shelf, be sure to check the Acknowledgments page in the front of the book. As we discussed earlier, authors will often thank their agent. If the agent knew how to sell this book, there's a good chance she'd know how to sell yours as well. Again, don't forget to mention in your query letter to the agent that you loved the other book. Tell her how yours is similar, but explain what distinguishes it from the book she sold.

Construct a list of all the agents who handle your type of writing and organize it so that your favorites are at the top. Once you begin to send out query letters, you'll want to note what day you sent it and what you included in the query package, and this list will keep you organized. Take the time to browse some of the books each agent has represented so you can personalize your query letter.

HAVE YOU FOLLOWED THE RULES? Notice that each agent specifies what he wants to see in a submission. Make sure you follow this to the letter. One common mistake agents mention is writers who should send in the first three chapters, but instead send the first chapter, another chapter from the middle of the book, and the last chapter. If the agent asks for three chapters, he means the first three. Make sure you include sufficient postage for the return of your materials. Check with the post office for Canadian or international submissions. Regular U.S. postage won't be sufficient, so it's best if you purchase International Reply Coupons (IRCs) for these agents from the post office. Or simply notify the agent in your query letter that your materials can be recycled rather than returned.

Never call an agent to check on a query submission.

ARE YOU CONFIDENT IN YOUR WORK'S MERIT? Some authors actually do try to bribe or threaten agents to request their manuscript or offer them representation. This always looks unprofessional and comes across as desperate. When you're confident in the merits of your manuscript, you'll let your work speak for itself. You don't need clever bargaining tactics or groveling to find representation. If you did, you wouldn't be sure whether the agent truly liked your work enough to put a strong effort into marketing it, or if he were simply trying to appease you. So leave your desperation at the door, and write a confident query letter that's free of any hint of defeat—even if it's your twenty-eighth submission. Remember, you have to believe in your writing talent and your work first before anyone else will.

ARE YOU DETERMINED? Despite the success stories you've heard about first-time authors selling their books for large advances, most writing careers don't happen overnight. No one expects to sit down at a piano and play beautifully the first time. It takes years of lessons and analyzing music theory before someone can become a great pianist. Likewise, writing is an occupation that requires patience and practice. Those who give up early will wonder at your determination.

And when you finally do sell your book, they'll promptly forget all the hard work it took you to get there, and they'll ask you how you managed to become an overnight success yourself.

And you'll just smile.

SUBMITTING YOUR WORK

When it comes time to submit your work, a professional submission is key. This process goes far beyond using the right paper and font size. Make sure your submission is the best it can be by reviewing the most common questions about submissions.

Q: How can I make sure my work looks professional?

A: Make sure you use clean, unwrinkled, white bond paper. Use a normal font typeface like Times New Roman, Courier, or Courier New. Double space between lines. Make sure your last name and your title appears on the top left side of every page. In the top right corner, type the page number. Make sure each page is free of printing errors and that the type is dark and easily readable. There's no need to be fussy about using a cover sheet or to panic about how wide your margins should be. As long as your type looks pleasing on the page without looking cramped, no one's going to get out a ruler and measure your margins. Do make sure that you proofread everything carefully before submitting.

Q: How will I know when my work is ready to submit?

A: Some writers agonize for years over whether their work is ready to send out into the world. Make sure you have had other writers read your work first to catch any inconsistencies or spelling or grammatical errors you may have missed. For this, you should join a critique group or start one with a few fellow writers in your area. Contact your local bookstore to find groups in a city near you or join one of the many writer's organizations that can hook you up with writers you can communicate with online.

Q: What if I submit my work even though I'm still revising and polishing it?

A: It's an editor's and agent's nightmare to have an author call up and say they're sending a revision to something they've already sent. Don't submit your work until it's complete and finished and it's your best work. If you catch spelling errors later or decide to redo the second half of your book, don't try to catch an agent before he's read what you've already sent. If it's a minor change, it won't make or break a deal. If it's something major, you should wait until the agent offers you representation to mention your proposed adjustments or save it for the next agent on your list in the event of a rejection.

Q: What is the basic submission process for contacting an agent?

A: First you should get your manuscript, script, or proposal package in its best shape. Then you should submit a query letter describing yourself and your work. Keep this as short as possible. Always include a self-addressed stamped envelope (SASE) if you'd like a reply. If you have an e-mail address, include that as well. Some agents will also take a query letter via e-mail; check individual listings to confirm each agent's preferences. Some agents will want you to include a synopsis or sample pages with your query letter, so be sure to read the specifications. You may send out query letters to more than one agent at a time.

   If the agent likes your idea based on the query, she'll ask for you to submit more, either your entire manuscript or several chapters. Many agents will not request an exclusive look at your manuscript unless they are seriously considering to offer representation.

Q: How many query letters should I send out at a time?

A: I recommend sending out batches of eight to ten at a time. More than that, and you could run into the problem of too many agents requesting a full submission. If they ask to see your manuscript on an exclusive basis, and you have to submit it to one agent at a time, the final agents on your list may forget they've requested your manuscript by the time you get around to submitting to them. More likely, you won't get a 100% positive response rate, so multiple query submissions are a good idea.

Q: What if I never get a reply from a query letter even though I've included an SASE?

A: Simply cross the agency off your list and continue to submit elsewhere. Do not call the agent to ask if they received your query. Most agents will reply with at least a form letter if you send an SASE, but some agents reply only if interested.

Q: How many manuscript submissions may I send out at a time?

A: More and more agents are asking for exclusive submissions, and here's why. An agent gets paid only when he sells your work. He does not get paid to read your manuscript, but it takes valuable time from his schedule to do so. Imagine his disappointment if he spends hours reading your manuscript, loves it, and calls to offer you representation only to find out that you've already found another agent in the meantime.

Q: What if more than one agent requests an exclusive look?

A: Let's say you've submitted ten query letters, and you've been lucky enough to get a request for your manuscript from five of them. Three of them ask for an exclusive look, and two simply ask to see more. At this point, you have some options. Find out each agent's usual response time by consulting his or her listing in this book. Some agents will get back to you within a week or a month, while others can take up to four months. Before you decide to grant an exclusive submission, you might want to submit first to the agents who have not requested your manuscript exclusively. Or you can arrange to submit first to the agent with the quickest response time down to the slowest. You can submit to the agent who showed the quickest, most enthusiastic response to your query letter. It's up to you.

In the cover letter you submit with your manuscript for further consideration, mention that you're granting an exclusive look at your manuscript for one month, and remind the agent they have requested to see what you're submitting. Remember that agents request several manuscripts every week, so include a brief reminder of what your book is about. If you don't hear from the agent within a month, you may submit elsewhere. But before you do, it doesn't hurt to send an e-mail or follow-up letter to the first agent to give them a polite nudge—"I just wanted to see if you had a chance to read my manuscript that you requested on November 15. On November 17 I sent you THE BLUE TOURNAMENT, my romance novel about a mysterious knight with unusual skills as a swordsman who turns out to be a woman."

If you accept representation from an agent, and your manuscript has been submitted to other agencies, you should inform them that you've found an agent and regrettably have to withdraw your work from their consideration.

Q: What if I receive more than one offer for representation?

A: This doesn't happen very often, but most writers who find themselves in this enviable position choose to work with the first agent who responds, or the one who responds most enthusiastically to their work.

Q: What if the agent asks me to make revisions?

A: Agents are tuned into publishing and what makes a book salable. Often they'll give some editorial suggestions. Remember that their advice may help improve your book, but ultimately the decision to revise is up to you. Regardless of whether you choose to make changes to your book, thank the agent for taking the time to make suggestions before you respond in a defensive way. Consider each suggestion carefully before you get back to the agent with your decision on why or why not this would improve the book.

Especially regarding nonfiction, taking editorial guidance from an agent can mean the difference between a bestseller and a no-seller.

Q: Should I submit to editors and agents at the same time?

A: It's a better idea to submit only to agents. Remember that once you have an agent, she'll submit your work to editors. If some of them have already seen your manuscript and rejected it, the door at those publishing houses may already be permanently closed to considering your manuscript, even after you make revisions under an agent's direction. It's best to work with an agent before sending your manuscript to publishers on your own.

Q: I write in more than one genre. Can I to submit to an agent who only handles one of those genres?

A: It's best to first find an agent for your strongest or most recent work. Once you have an agent, he may be willing to make an exception for your other manuscripts or at least refer your work to another agent who has more interest and skill in handling that category of writing.

WORKING WITH AN AGENT

Once you have an offer of representation, an agent may send you a contract or an agreement letter to specify the terms of your arrangement. In essence, this letter states that the agent is entitled to commission on projects he has sold for you, outlines what reimbursements (if any) are expected from you, and says how much notice you must give for terminating the relationship—usually thirty or sixty days.

Some agents work on a handshake agreement and won't ask you to sign anything. Either way, make sure you feel comfortable with the terms of the agreement. If there's any part you don't understand, ask questions. Your agent should be more than happy to answer all of your questions. Only a bad agent would be abrupt or rude to you at this point, and he isn't the type of agent you want.

Once you've signed with an agent, you may spend some time working with him on revisions before your work is ready to submit.

Once the submission process has begun, your agent should give you updates on where your work has been submitted and the responses he's received. He should make you aware of any offer that comes in, even if he feels it would be in your best interest to decline it and hold out for something better. Sometimes an editor will make a low offer or request changes that wouldn't be in the author's best interest to immediately accept, but an agent should keep you informed of these communications regardless.

While you don't want to call your agent every week for a progress report, your agent should keep you informed and return your phone calls and e-mails when they're necessary.

Once an agent receives an offer that you both agree is acceptable, the agent will negotiate the contract on your behalf. He'll keep as many subsidiary rights for you as he can and negotiate a fair amount of advance money and royalties.

SUBSIDIARY RIGHTS

So what exactly are these mysterious rights that the agent negotiates for you, and why can't you do that for yourself?

SERIAL RIGHTS
Serial rights are for excerpts of your book. First-serial rights are for excerpts that are published before your book is printed. Second-serial rights refer to excerpts after the book is printed, and usually the publisher holds those rights. Serial rights are great tools for publicity. I recently read a story in a women's magazine that was published in two parts, and I noticed it was an excerpt from a book that was coming soon. The story ends on a hopeful note, but readers of the magazine who are pulled into the story and interested in the characters will want to buy the book immediately when it hits the shelves.

FOREIGN RIGHTS
These rights refer to selling your book outside the United States or, in some cases, outside North America. Every good agent has a network of co-agents who they deal with to help sell your book abroad. It's an agent's job to know the trends in these markets and to know where your book is likely to have a strong chance of selling.

REPRINT RIGHTS
After a book has made a splash as a hardcover, the publisher will publish a less expensive paperback version of the book, usually six months to a year later. If the book originally comes out as a trade paperback that sells for around fifteen dollars, and the book does well, it might

be reprinted as a rack-size book with less expensive paper—called a mass-market paperback—and will sell for about half of the original price. Usually the publisher will negotiate to keep this right.

DRAMATIC/PERFORMANCE RIGHTS

These rights include television, film, theater, and radio. Sometimes these rights will sell before the hardcover rights do.

AUDIO RIGHTS

This includes cassette tapes or compact discs.

ELECTRONIC RIGHTS

Negotiating electronic rights in the contract is a newer consideration now that technology makes this a practical reality. Some of the older contracts don't include them, but nowadays, they're getting plenty of attention. While most publishers don't expect to exploit those rights imme-diately, there's still plenty of interest in them. Right now most readers prefer printed and bound books to the elec-tronic version, but who knows what the future will bring?

MERCHANDISING RIGHTS

Think of the Harry Potter phenomenon, and you'll begin to see how lucrative merchandising rights can be for an author. Action figures, t-shirts, statues, calendars, stick-ers, lunch boxes, and any other products affiliated with characters from the book fall under this category.

OTHER CONTRACT POINTS

Besides negotiating to keep your subsidiary rights, an agent will also negotiate when your manuscript is due to the editor, how much advance money you will be paid (and when you'll receive it), your royalty percentage rate, and other specifics that relate to your book. Sometimes an agent can ensure that you have meaningful input on the title or cover of your book, or even final approval, though such arrangements are unusual, especially with first-time authors.

If your book has bestseller potential, your agent can also negotiate bonus money for you. If your book makes a bestseller list or is chosen for a book club, for example, or if you're invited to appear on a popular television show, the publicity will sell more books, and the agent can negotiate an arrangement in which you will receive a share of the publisher's increased profit.

There are even more special clauses an agent can negotiate for you, including complimentary copies of the book. Your agent will be glad to go over the contract with you in detail, and if there are any special considerations you would like taken into account, remember that your agent is on your side and will fairly represent your needs to the editor.

MEMBERSHIPS & ETHICS

How can legitimate agents set themselves apart from the frauds? Any crook can hang out a shingle and call himself an agent, whether he knows a thing about publishing or not. But only legitimate agents qualify for membership in the Association of Author's Representatives (AAR).

This union for agents was formed in 1991 when the Society of Authors' Representatives (founded in 1928) merged with the Independent Literary Agents Association (founded in 1977). Before an agent can become a member of the AAR, an agent must meet certain professional qualifications and agree to the AAR's Canon of Ethics.

To qualify for membership, an applicant must have been an agent for two years and must have sold the rights to at least ten different books within eighteen months or five play productions within two years prior to applying.

AAR CANON OF ETHICS

Whether they are members of the AAR or not, all good agents should adhere to the code of appropriate behavior for author representatives that the AAR has established. Members must agree to:

1. Conduct their business honestly without any conflicts of interest.

2. Maintain separate bank accounts for their clients' funds and their own and promptly remit payment due their clients.

3. Charge clients only for reimbursement for expenses made on the client's behalf, such as copyright fees, manuscript retyping, photocopies, long distance calls, etc., and only if the client has agreed.

4. Keep each client apprised and furnish information the client requests pertinent to the agent's work on his behalf.

5. Limit his representation to the author and not the seller. He may not represent both in the same transaction.

6. Not make a secret profit in connection with any transaction involving a client. This includes receiving a kickback for referring an author to an editorial service.

7. Keep their client's financial affairs private and confidential.

8. Never charge reading fees or receive any payment for evaluating manuscripts.

As you look through the listings of agents, you should note whether the agent is a member of the AAR. Many qualifying agents choose not to join, but if any non-members offer you representation, you should ask if they agree to the AAR's code of ethics.

As of this writing, there are 343 members of the AAR. The AAR's objective is not to police their members, but to keep them informed about conditions in publishing, the theater, motion picture and television industries, and related fields, and to assist their members in representing their clients' interests. For more information about the AAR, visit their Web site at www.aar-online.org.

WGA

Another union for agents is the Writer's Guild of America (WGA), primarily for those agents who handle scripts. As with the AAR, members of the WGA must agree to not charge any reading or evaluation fees to consider a writer's work and must have made a certain type and number of sales within a three year period before qualifying for membership.

The WGA also offers a list of member agents and whether they're open or closed to receiving submissions from writers. For their free e-mail newsletter *Now Playing,* send an e-mail to: join-wga@laser.sparklist.com. The guild also publishes a magazine called *Written By.* For more information about the WGA, go to their Web site at www.wga.org.

CONFERENCES

The conference section of the directory lists conferences across the United States and Canada. Conferences are excellent ways to network and meet agents and editors face-to-face. Many agents and editors who normally don't invite unsolicited submissions will open their doors to you after meeting you personally. For this reason, you should consider conferences as networking opportunities, especially if your query letters have not led to any manuscript requests.

Usually conferences will have workshops on a variety of publishing topics led by industry professionals. These instructive sessions range from basic to advanced topics, so it's a good idea to get a brochure ahead of time and decide which workshops you're most interested in attending. At the end of each workshop, the speaker will often take questions from attendees and may meet with individuals for a few minutes afterward.

Use this time after the workshop to thank the speaker, introduce yourself, and exchange business cards. Agents usually will not accept query letters or manuscripts at conferences, but they often invite conference attendees to submit work to them afterward, even if they don't accept unsolicited manuscripts under normal circumstances.

Conferences often host mixers, lunches, and dinners where you can mingle with other attendees and the speakers. Don't let this time go to waste! Exchange as many business cards as you can, and jot some notes on the back of each card you receive to help you remember something about the person who gave it to you. Don't forget to follow up afterward as quickly as you can with a query letter or an e-mail. Remind them who you are and where you met, and include all of your contact information again in case they've misplaced your card.

Some conferences also allow you to sign up for one-on-one sessions with editors and agents. These sessions are usually ten to fifteen minutes long, which is just enough time for you to pitch your writing project and get some feedback. If you're an outgoing person who is comfortable having a conversation with a friendly stranger, prepare a quick pitch for your project, describing it in a few sentences, and then be prepared to describe it in a little more detail and answer questions about it. If you're more of an introvert, you can bring a query letter and let the agent look it over and give you some feedback. This is an excellent way to get tips on how to improve your query letter or synopsis, and sometimes an agent or editor will invite you to submit your manuscript after these sessions if they like your idea and your writing.

Make sure you come across as a professional at all times. This means you should be dressed nicely and on your best behavior. Personality goes a long way, so make sure you're gracious, friendly, and polite. You may receive some constructive criticism, but even if you don't agree with it, resist the urge to argue with the agent or editor, and accept the comments graciously. It's okay to ask questions, and you may even want to use a note pad or tape recorder so that you can remember everything later. Always ask the agent, "May I take notes?" or "Do you mind if I record this?" before you do so.

Many conferences will allow you to submit your work ahead of time, sometimes a month before the conference begins. This gives the editors and agents a chance to read your work more thoroughly so that you'll get more productive feedback during your session. Again, it's best to consult the conference Web site or brochure to find out if these meetings are available and what they entail.

Writer's conferences are well worth the time and expense for the valuable information and networking opportunities you'll gain.

RESOURCES DIRECTORY

You don't have to live next door to a bestselling novelist in order to get a referral. Instead you can network by joining a writer's club. The Resources Directory lists writer's organizations with local chapters across the country. You may even choose to join an online community where you can offer each other editing advice and share marketing tips. Some of these groups have published authors who are members, and they can be valuable contacts for new writers.

ORGANIZATIONS FOR AGENTS

ASSOCIATION OF AUTHORS' REPRESENTATIVES (AAR)
P.O. Box 237201 Ansonia Station
New York, NY 10003
www.aar-online.org
You can access the membership list of agents and their addresses through the Web site and read more about this union and its membership requirements.

ASSOCIATION OF AUTHORS' AGENTS (AAA)
62 Grafton Way
London W1P 5LD
England
(011) 44 7387 2076
www.agentassoc.co/uk
You can find a list of members on their Web site along with their code of practice and frequently asked questions.

ORGANIZATIONS FOR WRITERS

ACADEMY OF AMERICAN POETS
588 Broadway, Suite 604
New York, NY 10012-3210
212.274.0343
www.poets.org

AMERICAN MEDICAL WRITERS ASSOCIATION
40 W. Gude Dr., Suite 101
Rockville, MD 20850-1192
301.294.5303
www.amwa.org

**AMERICAN SOCIETY OF JOURNALISTS
& AUTHORS**
1501 Broadway, Suite 302
New York, NY 10036
212.997.0947
www.asja.org

AMERICAN TRANSLATORS ASSOCIATION
225 Reinekers Lane, Suite 590
Alexandria, VA 22314
703.683.6100
www.atanet.org

**THE ASSOCIATION OF WRITERS
& WRITING PROGRAMS**
The Tallwood House, Mailstop 1E3
George Mason University
Fairfax, VA 22030
703.993.4301
www.awpwriter.org

THE AUTHORS GUILD INC.
31 E. 28th St., 10th Floor
New York, NY 10016
212.563.5904
www.authorsguild.org

THE DRAMATISTS GUILD
1501 Broadway, Suite 701
New York, NY 10036
212.398.9366
www.dramaguild.com

EDUCATION WRITERS ASSOCIATION
2122 P St., NW, Suite 201
Washington D.C. 20037
202.452.9830
www.ewa.org

HORROR WRITERS ASSOCIATION
P.O. Box 50577
Palo Alto, CA 94303
www.horror.org

**INTERNATIONAL ASSOCIATION OF CRIME
WRITERS INC./NORTH AMERICAN BRANCH**
P.O. Box 8674
New York, NY 10016
212.243.8966
www.crimewritersna.org

**THE INTERNATIONAL WOMEN'S
WRITING GUILD**
P.O. Box 810, Gracie Station
New York, NY 10028-0082
212.737.7536
www.iwwg.com

**MEDIA COMMUNICATIONS
ASSOCIATION–INTERNATIONAL**
401 N. Michigan Ave.
Chicago, IL 60611
312.321.5171
www.mca-i.org

MYSTERY WRITERS OF AMERICA
17 E. 47th St., 6th Floor
New York, NY 10017
212.888.8171
www.mysterywriters.org

**NATIONAL ASSOCIATION OF SCIENCE
WRITERS**
P.O. Box 890
Hedgesville, WV 25427
304.754.5077
www.nasw.org

**NATIONAL LEAGUE OF AMERICAN
PEN WOMEN**
1300 17th St., NW
Washington, D.C. 20036-1973
202.785.1997
www.americanpenwomen.org

NATIONAL WRITERS ASSOCIATION
3140 S. Peoria, #295 PMB
Aurora, CO 80014
303.841.0246
www.nationalwriters.com

NATIONAL WRITERS UNION
113 University Place, 6th Floor
New York, NY 10003
212.254.0279
www.nwu.org

PEN AMERICAN CENTER
568 Broadway, 4th Floor
New York, NY 10012-3225
212.334.1660
www.pen.org

POETS & WRITERS, INC.
72 Spring St., Suite 301
New York, NY 10012
212.226.3586
www.pw.org

POETRY SOCIETY OF AMERICA
15 Gramercy Park
New York, NY 10003
212.254.9628
www.poetrysociety.org

ROMANCE WRITERS OF AMERICA

16000 Stuebner Airline Dr., Suite 140
Spring, TX 77379
832.717.5200
www.rwanational.com

SCIENCE FICTION AND FANTASY WRITERS OF AMERICA

P.O. Box 171
Unity, ME 04988-0191
www.sfwa.org

SOCIETY OF AMERICAN TRAVEL WRITERS

1500 Sunday Dr., Suite 102
Raleigh, NC 27607
919.861.5586
www.satw.org

SOCIETY OF CHILDREN'S BOOK WRITERS & ILLUSTRATORS

8271 Beverly Blvd.
Los Angeles, CA 90048
323.782.1010
www.scbwi.org

WESTERN WRITERS OF AMERICA

1012 Fair St.
Franklin, TN 37064
615.791.1444
www.westernwriters.org

WRITERS GUILD OF AMERICA-EAST

555 W. 57th St., Suite 1230
New York, NY 10019
212.767.7800
www.wgaeast.org

WRITERS GUILD OF AMERICA-WEST

7000 W. Third St.
Los Angeles, CA 90048
323.951.4000
www.wga.org

CANADA
WRITERS GUILD OF ALBERTA

Main Floor, Percy Page Centre
11759 Groat Rd., Edmonton
Alberta T5M 3K6, Canada
780.422.8174
http://writersguild.ab.ca

ENGLAND
ALCS (THE AUTHORS' LICENSING AND COLLECTING SOCIETY LIMITED)

Marlborough Court, 14-18 Holborn
London EC1N 2LE
tel: +44 (0) 20 7395 0600
fax: +44 (0) 20 7395 0660
www.alcs.co.uk

THE SOCIETY OF AUTHORS

84 Drayton Gardens
London SW10 9SB
tel: +44 (0) 20 7373 6642
www.societyofauthors.net

THE WRITERS' GUILD OF GREAT BRITAIN

15, Britannia St., London WC1X 9JN
tel: +44 (0) 20 7833 0777
fax: +44 (0) 20 7833 4777
http://cgi.writersguild.force9.co.uk/

CONFERENCE DIRECTORY

ASA INTERNATIONAL SCREENWRITERS CONFERENCE

AMERICAN SCREENWRITERS ASSOCIATION
269 S. BEVERLY DR., SUITE 2600
BEVERLY HILLS CA 90212-3807

PHONE/FAX   **E-MAIL**   **WEB SITE**
866.265.9091   asa@goasa.com   www.goasa.com

Coordinator:	John E. Johnson
Held:	August
Description:	Provides workshops on screenwriting and marketing/selling scripts for feature film and TV
Focus:	Scripts
Number of attendees:	250
Number of speakers:	40
Location:	Hollywood, CA
Cost:	$400–$600 includes registration, breaks, meals, workshops, pitching to producers
Past speakers include:	Aaron Sorkin, Gary Ross, Shane Black, Michael Hauge, Syd Field, Linda Seger, Madeline DiMaggio, Lew Hunter, Richard Walter

ASJA 2004 WRITERS CONFERENCE

AMERICAN SOCIETY OF JOURNALISTS AND AUTHORS
1501 BROADWAY, SUITE 302
NEW YORK NY 10036

PHONE/FAX   **E-MAIL**   **WEB SITE**
212.997.0947   staff@asja.org   www.asja.org
212.768.7414

Coordinator:	Robert Bittner
Held:	April
Description:	Leading editors, publishers, agents, and successful writers provide expert advice on current book and magazine markets, literary journalism, marketing and promoting your book, negotiating skills, online writing opportunities, and more. Personal mentoring sessions with ASJA members also available.
Number of attendees:	600–700
Number of speakers:	80–85
Location:	Grand Hyatt Hotel, New York City
Cost:	$195 includes 20–25 panels, banquet luncheon, reception
Past speakers include:	Assigning editors, publishers, agents, successful writers, prominent writer as keynote speaker

ASPEN SUMMER WORDS WRITING RETREAT & LITERARY FESTIVAL

ASPEN WRITERS' FOUNDATION
110 E. HALLAM ST., SUITE 116
ASPEN CO 81611

PHONE/FAX	E-MAIL	WEB SITE
970.925.3122	info@aspenwriters.org	www.aspenwriters.org
970.920.5700		

Executive Director:	Julie Comins
Held:	May
Description:	4-day writing retreat (mornings) and concurrent 5-day literary festival (afternoons and evenings). Retreat includes intensive workshops in advanced fiction, fiction, creative nonfiction, poetry, and children's literature. Offerings for participants include craft workshops, readings and talks, publishing panels, and agent/editor meetings.
Focus:	Literary Festival is a booklover's buffet, featuring 17 events for readers and writers
Number of attendees:	72 for the retreat, 200+ for the festival
Location:	The Given Institute and Paepcke Auditorium in Aspen, CO
Cost:	$375 for writing retreat; $195 for magazine symposium; $150 for literary festival. $30 discount for registering for both the festival and retreat or symposium. Complimentary morning coffee and pastries for students and 2 wine and hors d'oeuvres receptions for ASW registrants; other meals and services charged separately. Overnight accommodations available for registrants. Cost of accommodations start at $110/double; see Web site for more information.
Admissions deadline:	April 1 (for Workshops)
Past faculty includes:	Amy Bloom, Ron Carlson, Pam Houston (fiction); James Houston (creative nonfiction); Christopher Merrill (poetry); Laura Fraser (magazine writing)
Past speakers include:	Ann Patchett, Patricia Schroeder, Adrienne Miller

BALTIMORE WRITERS' ALLIANCE CONFERENCE

P.O. BOX 410
RIDERWOOD MD 21139

PHONE	WEB SITE
410.377.5265	www.baltimorewriters.org

Held:	November
Focus:	All areas
Additional information:	Please see Web site for more details
Past speakers include:	Kristen Auclair (agent with Graybill and English), other agents, editors, writers, teachers

THE BAY AREA WRITERS LEAGUE ANNUAL CONFERENCE

P.O. BOX 580007
SEABROOK TX 77586

FAX
409.762.4787

E-MAIL
con@bawl.org

WEB SITE
www.bawl.org

Coordinator:	Terri Richison
Held:	May
Description:	Introduces beginning and experienced writers to a variety of topics
Focus:	Fiction, nonfiction, poetry
Number of attendees:	150
Number of speakers:	27
Location:	University of Houston-Clear Lake, NASA area southeast of Houston, university campus setting, hotels available nearby
Cost:	$85 for 2 days includes lunch, Friday evening reception; $50 for 1 day; $50 for full-time students; add $25 for B.A.W.L. membership if not already a member
Additional information:	Includes a contest for novice writers and an open contest for all attendees
Past speakers include:	Authors, editors, agents, writing teachers; last year's list is at www.bawl.org/bios.htm

BLOODY WORDS MYSTERY CONFERENCE

CARO SOLES (CHAIR—BOARD OF DIRECTORS)
2 ROUNDWOOD CT.
TORONTO ON
CANADA M1W 1Z2

PHONE
416.497.5293

E-MAIL
info@bloodywords.com

WEB SITE
www.bloodywords.com

Coordinator:	Cheryl Freedman
Held:	June
Description:	A gathering of readers and writers of the mystery genre, for the discussion of mysteries and the craft of crime writing; includes panels, workshops, interviews, agent "pitch" sessions
Focus:	Mystery
Number of attendees:	275–350
Location:	Toronto; check Web site for information
Cost:	$175 (approximately) for all panels, workshops, discussions, banquet; discount for early registration
Past speakers include:	Peter Robinson, Val McDermid, Donald Maass (agent, NYC), Anne Perry (International Guest of Honor), Maureen Jennings (Canadian Guest of Honor)

BREAD LOAF WRITERS' CONFERENCE

MIDDLEBURY COLLEGE
MIDDLEBURY VT 05753

PHONE/FAX
802.443.5286
802.443.2087

WEB SITE
www.middlebury.edu/~blwc

Coordinators:	Michael Collier, director; Devon Jersild, associate director; Noreen Cargill, administrative manager
Held:	August
Description:	For more than 75 years, the workshops, lectures, and classes, held in the shadow of the Green Mountains, have introduced generations of participants to rigorous practical and theoretical approaches to the craft of writing, and given America itself proven models of literary instruction. Bread Loaf is not a retreat—not a place to work in solitude. Instead it provides a stimulating community of diverse voices in which we test our own assumptions regarding literature and seek advice about our progress as writers.
Focus:	Fiction, poetry, nonfiction
Number of attendees:	200+
Location:	The Bread Loaf Inn and its cottages and buildings at Middlebury College in Ripton, VT; most rooms are doubles; smoke-free facilities
Cost:	$1,260 for tuition; $673 for room and board; some financial aid available. See Web site for details.
Additional information:	Volleyball and clay tennis courts, a softball and soccer playing field, and jogging and hiking trails. A beach at Lake Dunmore is 12 miles away, and Lake Pleiad is a quarter-mile down the Long Trail. In nearby Middlebury you can find country auctions, antique shops, a state crafts center, a fine museum, a movie theater, and riding and golf facilities.
Past speakers include:	Many agents, as well as editors from major publishing houses

CENTRAL OHIO FICTION WRITERS

P.O. BOX 1981
WESTERVILLE OH 43086-1981

PHONE/FAX
614.764.2200

E-MAIL
dmacmean
@columbus.rr.com

WEB SITE
www.cofw.org

Coordinator:	Donna Mac Means
Held:	October
Focus:	All fiction
Location:	Wyndham Hotel, 600 Metro Place North, Dublin, OH 43017
Cost:	$75 (Saturday conference); Friday night dinner, $20; Friday panel, $10; Friday late-night networking, $10; Saturday night dinner, $23
Past speakers include:	Elaine English (agent with Graybill and English), agents, authors, editors

THE COLORADO GOLD WRITERS CONFERENCE

ROCKY MOUNTAIN FICTION WRITERS
CONFERENCE REGISTRATION
PMB 183
17011 LINCOLN AVE.
PARKER CO 80134-8815

WEB SITE
www.rmfw.org

Held:	September
Description:	Brings New York to Colorado by inviting editors from major publishing houses, agents, and best-selling authors
Focus:	Novel-length fiction
Number of attendees:	Limited to 350
Location:	The Renaissance Denver Hotel (www.renaissancehotels.com), 3801 Quebec Street, (I-70 and Quebec near old Stapleton), Denver, CO 80207
Cost:	$189 (early registration). A discounted hotel rate of $59 for single and double occupancy is available to attendees. To make hotel reservations, please call 1.888.238.6762 or 303.399.7500 and ask for the conference rate.
Past speakers include:	Authors, editors, and agents; agents have included Michelle Grajkowski, Irene Kraas, Kristin Nelson, Janet Reid, Pam Strickler

COLORADO MOUNTAIN WRITERS' WORKSHOP

P.O. BOX 85394
TUCSON AZ 85754

PHONE/FAX	E-MAIL	WEB SITE
520.465.1520	mfiles@cs.com	www.sheilabender.
520.572.0620		com

Coordinator:	Meg Files
Held:	June
Description:	This small workshop/retreat, featuring lots of individual attention and hands-on activity, aims to lift writers to their next level in personal writing
Focus:	Poetry, fiction, creative nonfiction
Number of attendees:	40
Number of speakers:	3
Location:	Colorado Mountain College dormitory in Steamboat Springs, CO
Cost:	$400 tuition includes all sessions, workshops, individual consultations, and readings for the week; $375 for room and board package
Past speakers include:	Meg Files, Sheila Bender, Jack Heffron

THE COLUMBUS WRITERS CONFERENCE

P.O. BOX 20548
COLUMBUS OH 43220

PHONE/FAX	E-MAIL	WEB SITE
614.451.3075	AngelaPL28@aol.com	www.creativevista.com
614.451.0174		

Coordinator:	Angela Palazzolo, director
Held:	Late August or September
Focus:	Poetry, fiction, nonfiction
Location:	The Fawcett Conference Center, 2400 Olentangy River Road, Columbus, OH. Accommodations available at Marriott Fairfield Inn & Suites, 3031 Olentangy River Road. 1.800.214.5542. Ask for the conference special rate.
Cost:	$235 (early registration) for full conference (includes Friday dinner program, all other meals, and open mike); $165 for Saturday conference only; $145 for Friday only; $38 for Friday night dinner and program only (agent/editor panel)
Past speakers include:	Jennifer DeChiara (fiction agent), Jeff Kleinman (nonfiction agent at Graybill and English), Nancy Ellis-Bell (agent at LitWest Group), editors, authors, other publishing professionals

FESTIVAL OF THE WRITTEN ARTS

P.O. BOX 2299
SECHELT, BC V0N 3A0
CANADA

PHONE/FAX
604.885.9631
604.885.3967

TOLL FREE PHONE
1.800.565.9631

WEB SITE
www.writersfestival.ca

Coordinator:	Gail Bull
Held:	August
Description:	A literary festival where authors give readings to audiences of eager readers and writers
Focus:	All genres
Number of attendees:	10,000
Number of speakers:	20–25
Location:	Rockwood Centre, Sechelt, BC. Local accommodations used for authors; audience members are responsible for their own lodgings.
Cost:	$125 for weekend pass (admission to all 21 events except the salmon BBQ); individual events are $12 general admission, $10 for students; salmon BBQ dinner, $12
Additional information:	See Web site, or call our office
Past speakers include:	Nino Ricci, Maria Coffey & Dag Goering, P.K. Page, Pierre Berton, Sandra Birdsell, Leon Rooke, Margaret Atwood, Susan Musgrave, Dennis Lee, Stuart McLean, Andreas Schroeder, Sheree Fitch, L.R. Wright, Myrna Kostash

FLORIDA CHRISTIAN WRITERS CONFERENCE

2344 ARMOUR CT.
TITUSVILLE FL 32780

WEB SITE
www.flwriters.org

Coordinator:	Billie Wilson
Held:	March
Location:	The Christian Retreat Conference Center in Bradenton, FL
Cost:	$525 for double occupancy, meals, and tuition; single occupancy, add $250; meals and tuition only, $400; tuition only, $310. Early registration, save $15.
Past speakers include:	Professional editors, agents, freelance writers

FLORIDA FIRST COAST WRITERS' FESTIVAL

9911 OLD BAYMEADOWS RD., ROOM C1301, FCCJ
JACKSONVILLE FL 32256

PHONE/FAX	E-MAIL	WEB SITE
904.997.2669	kclower@fccj.edu	www.fccj.org/wf
904.997.2746		

Coordinator:	Kathleen Clower
Held:	May
Description:	Provides opportunities for aspiring and published writers to improve their craft, network and mingle, learn from each other, and meet with editors and agents
Focus:	Fiction, nonfiction, poetry, screenwriting, mystery, writing for children, essays, romance
Number of attendees:	250–300
Number of speakers:	25–28
Location:	The Sea Turtle Inn, Atlantic Beach (just outside of Jacksonville), FL. The hotel offers special rates for conference attendees.
Cost:	$50 for preconference workshops; 1 day (with lunch), $110; 2 days (with lunches), $200; Friday night banquet, $50
Past speakers include:	Robert Bly, Tim O'Brien, Robert Morgan, Doug Marlette, James Hall, Tim Dorsey, John Dufresne, Elizabet Lund, Kitty Oliver, David Poyer, Cassandra King, S.V. Date, Scott Morris, Eddie Bell, Les Standiford, Ray McNiece, Kathy Pories (Algonquin), Jacky Sach

FLORIDA SUNCOAST WRITERS' CONFERENCE

UNIVERSITY OF SOUTH FLORIDA
DIVISION OF PROFESSIONAL & WORKFORCE DEVELOPMENT
4202 E. FOWLER AVE., CPR 107
TAMPA FL 33620

PHONE/FAX	WEB SITE
813.974.1711	http://english.cas.usf.
813.974.2270	edu/fswc/

Coordinators:	Dr. Betty Moss, Dr. Lagretta T. Lenker, Dr. Steven J. Rubin
Held:	February
Cost:	$125 (early); $145 (late)

FRONTIERS IN WRITING

P.O. BOX 19303
AMARILLO TX 79114

PHONE/FAX
806.379.7842
806.354.5471

E-MAIL
pcs@arn.net

WEB SITE
www.users.arn.net/
~ppw/

Coordinators:	Cindy Rios, chair; Phyliss Miranda, co-chair
Held:	June
Description:	Promotes, educates, and encourages writers of all levels and genres
Number of attendees:	150
Number of speakers:	2 keynote and 8–10 breakout session speakers
Location:	Ambassador Hotel
Cost:	$150 includes Friday night banquet, Saturday sessions and luncheon; $50 for all-day Friday session; $40 for tickets to *Texas Legacies* (outdoor musical drama & BBQ dinner)
Additional information:	We try not to focus on any one specific type of writing. We have a contest in conjunction with FIW Conference with categories for mystery, romance, sci-fi, poetry, children's, nonfiction, novel, short story, screenplay. Contact Cindy Rios, P.O. Box 52244, Amarillo, TX 79159 or see Web site for more information.
Past speakers include:	Deborah Elliott-Upton, Kimberly Willis Holt, Tony Hillerman, Diane Curtis Regan, Melanie Rigney, Donald Maass, Michael Cunningham, Patricia Lorenz, Colleen Sell, Elmer Kelton

HARDBOILED HEROES AND COZY CATS

SOUTHWEST CHAPTER, MYSTERY WRITERS OF AMERICA
C/O LAURA ELVEBAK
5837 VILLAGE FOREST CT.
HOUSTON TX 77092

PHONE	E-MAIL	WEB SITE
713.797.8464	info@mwasw.org	www.mwasw.org

Coordinator:	TBA
Held:	June
Description:	Covers how to write, publish, and sell in the mystery and crime genres
Focus:	Fiction (mysteries), nonfiction (true crime)
Number of attendees:	80
Number of speakers:	6–10
Location:	Houston, TX
Cost:	$75–$90 based on membership status and early or late registration; includes continental breakfast and hot lunch
Additional information:	Pre-conference networking dinner with the speakers (not included in conference fee). Short story contest with cash award in 2 categories: *Hardboiled Heroes* (gritty, hard-boiled stories) and *Cozy Cats* (traditional mysteries or cozies). Launched in 1984, HHCC is the Southwest's longest-running annual mystery-writing conference.
Past speakers include:	Editors, agents, writers, and forensics experts, including Rachel Vater, Nancy Love, Rick Riordan, Laura Joh Rowland, Chris Rogers, Dean James, Jeff Abbott, Casey Kelly, Malcolm Shuman, Bill Crider, Jay Brandon, Susan Wittig Albert, Vanessa Leggett, Al Alexander, Kate Stine, Genny Ostertag , Carolyn Hart, Peter Rubie, Amanda Powers, Gail Fortune

HEARTLAND WRITERS CONFERENCE

P.O. BOX 652
KENNETT MO 63857

PHONE / FAX	E-MAIL	WEB SITE
573.297.3325	ihwg@heartlandwriters.	www.heartlandwriters.
573.297.3352	org	org

Coordinator:	Harry Spiller
Held:	June
Description:	A multi-genre, fiction and nonfiction conference with both published and unpublished attendees
Number of attendees:	150
Number of speakers:	20
Location:	Best Western Coach House Inn, Sikeston, MO
Cost:	$190
Additional information:	2 full days of workshops and speakers. Contest. Open mike night. Banquet.
Past speakers include:	Chris Vogler, Evan Marshall, Robert Vaughan, Rita Clay Estrada, Bobbi Smith, Laurell Hamilton, Doris Booth; many editors, authors, agents

HIGHLAND SUMMER CONFERENCE

APPALACHIAN REGIONAL STUDIES CENTER
BOX 7014 RADFORD UNIVERSITY
RADFORD VA 24142-7014

PHONE / FAX	E-MAIL	WEB SITE
540.831.5366	jasbury@radford.edu	www.radford.edu/
540.831.5951		~arsc

Coordinator:	Dr. Grace Toney Edwards, director; JoAnn Asbury, assistant to the director
Held:	June
Description:	Writing-intensive workshop focusing on Appalachian literature and culture.
Focus:	Writer's choice
Number of attendees:	Limited to 20
Number of speakers:	2 well-known guest lecturers (for each week) and 2 guest speakers
Location:	Radford University campus, Radford, VA 24142; dorm rooms available upon request
Cost:	Regular tuition for a 3 hour class (graduate and undergraduate) plus $25 conference fee
Past speakers include:	Robert Morgan, Wilma Dykeman, Sharyn McCrumb, Nikki Giovanni, Jim Wayne Miller, David Huddle, Jeff Daniel Marion, George Ella Lyon, Denise Giardina, Gurney Norman

IWWG BIG APPLE WORKSHOPS: MEET THE AUTHORS/MEET THE AGENTS

INTERNATIONAL WOMEN'S WRITING GUILD
P.O. BOX 810 GRACIE STATION
NEW YORK NY 10028-0082

PHONE / FAX	E-MAIL	WEB SITE
212.737.7536	iwwg@iwwg.org	www.iwwg.org
212.737.9469		

Coordinator:	Hannelore Hahn
Held:	October
Description:	1-day writing workshop; next day, Meet the Authors panel (10 recently published IWWG authors discuss how they got themselves published and tricks of the trade) and Meet the Agents (each agent speaks briefly and members of the audience can introduce themselves)
Number of attendees:	200
Location:	New York Genealogical Society, 122 East 58 Street, New York City
Cost:	$130 both days (nonmembers); $110 both days (IWWG members). Does not include lunch or accommodations. Attendees can pay separately for each section.

IWWG EARLY SPRING IN CALIFORNIA CONFERENCE

INTERNATIONAL WOMEN'S WRITING GUILD
P.O. BOX 810 GRACIE STATION
NEW YORK NY 10028-0082

PHONE / FAX	E-MAIL	WEB SITE
212.737.7536	iwwg@iwwg.org	www.iwwg.org
212.737.9469		

Coordinator:	Hannelore Hahn
Held:	March
Number of attendees:	65
Number of speakers:	4
Location:	Bosch Bahai Center, Santa Cruz, CA
Cost:	$345 (nonmembers); $325 (IWWG members) inclusive of weekend room, board, and program

IWWG ONE-DAY WORKSHOPS

INTERNATIONAL WOMEN'S WRITING GUILD
P.O. BOX 810 GRACIE STATION
NEW YORK NY 10028-0082

PHONE / FAX	E-MAIL	WEB SITE
212.737.7536	iwwg@iwwg.org	www.iwwg.org
212.737.9469		

Held:	February, March, April, May
Additional information:	Please call

IWWG REMEMBER THE MAGIC, ANNUAL SUMMER CONFERENCE

INTERNATIONAL WOMEN'S WRITING GUILD
P.O. BOX 810 GRACIE STATION
NEW YORK NY 10028-0082

PHONE / FAX	E-MAIL	WEB SITE
212.737.7536	iwwg@iwwg.org	www.iwwg.org
212.737.9469		

Coordinator:	Hannelore Hahn
Held:	June
Number of attendees:	400–500
Number of speakers:	70
Location:	Skidmore College, Saratoga Springs, NY
Cost:	$900 (non-IWWG member, single occupancy); $800 (non-IWWG member, double occupancy); $885 (IWWG member, single occupancy); $775 (IWWG member, double occupancy). Includes 7 days' room, board, and program. 5-day, weekend, and commuter rates are available.

KENTUCKY WOMEN WRITERS CONFERENCE

114 BOWMAN HALL
LEXINGTON KY 40506-0059

PHONE / FAX
859.257.8734
859.323.1932

E-MAIL
kywwc@hotmail.com

WEB SITE
www.uky.edu/
conferences/kywwc

Coordinator:	Rebecca Howell
Held:	March
Description:	Presents contemporary women writers in a series of readings, writing workshops, performances, and discussions. Dedicated to advancing opportunities for well-known and promising new talents, scholars, and performers to meet directly with readers and writers in a forum that facilitates the exchange of views, concerns, and inspirations. The KWWC prides itself on a diversity of authors and attendees.
Focus:	Nonfiction and memoir writing with numerous genres represented
Number of attendees:	250
Number of speakers:	10
Location:	Lexington, KY
Cost:	$120 regular admission for all 3 days; $30 for Thursday only; $65 for Friday or Saturday only; $40 student admission for all 3 days or $20 per day
Additional information:	The KWWC celebrated its 25th anniversary in 2004
Past speakers include:	Alice Walker, Maya Angelou, Audre Lorde, Margaret Atwood, Toni Cade Bambara, Gloria Steinem, Vandana Shiva

LOST STATE WRITERS CONFERENCE

P.O. BOX 1442
GREENEVILLE TN 37744

PHONE	E-MAIL	WEB SITE
423.639.4031	loststate@hotmail.com	www.loststatewriters.com

Coordinator:	Tamara Chapman
Held:	September
Description:	Conducts classes and workshops in writing, educates writers about the publishing industry, aids in their professional development, and establishes awards and scholarships for creative writing
Focus:	Fiction, nonfiction, poetry, children's writing, songwriting, screenwriting
Number of attendees:	200
Number of speakers:	25
Location:	General Morgan Inn, Greeneville, TN
Cost:	$250 includes panel discussions, workshops, dinners, entertainment
Additional information:	Scholarships and critiques available
Past speakers include:	Lee Smith, Winston Groom, Charles Wright, Sharyn McCrumb, Wilma Dykeman, Ellen Douglas, Ron Howard, Jacki Collins, Dave Barry, Frank McCourt, Nicholas Sparks, Bellie Letts, Elizabeth George, Dorothy Allison, Jack Canfield, Terry Brooks, James McBride, Mitch Albom, Catherine Coulter, Ann Rule, Paula Danziger, Marianne Williamson

MARK TWAIN CREATIVE WRITING WORKSHOP

UNIVERSITY OF MISSOURI-KANSAS CITY
COLLEGE OF ARTS AND SCIENCES ENGLISH DEPARTMENT
5100 ROCKHILL RD.
KANSAS CITY MO 64110-2499

PHONE / FAX	E-MAIL	WEB SITE
816.235.1305	newletters@umkc.edu	www.newletters.org/
816.235.2611		writingconferences.asp

Coordinators: Michael Pritchett, Robert Stewart

Held: June

Description: 3-week, 3-hour/day workshop for beginning and advanced writers. Professional writers instruct participants on how to write and promote their work. Participants receive workshop analysis and private manuscript consultations.

Focus: Poetry, fiction, nonfiction, journaling, stage- and screenwriting

Number of attendees: 45

Number of speakers: 10

Location: Cockefair Hall on the University of Missouri-Kansas City's campus, located southeast of the Kansas City Plaza. Participants will be provided with a list of hotels near the campus.

Cost: $150 non credit. Students can attend for 1–3 hours of graduate or undergraduate credit. Out-of-state tuition is waved. Graduate cost is $210 per credit hour and undergraduate cost is $167 per credit hour.

Additional information: Course requirements: Regular attendance of lectures, workshops, and appropriate individual conferences, and the successful preparation of a portfolio of work

Past speakers include: Poets Jo McDougal, Michelle Boisseau, Dan Jaffe, Patricia Cleary Miller; novelists Trudy Lewis, James McKinley; journalist Steve Paul; playwright Catherine Browder; book critic Mark Luce; radio producer Angela Elam; filmmaker Don Maxwell; faculty members Michael Pritchett, Robert Stewart

MAUI WRITERS CONFERENCE

P.O. BOX 1118
KIHEI HI 96753

PHONE / FAX	E-MAIL	WEB SITE
808.879.0061	writers@mauiwriters.	www.mauiwriters.com
808.879.6233	com	

Coordinators:	John and Shannon Tullius, directors
Held:	September
Description:	While the conference offers sessions, workshops, and lectures about all aspects of writing, there are many opportunities to network with agents, editors, and publishers. Special one-on-one sessions and Agents Day are 2 venues where writers meet with these professionals to discuss their works-in-progress. Marketing and selling of one's work is a vital component of this event.
Focus:	Fiction, nonfiction, screenwriting, children's, poetry, journalism, travel writing, business of publishing, self-publishing, marketing
Number of attendees:	800
Number of speakers:	100
Location:	Wailea Marriott, an Outrigger Resort, Maui, HI
Cost:	$495–$695 conference fee only. (Fee depends on attendee's sign-up date.) Air, hotel, and food not included in price. Special pricing available to attendees from Marriott Resort.
Additional information:	See Web site for information about all of our programs; toll free phone: 888.974.8373; online registration also available

MAUI WRITERS CONFERENCE, PANAMA CANAL CRUISE

P.O. BOX 1118
KIHEI HI 96753

PHONE / FAX	**E-MAIL**	**WEB SITE**
808.879.0061	writers@mauiwriters.	www.mauiwriters.com
808.879.6233	com	

Coordinators:	John and Shannon Tullius, directors
Held:	March
Description:	Choose from the following 3 programs:
	· BOOK LOVERS Discuss the latest *New York Times* best-sellers, book club-style, with the authors.
	· MASTERS PROGRAM An intimate conference at sea includes hands-on writing classes, editing clinics, and intensive workshops by our faculty of *New York Times* best-selling authors.
	· WRITERS CHALLENGE AT SEA Learn how to write like a pro while working in small, intimate groups with best-selling authors. Learning how to write on demand will be the focus of this program. The best of each student's stories will be published in a book from this program.
Number of attendees:	300
Number of speakers:	7
Location:	*MS Rotterdam* sails out of Ft. Lauderdale, FL; 10-day southern Caribbean and Panama Canal cruise
Cost:	Varies depending on program and lodging. Program, food, and lodging included in price. Airfare not included.
Additional information:	Please visit Web site; toll free phone: 888.974.8373
Past speakers include:	Janet Evanovich, John Saul, Dorothy Allison, Elizabeth George, Terry Brooks, Susan Wiggs, Gail Tsukiyama

MAUI WRITERS RETREAT

P.O. BOX 1118
KIHEI HI 96753

PHONE / FAX
808.879.0061
808.879.6233

E-MAIL
writers@mauiwriters.com

WEB SITE
www.mauiwriters.com

Coordinators:	John and Shannon Tullius, directors
Held:	August (precedes the Maui Writers Conference)
Description:	6 intense, inspiring days of learning the art and craft of writing. In small, intimate, hands-on groups, the emphasis will be on how to shape and present a salable manuscript. Manuscripts will be written and revised to that end. Various levels of writing in tracks for fiction, nonfiction, and screenwriting (no poetry). A writing sample is required at the time of reservation and enrollment is limited.
Number of attendees:	175
Number of speakers:	30
Location:	Wailea Marriott, an Outrigger Resort, Maui, HI
Cost:	$975–$1075 based on date of registration
Additional information:	Registration and program information is available on our Web site; toll free phone: 888.974.8373
Past instructors include:	John Saul, Terry Brooks, Dorothy Allison, Elizabeth George, Katherine Ramsland, Susan Wiggs

THE MID-AMERICA CRIME WRITING FESTIVAL

MAGNA CUM MURDER
THE E.B. BALL CENTER
BALL STATE UNIVERSITY
MUNCIE IN 47306

PHONE / FAX
765.285.8975
765.747.9566

E-MAIL
kennisonk@aol.com

WEB SITE
www.magnacummurder.com

Coordinator:	Kathryn Kennison
Held:	October
Description:	A celebration of crime fiction, the people who write it, and the people who read it
Focus:	Crime writing
Number of attendees:	300
Number of speakers:	40
Location:	Radisson Hotel Roberts, Muncie, IN
Cost:	$185 includes Friday evening reception; Saturday and Sunday continental breakfasts and box lunches; Saturday evening banquet
Additional information:	Festival began in 1993
Past speakers include:	Mary Higgins Clark, Michael Connelly, Sue Grafton, Sara Paretsky, Donald Westlake, Ralph McInerny, Lawrence Block, Anne Perry

MIDLAND WRITERS CONFERENCE

GRACE A. DOW MEMORIAL LIBRARY
1710 W. ST. ANDREWS
MIDLAND MI 48640-2698

PHONE / FAX
989.837.3430
989.837.3468

E-MAIL
ajarvis@midland-mi.
org

WEB SITE
www.midland-mi.
org/gracedowlibrary

Coordinator:	Ann Jarvis
Held:	May
Description:	Provides a forum for beginning and established writers to exchange ideas with professionals
Focus:	Various topics
Number of attendees:	60–100
Number of speakers:	2–6
Location:	Grace A. Dow Memorial Library
Cost:	$60 includes continental breakfast and lunch
Past speakers include:	Michael Beschloss (keynote), Cynthia LaFerle, Margo LaGattuta, Boyd Miller, John Smolens

MOUNT HERMON CHRISTIAN WRITERS CONFERENCE

P.O. BOX 413
MOUNT HERMON CA 95041-0413

PHONE / FAX
831.335.4466
831.335.9413

E-MAIL
dtalbott@mhcamps.
org

WEB SITE
www.mounthermon.
org/writers

Coordinator:	David R. Talbott, Director of Adult Ministries
Held:	April
Description:	Trains beginning through advanced writers for the Christian market and provides a venue for inspiration, fellowship, networking, and instruction
Focus:	Fiction, nonfiction, children's, youth, special teen track (for teens only), poetry, scriptwriting, screenwriting, magazine articles, books
Number of attendees:	400–425
Number of speakers:	50, plus 13 hospitality and critique staff
Location:	Mount Hermon Christian Conference Center, Mount Hermon, CA, 35 miles southwest of San Jose, CA
Cost:	$350 tuition, plus room and board, depending on level of accommodations: $210 for student dormitory; $285 economy dormitory; $430 for standard hotel; $590 for deluxe double occupancy. Includes 13 meals, morning coffee breaks, afternoon fruit bowls, evening refreshments.
Additional information:	Includes free manuscript critique service in advance of conference, with follow-up appointments by faculty/staff, as needed. Meals are taken together with faculty/staff, family-style. Toll free phone: (888) MH-CAMPS
Past speakers include:	Calvin Miller, T. Davis Bunn, Sally Stuart, Gayle Roper, Lauraine Snelling, Karen Ball

NATIONAL CONFERENCE ON WRITING & ILLUSTRATING FOR CHILDREN

SOCIETY OF CHILDREN'S BOOK WRITERS AND ILLUSTRATORS
8271 BEVERLY BLVD.
LOS ANGELES CA 90048-4515

PHONE / FAX	E-MAIL	WEB SITE
323.782.1010	scbwi@scbwi.org	www.scbwi.org
323.782.1892		

Coordinator:	Lin Oliver
Held:	February
Description:	Writers and illustrators conference in children's literature
Focus:	Children's books
Number of attendees:	900
Number of speakers:	30
Locations:	Roosevelt Hotel (New York), Century Plaza Hotel (Los Angeles)
Cost:	For New York: $275 for 2 days, 1 meal, all sessions. For Los Angeles: $400 for 4 days, 3 meals, all sessions.
Additional information:	For updates on all our conferences, visit our Web site
Past speakers include:	Garth Williams, Judy Blume, Jane Yolen, Madeline L'Engle

THE NEW LETTERS WEEKEND WRITERS CONFERENCE

UNIVERSITY OF MISSOURI-KANSAS CITY
COLLEGE OF ARTS AND SCIENCES CONTINUING ED. DIVISION
5100 ROCKHILL RD.
KANSAS CITY MO 64110-2499

PHONE / FAX	E-MAIL	WEB SITE
816.235.2736	newletters@umkc.edu	www.newletters.org
816.235.2611		

Coordinator: Robert Stewart

Held: June

Description: Brings together talented writers in many genres for lectures, seminars, readings, workshops, and individual conferences. Attendees will learn about marketing their work and the opportunities and obstacles of a successful writing career.

Focus: The creative process in poetry, fiction, nonfiction, stage- and screenwriting, journalism

Number of attendees: 50

Number of speakers: 15

Location: Diastole, the UMKC scholars center, 2501 Holmes Street, Kansas City, MO. Participants will be provided with a list of the many hotels convenient to Diastole.

Cost: Registrants can attend the conference for 1–3 hours of graduate or undergraduate credit. Out-of-state tuition is waived. Credit students must prepare manuscripts prior to the conference. Graduate cost is $210 per credit hour and undergraduate cost is $167 per credit hour. $150 for non-credit attendance at all sessions, readings, and receptions. Non-credit students electing to have a manuscript evaluation will pay an additional $40 per manuscript. Limited financial aid is available to for-credit students only.

Additional information: See Web site for conference schedule. This midtown center houses unique art and other collections by the Diamond family.

Past speakers include: Poetry, Stanley Banks; fiction, Whitney Terrell; nonfiction, Conger Beasley; stage, Frank Higgins; screen, Mitch Brian; journalism, C.W. Gusewelle. Others include Chip Fleischer, Trish Reeves, Debra Di Blasi, Suzanne Rhodenbaugh, Loring Leifer.

NORTH CAROLINA WRITERS' NETWORK FALL CONFERENCE

P.O. BOX 954
CARRBORO NC 27510-0954

PHONE / FAX	E-MAIL	WEB SITE
919.967.9540	mail@ncwriters.org	www.ncwriters.org
919.929.0535		

Coordinator:	Carol Henderson, conference director
Held:	November
Description:	Helps writers learn about craft and marketing, share resources, network, and have fun. Offers 5 sessions, with 8 concurrent classes per session, over 2 days. Also offers a Manuscript Mart where authors can meet 1-on-1 with New York editors and agents to discuss their work; master classes in fiction, creative nonfiction, poetry (competitive); a keynote address.
Focus:	Fiction, poetry, creative nonfiction, children's literature, screenwriting, marketing
Number of attendees:	300
Number of speakers:	40
Location:	Hilton Riverside Hotel, in downtown Wilmington, NC
Cost:	$200 for NCWN members; $255 for nonmembers, which includes membership for a year. Tuition covers all classes, readings, and two meals on Saturday. The Manuscript Mart has an additional fee. Hotel accommodations are $79/night for NCWN participants.
Additional information:	Bristol Books, the local bookstore handling all sales, will carry titles (self-published included) of participants as well as faculty and guest speakers. Cocktail party and book signing Saturday night.
Past speakers include:	Andrei Codrescu, Rick Bragg, Haven Kimmel, Clyde Edgerton, Philip Gerard, Phil Furia, Donald Maass

PIKES PEAK WRITERS CONFERENCE

4164 AUSTIN BLUFFS PKWY 246
COLORADO SPRINGS CO 80918

PHONE / FAX	E-MAIL	WEB SITE
719.531.5723	info@ppwc.net	www.ppwc.net
719.590.7480		

Coordinator: Charlie Rush, director

Held: April

Description: Teaches the craft of storytelling and how writers can be true professionals in this often-complex profession. Attendees choose between 45 workshops in 8 sessions, an opportunity to read before an editor or agent, roundtable discussions, and numerous opportunities throughout conference to talk with editors and agents.

Focus: Fiction is main emphasis, although workshops in screenwriting and nonfiction are offered

Number of attendees: 420 maximum

Number of speakers: 30

Location: Wyndham Hotel in Colorado Springs, CO

Cost: $215 for members; $235 for nonmembers; includes meals on Friday evening, Saturday evening banquet, Saturday and Sunday lunch, continental breakfast on Saturday and Sunday

Additional information: A number of attendees have met and signed contracts with editors and agents at this conference. Colorado Springs is at the foot of Pikes Peak, with many tourist attractions within a few minutes or so from the hotel. "This is our favorite conference to attend," say many of our speakers.

Past speakers include: Robert Vaughan, Robert Crais, Eileen Dreyer, David Morrell, Sharon Sala, Barry Maher, Joan Johnston, Bruce Holland Rogers

PIMA WRITERS' WORKSHOP

PIMA COLLEGE
2202 W. ANKLAM RD.
TUCSON AZ 85709-0170

PHONE	FAX	E-MAIL
520.206.6974	520.206.6020	mfiles@pima.edu

Coordinator:	Meg Files
Held:	May
Description:	Offers opportunities for all writers—beginning or experienced—to talk and consult with professional writers, editors, and agents, as well as to write
Focus:	Fiction, nonfiction, poetry, screenplays, children's literature
Number of attendees:	250
Number of speakers:	14
Location:	Pima College Center for the Arts, Tucson AZ; accommodations at nearby hotels and motels
Cost:	$70 for the 3-day conference and a manuscript critique with a writer, editor, or agent
Additional information:	This friendly, supportive conference features a generous, accessible faculty. The focus is on writing, but sessions on marketing are always included as well.
Past speakers include:	Barbara Kingsolver, Larry McMurtry, Joanne Greenberg, Ray Gonzalez

POLICE WRITERS CONFERENCE

POLICE WRITERS ASSOCIATION
P.O. BOX 738
ASHBURN VA 20146

PHONE / FAX	E-MAIL	WEB SITE
703.723.4740	leslye@policewriter.	www.policewriter.com
703.723.4743	com	

Coordinator:	LeslyeAnn Rolik
Held:	Late September-early October
Description:	Offers classes and networking opportunities
Focus:	All genres
Number of attendees:	Varies
Number of speakers:	8
Location:	Newport, RI
Cost:	$175 early bird rate for members; increases $50 each time deadline passes until a max of $300; non-members add $50 to each rate; spouses pay a flat rate for meals and can attend classes with paid attendee
Additional information:	Check Web site frequently for updates
Past speakers include:	Roger Fulton, Ed Dee, Armand Mulder, Paul Bishop

ROMANCE WRITERS OF AMERICA NATIONAL CONFERENCE

16000 STUEBNER AIRLINE RD., SUITE 140
SPRING TX 77379

PHONE / FAX	E-MAIL	WEB SITE
832.717.5200	info@rwanational.org	www.rwanational.org
832.717.5201		

Held:	July
Description:	Enhances writing skills and knowledge of the ins and outs of publishing at more than 100 workshops. Attendees can schedule a one-on-one pitch meeting with an acquiring editor or literary agent; attend parties and network with the stars of romance fiction; and be a part of RWA's massive, 350-author strong "Readers for Life" charity book signing.
Focus:	Romance fiction
Number of attendees:	2,000
Location:	Adams Mark in Dallas, TX
Additional information:	RITA and Golden Heart Awards

SAN DIEGO STATE UNIVERSITY WRITERS' CONFERENCE

SDSU COLLEGE OF EXTENDED STUDIES
SAN DIEGO CA 92182-1920

PHONE / FAX	E-MAIL	WEB SITE
619.594.2517	xtension@mail.sdsu.	www.ces.sdsu.edu/
619.594.8566	edu	writersconference.html

Held:	January
Focus:	Fiction, nonfiction, scriptwriting
Location:	Doubletree Hotel in San Diego, CA
Cost:	$295 early registration; $325 late registration. $35 each for advance reading or agent/editor appointments (maximum of 3).
Past speakers include:	Over 20 agents, including Kimberley Cameron (Reece Halsey North), Jandy Nelson (Manus & Associates), Greg Dinkin (Venture Literary), Julie Castiglia; editors; screenwriting specialists

SANTA FE SCREENWRITING CONFERENCE

P.O. BOX 29762
SANTA FE NM 87592-8423

PHONE
505.424.1501

FAX
505.424.8207

WEB SITE
www.scsfe.com

Held:	June
Focus:	Screenwriting
Location:	Santa Fe, NM; campus dorms, apartments, or hotels available
Cost:	$595 includes mentor selection for 9-hour class, workshops, panel discussions, live readings, margarita party

SELLING TO HOLLYWOOD INTERNATIONAL SCREENWRITERS CONFERENCE

269 S. BEVERLY DR., SUITE 2600
BEVERLY HILLS CA 90212-3807

PHONE
866.265.9091

E-MAIL
asa@goasa.com

WEB SITE
www.goasa.com

Held:	August
Description:	This conference is renowned for its panels, workshops, and pitching sessions with agents and producers
Focus:	Screenwriting
Location:	Los Angeles, CA
Additional information:	See Web site for more details
Past speakers include:	Richard Walter, Linda Seger, Michael Hauge, Lew Hunter

SEWANEE WRITERS' CONFERENCE

310 ST. LUKE'S HALL
SEWANEE TN 37383-1000

PHONE / FAX	E-MAIL	WEB SITE
931.598.1141	cpeters@sewanee.edu	www.sewaneewriters. org

Coordinator: Cheri Peters

Held: July

Description: Brings together a nationally and internationally acclaimed faculty with younger writers for purposes of instruction, criticism, and encouragement in the craft and practice of writing. Each attendee is a member of a workshop that meets for 5 2-hour sessions over the course of the conference. In addition, each writer has an hour-long individual manuscript conference with a member of the faculty. A full schedule includes readings; craft lectures; panel discussions/Q&A sessions featuring editors, publishers, and agents; and numerous social events designed for more informal exchange.

Focus: Fiction (novel & short stories), poetry, playscripts

Number of attendees: 110

Number of speakers: 37 (inclusive of faculty)

Location: University of the South in Sewanee, TN

Cost: $1,325 for tuition, room, and board

Additional information: Fellowships (covering tuition, room and board) and scholarships (covering tuition) are available on a competitive basis to those writers with publications (in the case of poets and fiction writers) or productions (in the case of playwrights). Additional forms are required.

Past speakers include: Russell Banks, Pinckney Benedict, Georges & Anne Borchardt, Edgar Bowers, John Bricuth, Robert Olen Butler, John Casey, Elizabeth Dewberry, Ellen Douglas, Tony Earley, Stanley Elkin, Morgan Entrekin, Gary Fisketjon, Mary Flinn, Daisy Foote, Horton Foote, Richard Ford, Peggy Fox, Carol Frost, Ernest Gaines, Jonathan Galassi, Robert Giroux, David Godine, Debora Greger, Emily Grosholz, Rachel Hadas, Wendy Hammond, Barry Hannah, Robert Hass, Anthony Hecht, Amy Hempel, Edward Hirsch, Gail Hochman, John Hollander, Ann Hood, Tina Howe, Andrew Hudgins, Mark Jarman, Andrew Hudgins, Diane Johnson, Jon Jory, Donald Justice, Randall Kenan, X.J. Kennedy, John Kulka, Maxine Kumin, Brad Leithauser, Wendy Leser, Romulus Linney, Margot Livesey, William Logan, Alison Lurie, David Lynn, Andrew Lytle, Charles Martin, J.D. McClatchy, Jill McCorkle, Alice McDermott, Jean McGarry, Erin McGraw, Claire Messud, Arthur Miller, Susan Minot, Rick Moody, Mary Morris, Kent Nelson, Howard Nemerov, Marsha Norman, Tim O'Brien,

Past speakers cont: Stewart O'Nan, Robert Pack, Joseph Parisi, Ann Patchett, Joe Ashby Porter, Padgett Powell, Francine Prose, Alice Quinn, Shannon Ravenel, Mark Richard, Robert Richman, Lois Rosenthal, Mary Jo Salter, Jay Schaefer, Bob Shacochis, Marc Smirnoff, Dave Smith, Monroe Spears, Brent Spencer, Jon Stallworthy, Robert Stone, Mark Strand, William Styron, John Sullivan, Peter Taylor, Nigel Thompson, Jarvis Thurston, Richard Tillinghast, Deborah Treisman, Lily Tuck, Chase Twichell, Mona Van Duyn, Ellen Bryant Voigt, Derek Walcott, Harriet Wasserman, Richard Wilbur, Mark Winegardner, Charles Wright, Stephen Wright

SINIPEE WRITERS' WORKSHOP

LORAS COLLEGE
1450 ALTA VISTA
DUBUQUE IA 52004-0178

PHONE / FAX	E-MAIL	WEB SITE
563.588.7139	Chris.Neuhaus@loras.	www.loras.edu
563.588.4962	edu	

Coordinator:	Chris Neuhaus, secretary
Held:	April
Description:	Provides general information for writers on how to get published
Focus:	Poetry, nonfiction, fiction
Number of attendees:	40–50
Location:	Loras College, 1450 Alta Vista, Dubuque, IA
Cost:	$65 ($75 at the door); discounts available for senior citizens and students
Additional information:	Sponsors the John Tigges Writing Contest for short fiction, nonfiction, and poetry as part of workshop. Requirements: $5 entry fee / $15 additional fee for written critique. Poetry must not exceed 40 lines; short fiction and nonfiction entries must be 1,500 words or less. Style and subject are open, and work by aspiring writers as well as seasoned professionals is welcome. See Web site for contest deadline.
Past speakers include:	Joanne Walker, Bill Pauly, Allan Ede, Bill Bottoms, Donna Bauerly

SOCIETY OF SOUTHWESTERN AUTHORS

WRANGLING WITH WRITING
P.O. BOX 30355
TUCSON AZ 85751-0355

PHONE / FAX	E-MAIL	WEB SITE
520.546.9382	wporter202@aol.com	www.azstarnet.com/
520.296.0409	*and* excalibureditor@	nonprofit/ssa
	earthlink.net	

Coordinator:	Al Petrillo, conference director
Held:	January
Description:	Promotes the art of writing through 30 workshops and the opportunity to interview with more than 25 agents, editors, and publishers
Focus:	All genres
Number of attendees:	425
Location:	Holiday Inn Palo Verde, 4550 S. Palo Verde Blvd., Tucson, AZ 85714
Cost:	$300 for all workshops (includes 5 meals); price increases after deadline; see Web site for details. Interviews are $20 for a 15-minute session.
Past speakers include:	J.A. Jance, Ray Bradbury, Tony Hillerman, Donald Maass

SOUTHWEST WRITERS CONFERENCE

8200 MOUNTAIN RD., NE, SUITE 106
ALBUQUERQUE NM 87110

PHONE / FAX	E-MAIL	WEB SITE
505.265.9485	swriters@aol.com	www.southwestwriters.
505.265.9483		org

Held:	Late summer/early fall
Description:	Encourages, supports, and inspires people to express themselves creatively through the written word
Focus:	Fiction (long and short), nonfiction (long and short), children's literature, poetry, screenplays
Number of attendees:	300
Number of speakers:	40
Location:	Albuquerque, NM; hotels TBA
Cost:	$300 includes choice of sessions Saturday-Sunday, at least 4 meals, 1 10-minute appointment with an editor, agent, producer, or publicist. Cost of lodging not included.
Past speakers include:	Debbie Macomber, David Guterson, Charles Johnson, David Morrell, Lois Duncan, Dean Wesley Smith, Kristine Kathryn Rusch, Bruce Holland Rogers, Ann Rule, Jonathan Sanger, Tom Schulman, Christopher Vogler, Thomas Colgan, Milton Kahn

UCLA EXTENSION WRITERS' PROGRAM

THE WRITERS STUDIO
10995 LE CONTE AVE., #440
LOS ANGELES CA 90024

PHONE / FAX	E-MAIL	WEB SITE
310.825.9415	writers@	www.uclaextension.
310.206.7382	uclaextension.edu	edu/writers

Coordinator:	ULCA Extension Writers' Program
Held:	February
Description:	Aims to significantly enhance fiction writing and screenwriting skills. Successful authors and screenwriters bring extensive experience and knowledge to each of the 10 workshops.
Focus:	Short stories, novels, feature film screenwriting, TV scriptwriting
Number of attendees:	165 maximum
Number of speakers:	10
Location:	1010 Westwood Blvd., Westwood, Los Angeles, CA. Attendees must find their own accommodations.
Cost:	$550 for early enrollment; $650 for late enrollment; includes materials, continental breakfast, luncheon
Additional information:	The UCLA Extension Writers' Studio is becoming one of the most esteemed and popular intensive writing seminars in southern California.
Past speakers include:	Susan Taylor Chehak, Tod Goldberg, Rachel Resnick, Lisa Seidman, Steven Wolfson, Janna Gelfand, Leslie Lehr Spirson, Billy Mernit, Hope Edelman, Steve Duncan, Paula Cizmar

WATERSIDE PUBLISHING CONFERENCE

2187 NEWCASTLE AVENUE, SUITE 204
CARDIFF CA 92007

PHONE / FAX	**E-MAIL**	**WEB SITE**
760.632.9190	admin@waterside.	www.waterside.com
760.632.9295	com	

Coordinator:	Kimberly Valentini
Held:	April
Description:	The premier annual gathering of the computer book publishing industry. It is 3 days of non-stop interaction with the leading publishers, authors, and buyers in computer book publishing, and features great speakers, panels, and workshops.
Focus:	Computer and technical books, some general nonfiction
Number of attendees:	200–300
Number of speakers:	25–30
Location:	Berkeley, CA
Cost:	$500 general fee; $450 additional registrant; $250 author fee. Includes all Waterside-sponsored events and food.
Additional information:	See Web site for more details
Past speakers include:	Alan Cooper, author of *About Face* and *The Inmates are Running the Asylum;* Bob Ipsen, VP-Executive Editor, Wiley Technology Publishing; Dr. Lee Sun, President, Multi-Lingua Publishing Int'l; Leo Laporte, Tech TV's "The Screen Savers"

WESLEYAN WRITERS CONFERENCE

WESLEYAN UNIVERSITY
279 COURT ST.
MIDDLETOWN CT 06459

PHONE / FAX	E-MAIL	WEB SITE
860.685.3604	agreene@wesleyan.	www.wesleyan.edu/
860.685.2441	edu	writing/conferen.html

Coordinator:	Anne Greene
Held:	June
Description:	Seminars, readings, workshops, and manu-script consultations, all designed to give new perspectives on attendees' work and the company of other writers with shared interests. Welcomes new writers, established writers, and anyone seeking a better understanding of the writer's craft.
Focus:	Fiction, poetry, literary journalism, memoir, autobiography
Number of speakers:	20
Location:	Wesleyan University in Middletown, CT. Students may stay on campus (dormitory rooms are plain, simply furnished, single rooms with a shared bath; a limited number of air-conditioned rooms available upon request when registering) or in local hotels.
Cost:	$550 for tuition; $200 for meals; $125 for room. Day student rate: $750, which includes the full program, day and evening events, and all meals; $875 includes a single dorm room for 5 nights (plus $30 for an air-conditioned room). Some financial aid available. See Web site for details.
Additional information:	Conference enrollment is limited, so register early. Faculty members will read a limited number of manuscripts. If you would like to have a manuscript consultation, register promptly. Later, send a representative sample of your work in 1 genre: 10 poems, the first chapters of a novel (plus an outline or summary), or several short stories or nonfiction pieces. Please do not send more than 25 pages of material.
Past speakers include:	Amy Williams (an agent with International Creative Management); other agents, editors, authors, publishing industry professionals

WHIDBEY ISLAND WRITERS CONFERENCE

WHIDBEY ISLAND WRITERS ASSOCIATION
P.O. BOX 1289
LANGLEY WA 98260

PHONE	**E-MAIL**	**WEB SITE**
360.331.6714	writers@whidbey.com	www.whidbey.com/writers

Coordinator:	Celeste Mergens, director
Held:	March
Description:	Provides world-class opportunities for quality writers networks, instruction, and creative interaction. Participants attend unique Fireside Chats; panels with agents, editors, authors, and publishers; intensive workshops, keynotes and classes; added bonus of option for personal consultations with agents, editors, publishers, and authors.
Focus:	Fiction, nonfiction, poetry, screenwriting, songwriting
Number of attendees:	275
Number of speakers:	40
Location:	Langley, Whidbey Island, WA. Group and retreat lodging, B&Bs, and inns available.
Cost:	$350 for the entire weekend, including luncheons and receptions; $200 for volunteers (commit to working as a volunteer for 8–10 hours before, during, or after the conference); early-bird registration for $300 with a deposit of $75
Additional information:	See Web site for registration details. This world-class, personable conference generally fills to capacity. Early registration is suggested.
Past speakers include:	Rick Bass, Marvin Bell, Catherine Coulter, Elizabeth George, Erik Larsen, Dan Millman, Pattiann Rogers, Ann Rule, Eva Shaw, Debbie Macomber

WILLAMETTE WRITERS CONFERENCE

9045 S.W. BARBUR, SUITE 5A
PORTLAND OR 97219

PHONE / FAX
503.452.1592
503.452.0372

E-MAIL
wilwrite@teleport.com

WEB SITE
www.willamettewriters.com

Held:	August
Description:	Opportunities for learning, pitching, and networking. Offers more than 50 workshops taught by industry professionals; individual and group pitch sessions with agents, editors, managers, and producers; private sessions with a professional screenwriter.
Focus:	Fiction, nonfiction, scriptwriting
Location:	Portland, OR
Cost:	$175–$450, based on number of days attending and date of registration; special events, pitch and consulting sessions, extra workshops, accommodations not included
Additional information:	Send a catalog-sized SASE for a brochure or see Web site for more details
Past speakers include:	Donald Maass, Angela Rinaldi, Frank Ahearn, Marjorie Reynolds, Elizabeth Lyon, Michael Larsen, Elizabeth Pomada

WRITERS' LEAGUE OF TEXAS

1501 W. 5TH STREET, SUITE E-2
AUSTIN TX 78703

PHONE / FAX
512.499.8914
512.499.0441

E-MAIL
wlt@writersleague.org

WEB SITE
www.writersleague.org

Held:	July
Focus:	Fiction and nonfiction
Additional information:	Brochures are available on request. Speakers include many well-respected agents.

WRITERS RETREAT WORKSHOP

5721 MAGAZINE ST,. #161
NEW ORLEANS LA 70115

PHONE	E-MAIL	WEB SITE
800.642.2494	wrw04@netscape.com	www.writersretreat-workshop.com

Coordinator:	Jason Sitzes, director
Core staff:	Author Elizabeth Lyon, editor-in-residence; Lorin Oberweger, author; Dr. Keith Wilson
Held:	Late May–early June
Description:	Participants spend 10 days immersed in their novel, taking daily instructional classes based on the late Gary Provost's acclaimed course; 1-on-1 meetings with writers and agents; diagnostic sessions; readings; workshops; and ample writing time. Optional classes begin at 7 a.m. and the last session begins at 10 p.m.
Focus:	All genres
Number of attendees:	30 maximum
Location:	Marydale Retreat Center in Erlanger, KY (just south of Cincinnati). Rooms are private with small writing areas, beautiful outdoor grounds available for walking, running, writing, etc.
Cost:	$1,695 ($1,595 for returning participants and early registrants); includes all lodging, 3 meals daily (plus all snacks and drinks), classes, materials—everything but travel and miscellaneous items
Additional information:	Robin Hardy New Student Scholarship available (full tuition) for first-time participants. Register early. See Web site for updates.
Past speakers include:	Best-selling mystery novelist Nancy Pickard and author Lynn Lott (co-authors of *The Seven Steps On the Writer's Path),* literary agents

WRITING FOR CHILDREN WORKSHOP AT CHAUTAUQUA

HIGHLIGHTS FOUNDATION
814 COURT STREET,
HONESDALE PA 18431

PHONE / FAX	E-MAIL	WEB SITE
570.253.1192	contact@	www.
570.253.0179	highlightsfoundation.org	highlightsfoundation.org

Coordinator: Kent L. Brown, Jr., executive director

Held: July

Description: Enhances the personal and professional development of the writers and illustrators of children's literature by providing support and guidance through workshops and educational programs. Attendees have the opportunity to work in individual and small-group sessions with some of the most accomplished and prominent authors, illustrators, editors, and publishers in the world of children's literature. Participants attend workshop sessions, lectures, and panel discussions on a variety of topics ranging from plot development and characterization to submitting a manuscript for publication and finding children's markets. The manuscript reader and mentoring program allows attendees to meet 1-on-1 with individual members of the Chautauqua Workshop faculty who review and critique their work. (Manuscripts are requested ahead of time for the program.)

Location: Chautauqua Institution in Chautauqua, NY. Conference planners coordinate accommodations and ground transportation to and from airports, trains, and bus stations in Erie, PA, and Jamestown/Buffalo, NY, area for conference attendees.

Additional information: See Web site for workshop history, background, and course listing

Past distinguished faculty: Dominic Barth, John Barth, Ray Bradbury, Pat Conroy, Hal Crowther, James Dickey, Andrea Early, Peter P. Jacobi, Rod Ebright, Jean Reynolds, Andrew Gutelle, Susan Campbell Bartoletti, Bernette Ford, William Taylor, Larry Dane Brimner, Pat Broderick, George Ford, Susan Taylor Brown, Patricia Lee Gauch, Pamela Munoz Ryan, Mary Lou Carney, James Cross Giblin, Steven Herb, Joy Cowley, Carolyn P. Yoder, Ben White, Bernice Cullinan, Marge Facklam, Neil Waldman, Rosanna Hansen, Laurence Pringle, Jay Heale, William Styron, Shelby Foote, Horton Foote, Anne Rivers Siddons, Lee Smith, Daniel Wallace, Peter Jenkins, Jill McCorkle

WRITING TODAY—BIRMINGHAM-SOUTHERN COLLEGE

BOX 549003
BIRMINGHAM AL 35254

PHONE / FAX	**E-MAIL**	**WEB SITE**
205.226.4921	dcwilson@bsc.edu	www.bsc.edu/special
205.226.4931		events/writingtoday

Coordinator: Annie Green

Held: March

Description: Teaches the craft of writing and the mechanics of becoming published to writers at every stage of their development, from the casually interested to the practicing professional; honors literary masters.

Focus: All genres (including short stories, essays, and magazine writing), researching, editing, publishing

Number of attendees: 250

Number of speakers: 12–15

Location: Birmingham-Southern College campus. Conference attendees stay at area hotels.

Cost: $120 for the 2-day event, including morning coffee and rolls, luncheon, and reception ($130 after deadline); $65 for 1 day's events, including morning coffee and rolls, luncheon, and reception; $35 for lunch only on either day. Individual manuscript critique for an additional $40 fee.

Additional information: Hackney Literary Awards, open to writers nationwide, are presented in conjunction with the conference. Annual competition awards $5,000 in prizes for poetry and short story, plus a $5,000 award for an unpublished novel.

AGENTS DIRECTORY

DOMINICK ABEL LITERARY AGENCY

146 W. 82ND ST., 1B
NEW YORK NY 10024

PHONE / FAX
212.877.0710
212.595.3133

E-MAIL
agency@dalainc.com

Background: Mr. Abel has been an agent since 1975. Member of AAR.
Represents: Adult fiction and nonfiction
Does not represent: Children's, poetry

| HOW TO SUBMIT | **Send proposal by mail; include the first 3 chapters (no more than 50 pages) and a synopsis. No e-mail queries.** |

AGENTS INC. FOR MEDICAL PROFESSIONALS

P.O. BOX 4956
FRESNO CA 93744

Agent: Sydney Harriet, Ph.D.
Background: Dr. Harriet has been an agent for 15 years and handles 13 clients. Sold 3 titles in the last year. Prior to becoming an agent, Dr. Harriet was an English professor.
Represents: Health-related nonfiction and fiction (mystery and literary)
Workshop topics: Craft; how to obtain an agent; book proposals; writing successful fiction.
Success story: George Neil's book *Infantry Soldier* was rejected by 23 publishers; went on to become a big seller.
Clients: Maureen Keane, Steven Bratman, M.D.
Recent sales: *Men Who Can't Lose Weight* (Random House); *Women Who Can't Lose Weight* (Random House)

✓ **TIPS**
Don't call. Submit the best damn query letter in the world.

| HOW TO SUBMIT | **Send query letter by mail.** |

THE AHEARN AGENCY

2021 PINE ST.
NEW ORLEANS LA 70118-5456

✓ TIPS
*For new writers—
send ONLY what is
requested, no more,
no less!*

Agent:	Pamela G. Ahearn
Background:	Ms. Ahearn has been an agent for 20 years and handles 25–30 clients. Sold 15-20 titles in the last year. Member of MWA, RWA. Prior to becoming an agent, Ms. Ahearn worked at Bantam as an editor. She works extensively with new authors editorially.
Represents:	Women's fiction, suspense
Does not represent:	Science fiction/fantasy, juvenile, inspirational, poetry, essays
Workshop topics:	How to approach/get an agent; how to work with agents
Conferences:	RWA, Malice Domestic
Success story:	*The Amber Room* was sold after several years and 19 rejections for a substantial sum.
Clients:	Steve Berry, Sabrina Jefferies, Michele Albert, Laura Joh Rowland, Carlene Thompson
Recent sales:	*Do Me, Do My Roots,* by Rendahl (Pocket); *Take the Bait,* by Hubbard (Pocket); *The Amber Room,* by Berry (Ballantine); *The Perfumed Sleeve,* by Rowland (St. Martin's)

HOW TO SUBMIT | **Send query letter by mail with SASE or e-mail (no samples or attachments).**

ALLRED AND ALLRED LITERARY AGENTS

7834 ALABAMA AVE.
CANOGA PARK CA 91304-4905

✓ TIPS
Be professional.

Agents:	Robert Allred, Kim Allred
Background:	Mr. Allred has been an agent for 15 years. The agency sold 4 titles last year and currently handles 6 clients. Before opening his own agency, Mr. Allred worked at other agencies.
Represents:	Fiction, nonfiction
Clients:	Mike Spence, Alicia Holbrooke
Recent sales:	*Treason Alliance,* by Mike Spence; *Myths and Markets,* by Alicia Holbrooke

HOW TO SUBMIT | **Send query letter, synopsis, and first 25 pages by mail. No fax or e-mail queries.**

THE ALPERN GROUP

15645 ROYAL OAK RD.
ENCINO CA 91436

E-MAIL
mail@alperngroup.com

Agents:	Jeff Alpern, Liz Wise, Jeff Aghassi
Represents:	Movie scripts, TV scripts, stage plays

HOW TO SUBMIT   **Send query letter only by mail with SASE or e-mail.**

MIRIAM ALTSHULER LITERARY AGENCY

53 OLD POST RD. N.
RED HOOK NY 12571

PHONE
845.758.9408

FAX
845.758.3118

Agent:	Miriam Altshuler
Background:	Ms. Altshuler currently handles 40 clients. Member of AAR.
Represents:	Nonfiction: biography, autobiography, memoir, multicultural, history, environmental, pop culture, psychology, sociology, women's issues; Fiction: literary, mainstream, multicultural, thriller
Does not represent:	Mystery, self-help, spiritual, sci-fi/fantasy, poetry
Conferences:	Bread Loaf Writers' Conference, Washington Writer's Conference

HOW TO SUBMIT   **Send query letter by mail with SASE. No e-mail or fax queries. Returns materials only with SASE. Most new clients are obtained through referral.**

MARCIA AMSTERDAM AGENCY

41 W. 82ND ST.
NEW YORK NY 10024-5613

PHONE
212.873.4945

Background:	Member of WGA.
Represents:	Nonfiction: parenting, pop culture, self-help; Fiction: action/adventure, crime, mystery, suspense, contemporary and historical romance, science fiction, thriller, young adult; Script (feature film, TV MOW, sitcom): comedy, mainstream, mystery, suspense, romantic comedy, romantic drama

HOW TO SUBMIT | **Send an outline and 3 sample chapters by mail with SASE.**

BART ANDREWS & ASSOCIATES INC.

7510 SUNSET BLVD., SUITE 100
LOS ANGELES CA 90046

PHONE   **FAX**
310.271.9916   310.271.9916

✓ **TIPS**
Pet peeve: *Bothering the agent. When he hears something, so will you!*

Agent:	Bart Andrews
Background:	Mr. Andrews has been an agent since 1982 and currently handles 22 clients. Sold 12 titles in the last year. Member of WGA. Prior to opening his agency, he was an author and has written 27 books.
Represents:	Nonfiction, biography
Does not represent:	Fiction
Workshop topics:	How to best deal with an agent
Conferences:	UCLA
Success story:	*Loving Lucy*—after 24 submissions we had a sale. So far, 85,000 hardcovers in print.
Clients:	J. Randy Taraborrelli

HOW TO SUBMIT | **Send simple 1-page query letter by mail with SASE.**

APPLESEEDS MANAGEMENT

200 E. 30TH ST., SUITE 302
SAN BERNARDINO CA 92404

PHONE
909.882.1667

Manager:	S. James Foiles
Represents:	Mystery novels with a detective who could sustain a continuing series

HOW TO SUBMIT | **Send query letter by mail with SASE. Reports in 2 weeks on queries, 2 months on manuscripts. Receives 15% commission on domestic sales.**

ARCADIA

31 LAKE PL. N.
DANBURY CT 06810

PHONE	**FAX**	**E-MAIL**
203.797.0993	203.730.2594	arcadialit@att.net

Agent:	Victoria Gould Pryor
Background:	Ms. Pryor has been an agent for 30+ years. Member of AAR, Authors Guild. Arcadia has represented many critical and commercial successes. "Although I accept very few new authors, if I believe in someone's work I'm willing to share my experience and tenacity to help that author reach his or her potential."
Represents:	High-quality nonfiction in the areas of science and medicine. I'm interested in new work in those subjects or other serious nonfiction that's intriguing and wonderful, especially books that change a reader's way of looking at the world.
Does not represent:	Children's/young adult, science fiction/fantasy, humor, horror, how-to books
Clients:	Dr. Bernie Siegel, Jonathan Weiner

HOW TO SUBMIT | **Send query letter by mail or e-mail without attachments; no phone calls, please. Query letters must include an SASE or e-mail address for a response. Ideally, a full proposal should contain an overview/synopsis, detailed chapter outline, and sample chapter(s).**

✓ **TIPS**
If you want your work to be treated with respect, you have to earn it. There are many excellent books available to teach you about the book business and help you hone your presentation. It's a rough, competitive world out there, and whatever you present has to be intelligent, well-developed and thoughtful. Anything less than superb is not good enough. Be prepared for a wild ride. You'll need strength, a high threshold for frustration and a well-developed sense of humor and adventure.

AUTHENTIC CREATIONS LITERARY AGENCY

875 LAWRENCEVILLE-SUWANEE RD.
SUITE 310-306
LAWRENCEVILLE, GA 30043

PHONE / FAX	E-MAIL	WEB SITE
770.339.3774	marylee@authentic	www.authenticcreations.
770.339.7126	creations.com *or*	com
	ron@authenticcreations.com	

Agents: Ronald E. Laitsch, Mary Lee Laitsch

Background: Mr. Laitsch has been an agent for 9 years and handles 40–50 authors. Sold 20 titles in the last year. Member of AAR, Authors Guild. "We provide our authors with strong marketing of manuscripts to potential publishers and continue to work with our authors after the book is published to maximize sales of the work. We have established a good reputation of representing authors who are willing to build a writing career by working closely with the publisher to put out a quality product edited to meet the demographics of the publishing house. We are actively working to expand our list of published authors." Prior to working at this agency, Ms. Laitsch was a librarian and Mr. Laitsch was an attorney.

Represents: Mainstream fiction, mystery, suspense, romance (historical and contemporary), women's fiction, and some literary and science fiction. We are very flexible in the area of nonfiction and have experienced great success in this area. Most notable is our continuing success with true crime and business-related books.

Does not represent: New Age, poetry, coming-of-age, children's

Workshop topics: Query letters to agents; process for publishing a book; trends in the book industry

Conferences: BEA

Success story: We recently sold a manuscript that a well-known New York agency could not place. We were able to make the sale after a number of submissions. Clearly, the author was quite pleased with our efforts to sell her work.

Recent sales: *Beauchamp Beseiged,* by Elaine Knighton (Harlequin); *Bayou Moon,* by Caren Bevill (St. Martin's); *This is the Zodiac Speaking,* by Michael Kelleher (Praeger/Greenwood)

HOW TO SUBMIT **Send query letter, synopsis or proposal, and information about the author's publishing experiences, if any, by mail For nonfiction, it is important to let us know why you are qualified to write the manuscript.**

THE AXELROD AGENCY

55 MAIN ST., P.O. BOX 357
CHATHAM NY 12037

PHONE	FAX	E-MAIL:
518.392.2100	518.392.2944	steve@axelrodagency.com

Agent:	Steven Axelrod
Background:	Mr. Axelrod has been an agent for 25 years and handles 25 clients. Member of AAR. Prior to opening his agency, he worked at 3 other major NYC agencies.
Represents:	Exciting commercial fiction
Does not represent:	Highly literary fiction, general nonfiction
Conferences:	RWA

HOW TO SUBMIT | **Send query letter or partial manuscript by mail with SASE.**

MALAGA BALDI LITERARY AGENCY

204 W. 84TH ST., SUITE 3C
NEW YORK NY 10024

PHONE	E-MAIL
212.579.5078	mbaldi@aol.com

Agent:	Malaga Baldi
Background:	Ms. Baldi has been an agent for 20+ years and handles approximately 25 clients. Sold 10 titles last year. She was self-employed and worked for 2 other agents before opening her own agency. Her agency is small, independent, eclectic, edgy. Actively building client list.
Represents:	Cultural history, memoir, quality adult fiction, gay and lesbian fiction and nonfiction, narrative nonfiction. Looking for the great American novel, narrative nonfiction that blends several disciplines, a memoir of the making of an architect (comparable to Scott Turow's *One L* about law school).
Does not represent:	Romance, science fiction, how to, self-help, New Age, Christian, fantasy, young adult
Clients:	Kate Bornstein, William J. Mann, Patty Dann, Robert Taylor, Jim Sullivan, Martin Moran, Mona Vold, Rick Whitaker, Yannick Murphy, Frank Urso
Recent sales:	*Sweet & Crazy,* by Patty Dann (St. Martins); *Whose Eye on Which Sparrow,* by Robert Taylor (Haworth); *The Edge of Midnite,* by William J. Mann (Random House UK); *The Tricky Part,* by Martin Moran (Beacon)

HOW TO SUBMIT | **Send a sharp query letter by mail. Referrals are wonderful. On the basis of the query letter I will request the manuscript along with a SAS jiffy bag.**

✓ **TIPS**

Be persistent. There are many agents. Always include postage and an envelope if you want the manuscript returned. Be patient—it takes time to read a manuscript. Do your research. Know what type of work the agent represents. Don't send a photo of yourself. Manuscripts should be typed on white paper, unbound, double-spaced, single-sided ALWAYS.

★ **MAGAZINE RECOMMENDATIONS**
Poets & Writers • Purple Crayon • Publishers Marketplace (It is worth every penny.)

BALKIN AGENCY, INC.

P.O. BOX 222
AMHERST MA 01004

PHONE
413.548.9835

FAX
413.548.9836

Agent:	Rick Balkin
Represents:	Nonfiction books, scholarly books, textbooks
Does not represent:	Children's, fiction, poetry, screenplays, computer books

HOW TO SUBMIT **Send query letter, proposal package, and outline by mail with SASE. Finds most new clients by referral.**

THE BARN HOUSE

244 WESTSIDE RD.
NORFOLK CT 06058

PHONE
860.542.5733

FAX
860.542.5469

E-MAIL
robertducas@aol.com

Agent:	Robert Ducas
Background:	Prior to opening his agency, Mr. Ducas ran the *London Times* and the *Sunday Times* in the U.S. from 1966 to 1981.
Represents:	Nonfiction: journalistic exposé, biography, history; Fiction: mystery, suspense, thriller, family saga, contemporary issues, sports, mainstream, literary
Does not represent:	Women's fiction

HOW TO SUBMIT **Send query letter by mail with SASE. Finds most clients by referral.**

THE BARRY-SWAYNE LITERARY AGENCY

4 MANITOU RD.
GARRISON NY 10524

PHONE / FAX	E-MAIL	WEB SITE
845.424.2448	sbarry@swayne	www.swayneagency.
845.424.2490	agency.com	com

Agents:	Susan Barry, Lisa Swayne
Background:	This agency has been in operation for 3^1/$_2$ years. Currently handles approximately 45 clients. Sold approximately 25 titles in the last year. The agents have 17 years' experience in publishing, including editorial director at McGraw-Hill, executive editor at John Wiley & Sons, and senior editor New York Institute of Finance (S&S imprint). "This agency has deep connections in business publishing at every major publisher. Also represents ghostwriters for the corporate writing market. Still actively building client list in history and trade science."
Represents:	Nonfiction only! Emphasis on business, history, literary nonfiction, trade science, horses (riding skills, horse care)
Does not represent:	Fiction, romance, science fiction, children's, spiritual
Clients:	Guy Consolmagno, S.J.; Adam Penenberg; Holly Firfer; Amey Stone; Mike Brewster; John Kador; David Collins; Ernest Dillon
Recent sales:	Multi-title business series, *The Manager's Bootcamp,* by Gartner Inc. (Harvard Business School Press); *Handwriting: A Sentimental History*, by Matthew Battles (W.W. Norton); *Bitter Medicine: How the FDA Has Abused its Power,* by Fran Hawthorne (John Wiley & Sons)

HOW TO SUBMIT	**By referral only.**

✓ TIPS
Use referrals—most agents don't respond to unsolicited queries; do not send multiple e-mails regarding the same proposal; try to bring an agent into the process early; unpublished just means you haven't had a book published—it doesn't mean you've never been published in a magazine or newsletter; try to build a portfolio of published materials before embarking on a book. For business books, make sure your client list is national (or international) rather than regional.

★ MAGAZINE
RECOMMENDATIONS
Harper's • Atlantic Monthly • The Economist • Wall Street Journal • Harvard Business Review • American Heritage • Practical Horseman • Dressage Today

109

BASKOW AGENCY

2948 E. RUSSELL RD.
LAS VEGAS NV 89120

PHONE
702.733.7818

FAX
702.733.2052

E-MAIL
jaki@baskow.com

Agent: Ms. Jaki Baskow
Represents: Feature film, TV movie-of-the-week; unique, all-American true stories; kids projects
Does not represent: Anything with heavy violence

HOW TO SUBMIT | **Send outline, proposal, and treatments.**

BEACON ARTISTS AGENCY

208 W. 30 ST.
NEW YORK NY 10001

PHONE
212.736.6630

FAX
212.868.1052

Agent: Patricia McLaughlin
Background: Ms. McLaughlin has been an agent for 14 years. Currently handles 25 clients. Sold 8–10 titles in the last year. Member of AAR, WGA. Prior to working at this agency, she got her MFA in theatre. She is still building her client list, has interest in young talent, has a strong reputation, and gives personal attention to her clients.
Represents: Plays, screenplays, TV
Does not represent: Novels, poetry, short stories

HOW TO SUBMIT | **By referral only!**

MEREDITH BERNSTEIN LITERARY AGENCY

2112 BROADWAY, SUITE 503A
NEW YORK NY 10023

PHONE	FAX
212.799.1007	212.799.1145

Agent:	Meredith Bernstein
Background:	Ms. Bernstein has been an agent for 27 years and represents approximately 65 clients. Member of AAR, RWA, WGA. Prior to working at this agency she was a story editor for film producers.
Represents:	Interesting fiction and nonfiction of all types, but it must be special
Does not represent:	Screenplays, poetry, military fiction
Workshop topics:	The agent/author relationship; how to promote your book
Success story:	A huge deal for Nancy Pickard, moving her from her longtime association with Pocket Books back to her "original" editor, Linda Marrow at Ballantine Books.
Clients:	Sharon Sala, Sandra Hill, Dinah Dinwiddie (Julia London), PC Cast, Dr. George Kessler, David Carroll, Michael Jahn, Robyn Freedman Spizman, Elizabeth Lyon, Martin Goldstein
Recent sales:	A 3-book deal for Nancy Pickard to Ballantine

✓ TIPS
Learn how to write a "stand out" query letter.

111

HOW TO SUBMIT **Send query letter, synopsis, and author's bio by mail only.**

DANIEL BIAL AGENCY

41 W. 83RD ST., SUITE 5-C
NEW YORK NY 10024-5246

PHONE	**FAX**	**E-MAIL**
212.721.1786	309.213.0230	dbialagency@juno.com

Agent:	Daniel Bial
Background:	Mr. Bial has been an agent for 12 years. "I'm a member of the OAG—The 'Other Agents Group.' It's an informal bunch of agents, most working on Manhattan's Upper West Side, and we get together once a month to talk over issues, gossip, etc. Often we invite an editor to address us and fill us in on what's happening at their house." Prior to opening his agency, Bial was an editor for 14 years—2 at Holt, 10 at HarperCollins, and 2 at Longmeadow Press, an imprint of Waldenbooks that, during his short time there, became a house that published material for bookstores across the nation, not just Walden stores. "My clients know they can count on my personal attention. I have excellent editing skills, so if their proposal needs some touch-up, I'm sure to help them."
Represents:	Adult nonfiction: business, current events, entertainment, gift, health, history, humor, language, New Age, psychology, reference, science, self-help, sports, travel
Does not represent:	Poetry, children's/young adult, genre fiction, screenplays, academic treatises

HOW TO SUBMIT

Send query letter by mail with SASE or e-mail (no attachments).

BIGSCORE PRODUCTIONS

P.O. BOX 4575
LANCASTER PA 17604

PHONE / FAX	E-MAIL	WEB SITE
717.293.0247	bigscore@bigscore	www.bigscore
717.293.1945	productions.com	productions.com

Agents:	David A. Robie, Sharon Hanby-Robie, Deb Strubel (associate agent)
Background:	All Bigscore agents have publishing and media experience and have been agents since 1995. Currently handles 30–50 clients. Sold approximately 20 titles in the last year.
Represents:	All fiction and nonfiction
Does not represent:	Erotic fiction, alternative lifestyles, poetry
Clients:	Stan Toler, Ruth Scofield, Brad Densmore, George Givens, Buddy Levy, Doug Connelly
Recent sales:	*Hot Bod Fusion,* by Robin Forward (Marlowe/Avalon); *Minute Motivators,* by Stan Toler (Honor/Cook); *The Great Bible Trivia Workout,* by Brad Densmore (Zondervan/HarperCollins)

HOW TO SUBMIT
Send query letter by e-mail first. See our Web site for guidelines.

113

DAVID BLACK LITERARY AGENCY, INC.

156 FIFTH AVE.
NEW YORK NY 10001

PHONE	FAX
212.242.5080	212.924.6609

Agent:	David Black
Background:	Mr. Black has been an agent for 15 years. Member of AAR.
Represents:	Narrative nonfiction
Does not represent:	Romance, science fiction, children's

HOW TO SUBMIT
Send query letter and synopsis by mail with SASE.

BLEECKER STREET ASSOCIATES, INC.

532 LAGUARDIA PL., #617
NEW YORK NY 10012

PHONE
212.677.4492

FAX
212.388.0001

✓ TIPS
*Please don't call,
e-mail, or fax about
your book. Don't send
any part of the man-
uscript or proposal
unless specifically
requested by agency.*

Agent: Agnes Birnbaum

Background: Ms. Birnbaum has been an agent for 20 years
and handles about 50 clients. Sold 30 titles
in the last year. Member of AAR, RWA, MWA.
Prior to working at this agency, she was an editor
at Simon & Schuster, NAL, and Dell. Her agency
is known for hands-on representation, and she
does particularly well with first-time authors.

Represents: History, women's interest, science, New Age,
parenting, relationship, chick lit, mysteries and
thrillers, how-to, cookbooks, sport psychology,
Judaica, African-American, current events

Does not represent: Westerns, science fiction, academic or scholarly
books, poetry

Clients: Bevin Alexander, Amy Wong Keltner, Brad &
Sherry Steiger, Dicey Deere

Recent sales: *Sailing Into the Abyss,* by W. Benedetto
(Kensington); *Mars On a Budget,* by Andrew
Mishkin (Berkley); *Handy Geology Answer
Book,* by Pat & Tom Svarney (Visible Ink).

114

| HOW TO SUBMIT |

**Send 1-page query letter summarizing
manuscript and author's background by
mail with SASE. Do not send text, outline,
proposal, etc.**

REID BOATES LITERARY AGENCY

69 COOKS CROSSROAD
PITTSTOWN NJ 08867

PHONE
908.730.8523

FAX
908.730.8931

E-MAIL
boatesliterary@att.net

Agent:	Reid Boates
Background:	Mr. Boates has been an agent for 18+ years and handles 30 clients. Prior to opening his agency, he was vice president and senior editor at Warner Books. This agency has a solid reputation, is actively building a client list, and offers personal service and editorial for clients.
Represents:	Adult general interest nonfiction
Does not represent:	Fiction
Workshop topics:	Craft of writing and preparation; the publishing process
Clients:	Coleman Barks, Joseph Goldstein, Stephen Singular, Jon Winokur
Recent sales:	*Anyone You Want Me to Be: A True Story of Romance and Death on the Internet,* by John Douglas & Stephen Singular (Simon & Schuster); *Ruling Your World,* by Sakyong Mipham Rinpoche (Riverhead/Putnam)

115

HOW TO SUBMIT	**By referral only.**

THE BOHRMAN AGENCY

8889 BEVERLY BLVD., SUITE 811
LOS ANGELES CA 90048

PHONE
310.550.5444

Agents:	Caren Bohrman, Angela Ryberg (sub-agent)
Background:	Ms. Bohrman has been an agent for 20 years. Member of WGA, DGA. The agency is known for personal contact, strategy, hard work and creativity.
Represents:	Feature films, teleplays, books, plays, pilots

HOW TO SUBMIT	**By referral only with postcard.**

BOOKENDS, LLC

136 LONG HILL RD.
GILLETTE NJ 07933

PHONE	E-MAIL	WEB SITE
908.604.2652	editor@bookends-inc.com	www.bookends-inc.com

116

Agents: Jessica Faust, Jacky Sach

Background: The agency currently handles around 50 clients, and sold approximately 35 books in the last year. BookEnds, LLC, is a literary agency cofounded by Ms. Faust and Ms. Sach. Established in 1999 as a book packaging company, BookEnds now operates primarily as a literary agency focusing on fiction and nonfiction books for adult audiences. Ms. Faust and Ms. Sach work closely with their authors to develop strong book proposals and careers. Still actively building a client list, they always look forward to bringing on new authors. Both Ms. Faust and Ms. Sach were editors prior to starting BookEnds. Ms. Faust was an acquisitions editor at Berkley Publishing and Macmillan, where she had the unique opportunity to work with both fiction and nonfiction. At Berkley she acquired romance, mystery, and nonfiction in all areas. At Macmillan she worked on the popular *Complete Idiot's Guide* series. Memberships include RWA, MWA. Ms. Sach was senior managing editor and managing editor of E Books at Berkley Books (a division of Penguin Group).

Represents: Adult nonfiction: pets, self-help, health, women's issues, parenting, finance; Adult fiction: mystery, romance, chick lit, women's issues

Does not represent: Sci-fi/fantasy, children's, poetry, military thrillers

Workshop topics: MS. FAUST: Writing a query letter; questions to ask an agent before signing on; understanding rejection; finding an agent
MS. SACH: Rejection; submission letters; query letters

Conferences: Bouchercon, Malice Domestic

Success story: We've had many successes—some unusual—from selling a book after 2 years, to selling a book the day we took it on. One title we had given up on, after more than 25 rejections, finally sold when an editor dug it out of her submissions pile 2 years after we first sent it in.

Clients: MS. FAUST: Barbara Gale, Gabriella Anderson Dara Girard, Dr. Rachel McClintock Franklin Dr. Patti Britton, Dr. Bernardo Carducci
MS. SACH: Kathy Brandt, Diana Killian, Marlene Browne, Dr. Laurie Helgoe, Libby Hellmann

Recent sales: **MS. FAUST:** *Dr. Rachel's Guide to Multiple Pregnancy*, by Dr. Rachel McClintock Franklin (St. Martins Press); *Resilience at Work*, by Salvatore R. Maddi and Deborah M. Khoshaba (Amacom); *Discover Your Inner Blueprint*, by Rev. Denny Daikeler (Rodale); *The Complete Guide to Mutts*, by Margaret H. Bonham (Wiley); *The Complete Idiot's Guide to Algebra*, by W. Michael Kelley (Alpha)

MS. SACH: *Our Empty Rooms*, by Jennifer Patrick (soho press); *Complete Idiot's Guide to Talmud*, by Rabbi Aaron Parry (alpha books); *Your Pocket Spell Guide*, by Kerri Connor (New Page); *Combat Ring Nerves*, by Diane Peters Mayer (Howell/Wiley books)

| HOW TO SUBMIT |

Send proposal by mail; include the first 3 chapters (no more than 50 pages) and a synopsis. E-mail queries accepted.

communication who you are, what your book is, what prior conversations you have had, etc. We receive a huge number of queries every day and cannot keep track of everyone we speak with. Make sure the agency represents the type of book you have written. Many queries contain much irrelevant information (such as family vacation history, unrelated hobbies, age, weight, etc.). We also receive a lot of strange gifts, which are completely unnecessary. Both advise that you join local and national writers groups— there's nothing better than the newsletters or magazines provided by both RWA and MWA. The best way to learn about the business is through these 2 organizations and their many chapters.

★ RECOMMENDATIONS
An educated writer is an invaluable asset, so investigate:
How to Be Your Own Literary Agent, by Richard Curtis; *Complete Idiot's Guide to Getting Published*, by Sheree Bykofsky; *Writer's Guide to Book Editors & Literary Agents*, by Jeff Herman; *Poets & Writers*; *Literary Marketplace*; *Publishers Weekly*; *Romantic Times*; *Writer's Digest*; Writers' boards on the Internet

BOOKS & SUCH

4788 CARISSA AVE.
SANTA ROSA CA 95405

PHONE	E-MAIL	WEB SITE
707.538.4184	janet@janetgrant.com	www.janetgrant.com

✓ TIPS
Realize that agents receive a large amount of queries and proposals. (I receive at least 100 each week.) Don't call an agent to ask what they do or for career advice. That isn't a professional way to approach an agent.

Agent: Janet Kobobel Grant

Background: Ms. Grant has been an agent since 1997 and handles 40 clients. Sold approximately 75 titles in the last year. Member of CBA, AAR, AWSA, Writer's View. Prior to opening her agency, she was an editor at Zondervan and a managing editor at *Focus on the Family*. "While a strong editorial view is part of the package, so is career planning, rather than just trying to place the current work."

Represents: Mostly spiritual or Christian-themed work; some placement in the general market. Children's, young adult, and adult fiction and nonfiction

Does not represent: Horror, thrillers

Conferences: Sandy Cover Writers Conference, Mt. Hermon Writers Conference

Success story: I sold a first-time novel I had submitted to publishers for 2 years and ended up with 2 publishers wanting it at the same time!

Clients: Robin Jones Gunn, BJ Hoff, Kathy Collard Miller

Recent sales: *Threads of Light* fiction series, by Rene Gutteridge (Tyndale); *Gardenias for Breakfast*, by Robin Jones Gunn (W Publishers)

HOW TO SUBMIT | **Send query letter by mail or e-mail. A referral puts you at the top of the stack.**

118

THE JOAN BRANDT AGENCY

788 WESLEY DR.
ATLANTA GA 30305-3933

PHONE
404.351.8877

Agent: Joan Brandt

Background: Ms. Brandt has been an agent for 28 years and currently handles 25 clients. Prior to opening her agency, she worked at Sterling Lord Literistic.

Represents: Nonfiction; Fiction (novels and short story collections): mainstream, literary, mystery, suspense, thriller, family sagas

Does not represent: Romance, horror, science fiction, historical, western, scientific, technical

HOW TO SUBMIT | **Send brief synopsis by mail with SASE.**

CURTIS BROWN LTD.

10 ASTOR PL.
NEW YORK NY 10003-6935

1750 MONTGOMERY ST.
SAN FRANCISCO CA 94111

PHONE
212.473.5400 (NY)

PHONE
415.954.8566 (CA)

Agents: Laura Blake Peterson; Ellen Geiger; Emilie Jacobson, Vice President; Maureen Walters, Vice President; Virginia Knowlton (literary, adult, children's); Timothy Knowlton (film, screenplays, plays); Ed Wintle (film, screenplays, plays); Mitchell Waters; Elizabeth Harding; Douglas Stewart; Kristen Manges; Dave Barber (translation rights)

Represents: A wide range of fiction, nonfiction, children's books, screenplays, plays

HOW TO SUBMIT

Send query letter by mail with SASE. Contacts: Perry Knowlton, Chairman; Timothy Knowlton, CEO; Peter Ginsberg, President.

119

KNOX BURGER ASSOCIATES

425 MADISON AVE.
NEW YORK NY 10017

PHONE
212.759.8600

FAX
212.759.9428

Agents: Knox Burger (literary), Pamela Malpas (translation rights)

Background: Founded in 1970 and merged with Harold Ober Associates in 2000. Members of AAR (affiliate of Harold Ober Associates Incorporated).

Represents: General fiction, nonfiction

Does not represent: Plays, film scripts

HOW TO SUBMIT

Send query letter by mail with SASE. No fax or e-mail queries. No unsolicited manuscripts. Most clients obtained through recommendations.

SHEREE BYKOFSKY ASSOCIATES, INC.

577 SECOND AVE., PMB 109
NEW YORK NY 10016

PHONE	E-MAIL	WEB SITE
212.244.4144	shereebee@aol.com	www.shereebee.com

120

Agent: Sheree Bykofsky

Background: Incorporated 1991, this agency handles over 100 clients. Sold 100 titles in the last year. Member of AAR, ABPA, WNBA. Prior to opening her agency, Ms. Bykofsky was Executive Editor at The Stonesong Press. Full service agency, wide-ranging experience, and excellent reputation. "I'm the author of *The Complete Idiot's Guide to Getting Published* and I teach publishing at NYU."

Represents: Nonfiction: self help, business, spirituality, women's issues, psychology, finance, music; Fiction: literary/commercial, mystery, women's

Does not represent: Sci-fi/fantasy, westerns, poetry, horror, screenplays

Workshop topics: The 6 secrets of getting published; finding and working with an agent

Success story: Taro Gold's *Open Your Mind, Open Your Life* is the bestselling book of Eastern wisdom.

Clients: Taro Gold, Richard Roeper, Andy Straka, Bob Berkowitz, Nicholas Boothman, Heather Swain, Supermodel Roshumba, Jeff Tamarkin

Recent sales: *Could It Be My Thyroid?,* by Dr. Sheldon Rubenfeld (M. Evans and Company); *10 Sure Signs a Movie Character is Doomed,* by Richard Roeper (Hyperion Press); *Heart and Sole,* by Jane Eldershaw (St. Martin's Press); *Decorating with Funky Shui,* by Jennifer & Kitty O'Neil (Andrews McMeel Publishing)

HOW TO SUBMIT	**Send query letter by mail with SASE.**

CASTIGLIA LITERARY AGENCY

1155 CAMINO DEL MAR, SUITE 510
DEL MAR CA 92014

PHONE	FAX	WEB SITE
858.755.8761	858.755.7063	www.publishersmarket-place.com/members/CastigliaAgency

Agents: Julie Castiglia, Winifred Golden

Background: Ms. Castiglia has been an agent for 15 years; Ms. Golden for 17 years. They represent approximately 50 clients. Prior to opening the Castiglia Agency, Ms. Castiglia "was an author [with] 3 published books to my credit plus poetry in literary anthologies. I also worked for 5 years with a large agency as their trade book agent." In 2003 we sold 19 books up to the end of July; 20 books in 2002.

Represents: MS. CASTIGLIA: Brilliant literary novels, ethnic fiction, chick lit, unusual thrillers and mysteries, cutting-edge science and health books, biography, unique parenting books with a different hook—same with women's issues, and narrative nonfiction with excellent credentials
MS. GOLDEN: Sci-fi, quirky nonfiction, high-profile true crime, mainstream fiction, suspense thrillers, narrative nonfiction

Does not represent: MS. CASTIGLIA: Horror, true crime, poetry, sci-fi/fantasy
MS. GOLDEN: Poetry, fantasy

Conferences: San Diego State University Writers' Conference

Recent sales: *Outwit Your Genes,* by Dr. Susan Mitchell and Dr. Catherine Christie (Simon & Schuster); *Maya Running,* by Anjali Banerjee (Random House); *Destined for the Throne,* by Julia Gelardi (St. Martin's); *Qi Gong For Staying Young,* by Shoshanna Katzman (Putnam); *Cereal for Dinner,* by Kristine Breese (St. Martin's); *One Foot in Love,* by Bil Wright (Simon & Schuster); *Bride in Overdrive,* by Jorie Green Mark (St. Martin's); *George Orwell A–Z,* by Kent Rasmussen and Philip Bader (Facts on File); *Classic Cottages,* by Douglas Keister and Brian Coleman (Gibbs Smith); *Young Black Rich and Famous,* by Todd Boyd (Doubleday)

121

HOW TO SUBMIT Send 1-page query letter by mail; with fiction, 1 or 2 pages of writing may be included. We prefer referrals. If an author includes no relevant information about him- or herself in the query letter, we reject.

CIRCLE OF CONFUSION LTD.

107-23 71ST RD., SUITE 300
FOREST HILLS NY 11375

E-MAIL
queries@circleofconfusion.com

Managers:	Lawrence Mattis, Trisha Smith, David Mattis
Background:	Circle of Confusion was formerly an agency but is now a management company representing screenwriters and directors. The company has 13 years of agent/management experience and 24 clients.
Represents:	Feature film, screenplays, comic books, video game properties for film and TV
Does not represent:	Novels
Clients:	The Wachowski Brothers, Gregg Chabot, Kevin Peterka, Simon Kinberg

HOW TO SUBMIT **Send query letter with short description of the project and author's background by mail or e-mail.**

WM CLARK ASSOCIATES

355 W. 22ND ST.
NEW YORK NY 10011

PHONE	E-MAIL	WEB SITE
212.675.2784	query@wmclark.com	www.wmclark.com

Agent: William Clark

Background: Mr. Clark has been an agent for 12 years and represents 35 clients. Sold more than 20 titles in the last year. Member of AAR. Prior to opening his agency, he worked at the William Morris Agency. "Offering individual focus and global presence, William Clark follows an innovative and broad-ranged approach to the representation of content and the talent that creates it, ranging from authors of first fiction and award-winning, best-selling narrative nonfiction, to international authors in translation, musicians, and artists. The agency mandate is to create new markets for existing clients, discover and nurture tomorrow's most interesting talent, and provide agency services to a new client base emanating from the digital media business wishing to expand into the print publication arena."

Represents: Nonfiction: biography, computers/technology, business /investing/finance, history, mind/body/spirit, health, travel, lifestyle, cookbooks, science, popular culture, current events; General and mainstream literary fiction

Does not represent: Horror, sci-fi/fantasy, detective, children's, young adult, Christian, screenplays

Clients: Peter Hessler, Dayle Haddon, Sarah Erdman, Björk, Keith Kachtick

Recent sales: *Falling Water Rising: Frank Lloyd Wright, E.J. Kaufmann, and America's Most Extraordinary House,* by Franklin Toker (Alfred A. Knopf); *City On Fire: Burning Man and the Post-Millennial Search for Meaning,* by Brian Doherty (Little, Brown & Co.); *The Bush-Hater's Handbook: An A–Z Guide to the Most Appalling Presidency of the Past 100 Years,* by Jack Huberman (Nation Books); *The Book of "Exodus": The Making and Meaning of Bob Marley's Album of the Century,* by Vivien Goldman (Crown)

HOW TO SUBMIT	Send query letter, concise description of work, synopsis/outline, biographical information, and publishing history, if any, by e-mail only. E-mails with attachments will be deleted unread. Responds in 4 weeks (usually). Does not respond to screenplay pitches.

123

RUTH COHEN, INC., LITERARY AGENCY

P.O. BOX 2244
LA JOLLA CA 92038

PHONE
858.456.5805

Agent:	Ruth Cohen
Background:	Ms. Cohen has been an agent for 20+ years. Member of AAR, RWA, Authors Guild. "We listen, we help, we offer advice, we work together, we're honest, and we respond within 3–4 weeks."
Represents:	Quality writing in women's fiction, historical romances, strong character-driven mysteries, juvenile fiction of all ages
Does not represent:	Sci-fi, film scripts, rhyming books, poetry

HOW TO SUBMIT   **Send synopsis or outline and first chapter or first 10 pages by mail with SASE.**

COLLINS MCCORMICK LITERARY AGENCY

10 LEONARD ST.
NEW YORK NY 10013

PHONE	**E-MAIL**	**WEB SITE**
212.219.2894	212.219.2895	http://collins mccormick.com

Agents:	Nina Collins, David McCormick, Leslie Falk
Background:	Member of AAR.
Represents:	Narrative nonfiction, literary and commercial fiction
Does not represent:	Children's, sci-fi, romance

HOW TO SUBMIT   **Send query letter by mail.**

COMMUNICATIONS AND ENTERTAINMENT, INC.

2851 SOUTH OCEAN BLVD., #5K
BOCA RATON FL 33432-8407

PHONE	FAX	E-MAIL
561.391.9575	561.391.7922	jlbearde@bellsouth.net

Agents:	James L. Bearden; Rosalind Ray, Esq.	✓ **TIPS**
Background:	Mr. Bearden has been an agent for 15 years and sold 5 titles in the last year. Member of WGA. Prior to working at this agency, he was a TV/film producer, director, and entertainment lawyer.	*Have patience.*
Represents:	Novels, movie scripts, television scripts	
Does not represent:	Children's or juvenile books and scripts	
Workshop topics:	Intellectual property issues; TV/film production; publishing	
Conferences:	AAR, RWA	

HOW TO SUBMIT	**Send query letter, synopsis, outline, or proposal by mail or e-mail.**

COMMUNICATIONS MANAGEMENT ASSOCIATES

1129 6 AVE., #1
ROCKFORD IL 61104-3147

PHONE	FAX
815.519.7740	815.964.3061

Agent:	Thomas R. Lee
Represents:	Horror, suspense, action, adventure, erotica

HOW TO SUBMIT	**Send query letter only by mail.**

DON CONGDON ASSOCIATES INC.

156 FIFTH AVE., SUITE 625
NEW YORK NY 10010-7002

PHONE	FAX	E-MAIL
212.645.1229	212.727.2688	dca@doncongdon.com

Agents: Don Congdon, Michael Congdon, Susan Ramer, Cristina Concepción

Background: Don Congdon Associates started in 1983 and handles over 100 clients. Members of AAR, Authors Guild. "We have a strong editorial reputation and are continuously adding to our client list."

Represents: Commercial and literary fiction and nonfiction

Does not represent: How-to, romance, religious, textbooks

HOW TO SUBMIT   **Send query letter by mail with SASE or e-mail (no attachments; all material must be copied and pasted into e-mail).**

CONNOR LITERARY AGENCY

2911 W. 71ST ST.
MINNEAPOLIS MN 55423

PHONE	FAX	E-MAIL
612.866.1426	612.869.4074	coolmkc@aol.com

Agents:	Marlene Connor Lynch, Deborah Coker
Background:	Ms. Connor Lynch as been an agent since 1985 and handles 20–30 clients. Prior to opening this agency, she was an editor with the Literary Guild, and an assistant editor for Simon & Schuster. Interested in writers with longevity. Special interest in and abilities with illustrated books. Works with all areas of publishing including multicultural titles and some children's books. Has had best-selling authors and has represented major corporations.
Represents:	Nonfiction: self-help, inspirational, relationships, astrology, political thought, history, current affairs, cooking, health, sexuality, parenting, pop psyche; Fiction: multicultural writers, some literary, historical, suspense, thrillers
Does not represent:	Romance, genre mysteries, young adult
Workshop topics:	The business in general; how to create a winning proposal; how to write a query letter
Clients:	Dr. Ronn Elmore, Thelma Balfour, Simplicity Pattern Company

HOW TO SUBMIT

Send query letter by e-mail. Responds only if interested in seeing ms. We're always seeking good new talent, but we tend to be overwhelmed with query letters so referrals are preferred.

✓ TIPS
Don't send a letter asking for information about the agency. Spend your postage on an actual query instead. Be confident, but don't sell yourself. Offer as much info as you can about your writing successes. Never be offended by a response you receive—not worth the energy.

127

THE DOE COOVER AGENCY

4509 INTERLAKE AVE., N. #256   P.O. BOX 668
WINCHESTER MA 01890   SEATTLE WA 98103

PHONE	FAX	WEB SITE
206.339.7183 (MA)	781.721.6727 (WA)	http://doecoover
781.721.6000 (WA)		agency.com

Agents: Doe Coover (nonfiction, Winchester office), Colleen Mohyde (fiction and nonfiction), Amanda Lewis (childrens), Frances Kennedy (assistant)

Background: The agency was founded in 1986 and has over 100 clients. This agency sold 25–30 titles in the last year. Prior to working at this agency, Ms. Coover and Ms. Mohyde both were editors for over a decade.

Represents: General nonfiction: cookbooks, social science, science, anthropology, business, finance, management, memoir/biography, women's health/parenting; Fiction: literary and contemporary (commercial)

Does not represent: Children's books, poetry

Conferences: BEA, IACP, Bread Loaf Writers' Conference

Clients: WGBH, *Gourmet* magazine, New England Aquarium, Peter Lynch, Jacques Pepin, Rick Bayless, Deborah Madison, Judy Rodgers, Sandra Shea, Robert Clark, Suzanne Berne

HOW TO SUBMIT

Send query letter and brief outline by mail with SASE. No e-mail or faxed queries. No unsolicited manuscripts. Returns material only with SASE.

RICHARD CURTIS ASSOCIATES, INC.

171 E. 74TH ST., SUITE 2
NEW YORK NY 10021

PHONE	FAX	WEB SITE
212.772.7363	212.772.7393	www.curtisagency.com

Agent: Richard Curtis

Background: Mr. Curtis has been an agent for 40 years. Currently handles about 100 clients. Sold approximately 100 titles in the last year, not counting foreign rights and film sales. Member of RWA, WWA, MWA, Authors Guild, Screenwriters Guild of America. Prior to opening this agency, Mr. Curtis was a freelance writer and had 50 books published. The agency is best known for building author careers via hands-on editorial input.

Represents: Sci-fi/fantasy, romance, thrillers, general nonfiction

Does not represent: First novels, self-published books, academic nonfiction, screenplays, children's literature

Workshop topics: Electronic rights and the future of publishing

Conferences: World Fantasy, RWA

Clients: Janet Dailey, Jennifer Blake, Dan Simmons, Harlan Ellison, Greg Bear, Barbara Parker

Recent sales: *Ilium and Olympus,* by Dan Simmons (HarperCollins); *Dead Lines,* by Greg Bear (Del Rey); *Suspicion of Madness,* by Barbara Parker (Dutton)

HOW TO SUBMIT | **Send query letter with 1-page synopsis by mail with SASE. For nonfiction, include information about author credentials and "platform." An SASE for reply is essential.**

THE CYPHER AGENCY

816 WOLCOTT AVE.
BEACON NY 12508

PHONE	FAX	E-MAIL
845.831.5677	845.831.5677	jimcypher@prodigy.net

Agent: James R. "Jim" Cypher

Background: Mr. Cypher has been an agent since 1994. He handles approximately 25 clients and provides strong, friendly editorial support to new writers. Member of AAR, Authors Guild. Before becoming an agent, he spent 28 years handling corporate communications and public relations at IBM.

Represents: Nonfiction: health and medical, true crime, sports (NASCAR, golf), public affairs, memoir/biography

Does not represent: Fiction, juvenile, cookbooks

Clients: Monte Dutton, Mark Horner, Toby Johnson, Former U.S. Ambassador Donald Petterson, M. William Phelps, Cal Orey

Recent sales: *September Sacrifice,* by Mark Horner (Kensington); *Killer with a Badge,* by Charles Hustmyre (Berkley); *Lethal Guardian,* by M. William Phelps (Kensington); *The Masters: A Hole-by-Hole History of America's Golf Classic,* by David Sowell (Brassey's)

HOW TO SUBMIT | **Send query letter and proposal with 2 sample chapters by mail or e-mail.**

DARHANSOFF, VERRILL, FELDMAN LITERARY AGENTS

236 W. 26TH ST., SUITE 802
NEW YORK NY 10001

PHONE	FAX
917.305.1300	917.305.1400

Agents: Liz Darhansoff, Charles Verrill, Leigh Feldman, Kristin Lang

Represents: Literary fiction

Does not represent: Genre fiction

HOW TO SUBMIT | **Send query letter and sample chapter only by mail.**

DH LITERARY, INC.

P. O. BOX 990
NYACK NY 10960-0990

PHONE
212.753.7942

E-MAIL
dhendin@aol.com

Agent:	David Hendin
Background:	Member of AAR since 1994.
Clients:	Judith Martin ("Miss Manners"), Elaine Viets, Abraham Twerski

HOW TO SUBMIT | **We are active agents, but we are NOT accepting submissions until further notice.**

SANDRA DIJKSTRA LITERARY AGENCY

1155 CAMINO DEL MAR, SUITE 515
DEL MAR CA 92014-2605

PHONE
858.755.3115

FAX
858.794.3115

Agent:	Sandra Dijkstra
Background:	Ms. Dijkstra currently handles 300 clients. Sold approximately 100+ domestic titles. This agency has strong editorial skill and success at developing new writers.
Represents:	All nonfiction; Fiction: mystery, thriller, mainstream, contemporary, cultural
Does not represent:	Sci-fi/fantasy
Workshop topics:	Agenting; how to get an agent
Clients:	Amy Tan, Diane Mott Davidson, Kate White, Chitra Divakaruni, Lisa See, Mike Davis, Ira Berlin, Veronica Chambers
Recent sales:	Untitled book by Diane Mott Davidson (Bantam); *Opposite of Fate,* by Amy Tan (Putnam); an untitled four-book deal by Kate White (Warner Books)

✓ **TIPS**
Never call the agency to pitch. Always send a SASE!

★ **WEB SITE RECOMMENDATIONS**
Publishersmarket place.com and *Literarymarket place.com*

HOW TO SUBMIT | **Send query letter by mail.**

JIM DONOVAN LITERARY

4515 PRENTICE ST., SUITE 109
DALLAS TX 75206

PHONE
214.696.9411

Agents:	Jim Donovan, Kathryn Lindsey
Background:	This agency has been in operation for 9 years and handles 30 clients. Sold 15 titles in the last year. Mr. Donovan was an editor prior to opening his agency. The agency is committed to helping its clients produce the best and most polished writing possible, with an emphasis on excellent proposal writing and editorial acumen.
Represents:	Nonfiction: sports, history, military history, biography, business, film, culture; Fiction: thrillers, mysteries
Does not represent:	Children's, poetry, short stories, romance, sci-fi/fantasy, religious, inspirational
Workshop topics:	How to write a great nonfiction proposal; do's and don'ts for query writers
Clients:	Jim Dent, Bill Sloan, Sam Staggs, Curt Sampson, Robert Solomon, Richard Bak, David A. Clary
Recent sales:	*The Killing Ground,* by Bill Sloan (Simon & Schuster); *The Great Atlantic Air Race of 1927,* by Richard Bak (Wiley); *The Tuna Went Down to Texas,* by Mike Shropshire (HarperCollins); *Dead Men Rise Up Never,* by Ron Faust (Bantam)

HOW TO SUBMIT **Send query letter, detailed synopsis/outline or full proposal, and first chapter by mail with SASE.**

DOYEN LITERARY SERVICES, INC.

1931 660TH ST.
NEWELL IA 50568-7613

PHONE
712.272.3300

WEB SITE
www.barbaradoyen.com

Agent:	B.J. Doyen (President)
Background:	Ms. Doyen formed the corporation in 1988 and currently handles nearly 100 clients. Prior to opening her agency, she was a published novelist, a public school teacher, and wrote and appeared in a commercial TV program for 1 year. "We offer outstanding service that starts with extensive advice about preparing a winning book proposal, and unlike many agents, our service doesn't end with the publisher's contract—we're there to assist the author through the whole process, to ensure a positive outcome: successful books!"
Represents:	Primarily nonfiction. Especially interested in acquiring excellent writers for all kinds of trade nonfiction books. Known for outstanding nonfiction authors who write knowledgeably and well and who deliver on deadline. Takes on the occasional novel that is too good to resist.
Does not represent:	Poetry, children's, pornography, textbooks, category romance, short story collections (unless author/compiler is already famous)
Workshop topics:	How to write salable material; the state of the current marketplace; what is selling and how to break in; marketing yourself to agents and editors; author/agent and author/editor relations; planning and achieving a successful book publishing career
Success story:	Once we commit to a client, we do not give up easily, even in the face of market resistance. Back when we were still selling children's books, one project collected many, many rejections. Every time we thought of giving up, we'd reread the text and know that it deserved a publisher. It got picked up by a major publisher—and it went on to sell over 100,000 copies.

✓ **TIPS**

Someone somewhere must have written something advising authors to call first to ask if an agent is accepting new clients—we get dozens of these calls each month, and they are a total waste of time. Just send your query letter with a SASE and you'll find out quickly.

Another time-waster is calling to verify the address—if you can get our phone number, you probably can get our address without bothering us, or buy this directory! Calling to query us about your book, unless you are a client, won't accomplish your goal of representation. We first need to know if you can write well— after all, that is what you are selling! Your letter is your sales piece—it gets you in the door.

133

HOW TO SUBMIT

Send a 1-page query letter by mail briefly telling us about your book, why it should be published, and why you are qualified to be an author. If querying about fiction, include the first 3 or 4 pages of the novel and a 1-page synopsis.

DUNHAM LITERARY, INC.

156 FIFTH AVE., SUITE 625
NEW YORK NY 10010-7002

WEB SITE
www.dunhamlit.com

✓ **TIPS**
*Don't e-mail query
letters to this agency.*

Agent:	Jennie Dunham
Background:	Ms. Dunham has been an agent for 11 years and handles 40 clients. Sold 30 titles in the last year. Member of AAR, SCBWI. Ms. Dunham worked at Russell & Volkening before opening her own agency 3 years ago. "I have a good track record at getting authors published for the first time."
Represents:	Literary fiction and nonfiction, some children's books
Does not represent:	Westerns, science fiction, poetry, romance
Workshop topics:	Narrative voice; elements of story; what agents do for writers; what writers need to know about book contracts
Clients:	Tod Goldberg, Mark Bowden, Margaret McMullan, Marlene Carvell, Barbara McClintock

HOW TO SUBMIT — **Send query letter by mail with SASE. See detailed submission information on the Web site.**

EDUCATIONAL DESIGN SERVICES, INC.

P.O. BOX 253
WANTAGH NY 11793-0253

PHONE
516.221.0995

Agents:	Bertram L. Linder, Edwin Selzer
Background:	Mr. Linder has been an agent for 23 years and sold 4 titles in the last year.
Represents:	Text materials for the K-12 market, educational administration and supervision
Does not represent:	Children's fiction
Clients:	Elaine Farran, Ann-Jean Paci, Harvey Singer, Harry E. Gunn, Jaswinder Singh

HOW TO SUBMIT — **Send query letter, table of contents, sample chapter, and proposal by mail.**

ETHAN ELLENBERG LITERARY AGENCY

548 BROADWAY, #5E
NEW YORK NY 10012

PHONE / FAX	E-MAIL	WEB SITE
212.431.4554	agent@ethanellenberg.	www.ethanellenberg.
212.941.4652	com	com

Agents: Ethan Ellenberg, Michael Psaltis

Background: Mr. Ellenberg has been an agent for 20 years. The agency currently handles approximately 85 clients and has sold more than 100 titles in the past year. Member of AAR. Before opening his own agency, Mr. Ellenberg was contracts manager for Berkley/Jove and assistant contracts manager for Bantam.

Represents: Nonfiction: health, science, psychology, history, current affairs, business, cookbooks, pop-culture, true crime, biography, memoir, New Age, spirituality; Fiction: thrillers, mysteries, action/ adventure, children's, romance, women's, ethnic, sci-fi/fantasy, literary

Does not represent: Poetry, short stories, screenplays

Clients: Eric Rohmann, Dallas Schulze, Laurie Breton, Marthe Jocelyn, Rebecca York, MaryJanice Davidson, Bertrice Small

Recent sales: *Dragonlance Adventurers,* by Dan Willis (Wizards); *Dakota Dreams,* by Madeline Baker (Dutton); *Taken by Storm: Whirlwind,* by Kathy DeNosky (Silhouette); *Not Tonight Honey,* by Susan Reinhardt (Kensington)

HOW TO SUBMIT

For nonfiction, send a book proposal that includes an outline, sample material, and an author bio by mail with SASE. For fiction, send a synopsis and first 3 chapters (50–100 pages) by mail with SASE. Accepts queries by e-mail (no attachments); responds to e-mail queries within 2 weeks if interested in reviewing the manuscript.

FELICIA ETH LITERARY REPRESENTATION

555 BRYANT ST., SUITE 350
PALO ALTO CA 94301-1700

PHONE	FAX	E-MAIL
650.375-1276	650.401.8892	feliciaeth@aol.com

136

Agent: Felicia Eth

Background: Ms. Eth has been an agent for 24 years. Currently handles 30 clients and sold 8–10 titles in the last year. Member of AAR. Prior to opening her agency, she worked as an agent in New York at Writers House, Inc., for 10 years. Before that she worked in the movie business on the West Coast. She is known for her personal attention, strong editorial know-how, and solid reputation.

Represents: Strong writing and original, provocative ideas— whether nonfiction in how-to or narrative genres, a small number of accessible literary novels

Does not represent: Romance, science fiction, fantasy, genre mystery or thriller, children's

Success story: Lots of stories of books that took many, many submissions—upward of 15—that eventually sold well (in excess of 25,000 copies), and then publishers that came back to us eager for the next book, or a 2-book contract.

Clients: Arlene Blum, Peggy Vincent, Cathryn Alpert, Linda Kohanov

Recent sales: *Jane Austen in Boca,* by Paula Marantz Cohen (St. Martin's); *Breaking Trail,* by Arlene Blum (Scribner); *Beyond Blue and Pink,* by Dr. Leonard Saxe (Doubleday); *The Ancestral Mind,* by Dr. Gregg Jacobs (Viking); *Baby Catcher,* by Peggy Vincent (Scribner/S&S)

HOW TO SUBMIT **Send query letter only by mail or e-mail. A referral is always a plus.**

FARBER LITERARY AGENCY INC.

14 E. 75TH ST., #2E
NEW YORK NY 10021

PHONE / FAX	E-MAIL	WEB SITE
212.861.7075	farberlit@aol.com	donaldfarber.com
212.861.7076		

Agents:	Ann Farber, Seth Farber, Donald C. Farber (attorney)
Background:	Ms. Farber has been an agent for 12 years. Currently handles 32 clients. Sold 9 titles in the last year. Prior to opening this agency, she taught college-level math. This agency has a distinguished reputation and offers the services of Mr. Donald C. Farber as attorney for all clients of the agency at no extra charge.
Represents:	Nonfiction, fiction, adult, children's, plays
Does not represent:	Short stories, short plays, film or TV scripts
Clients:	Ed Bullins; Colin Neenan; Kurt Vonnegut, Jr.; Charles Hicham; Marcia Leslie

✓ TIPS
Spell correctly in the cover letter.

HOW TO SUBMIT | **Send query letter, synopsis, and/or 3 chapters by mail with SASE.**

PETER FLEMING AGENCY

P.O. BOX 458
PACIFIC PALISADES CA 90272

PHONE
310.454.1373

Agent:	Peter Fleming
Background:	Mr. Fleming has been an agent for 40 years. Prior to opening his agency, he worked at the William Morris Agency.
Represents:	Nonfiction only

HOW TO SUBMIT | **Send query letter by mail with SASE.**

B.R. FLEURY AGENCY

P.O. BOX 149352
ORLANDO FL 32814-9352

PHONE	FAX	E-MAIL
407.895.8494	407.898.3923	brfleuryagency @juno.com

✓ **TIPS**
Common mistakes we see are passive action and bad grammar.

Agents: Blanche, Margaret, Bob
Background: The agents have 8–10 years of agenting experience and prior experience in writing and editing. Member of WGA.
Represents: Manuscripts, screenplays
Does not represent: Science fiction, sex, religious

HOW TO SUBMIT

Send 1-page query letter only by mail or e-mail. Anything with attachments or enclosures will not be considered.

THE FOGELMAN LITERARY AGENCY

7515 GREENVILLE AVE., SUITE 712
DALLAS TX 75231

E-MAIL
foglit@aol.com

Agent: Helen Brown
Background: Ms. Brown has been an agent for 2 years. Prior to that, she worked in banking, IT, and law. "Our agency has been around for 10 years. We have lots of experience and have handled a variety of books. The owner of the agency is also an entertainment lawyer and is a valuable resource for negotiating contracts."
Represents: Narrative nonfiction, self-help, biography
Does not represent: Children's, science fiction

HOW TO SUBMIT

Send 1-page query letter by mail or e-mail with SASE. No unsolicited manuscripts or chapters.

FORT ROSS INC.

26 ARTHUR PL.
YONKERS NY 10701-1703

PHONE / FAX
914.375.6448
914.375.6439

E-MAIL
fort.ross@verizon.net

WEB SITE
www.fortross.net

Agents:	Dr. Vladimir P. Kartsev, Olga Bovodyanskaya, Svetlana Kolmanovskaya, Konstantin Paltchikov
Background:	This agency has been in operation since 1992 and handles 25 clients. Sold 20 titles in the last year. Prior to working at this agency, Dr. Kartsev was director of MIR Publishing House in Moscow and Director of the United Nations Publishing Division, New York. This agency is known for having strong contacts with Russian authors and publishers and has a good editorial reputation.
Represents:	Russian-related fiction and nonfiction; best-selling fiction and nonfiction U.S. authors who want to be published in Russia; outstanding fiction and nonfiction authors from Russia
Workshop topics:	Translation rights
Conferences:	BEA
Clients:	Virginia Brown, Jerry Piasecki, George Vainer, Daniil Granin
Recent sales:	*Mastering Judo with Vladimir Putin,* by Vladimir Putin (North Atlantic Books); *Dream Journey*, by Vladimir Kush (Byron Preiss Visual Publications, NY); *In Rogue's Arms,* by Virginia Brown (AST, Moscow); *The Suitcase,* by Sergey Dovlatov (Amber, Warsaw)

★ **RECOMMENDATION**
Publishers Weekly

139

HOW TO SUBMIT

Send query letter, list of books, and some reviews by mail with SASE.

FORTHWRITE LITERARY AGENCY

23852 W. PACIFIC COAST HWY., SUITE 701
MALIBU CA 90265

E-MAIL
query@kellermedia.com

WEB SITE
www.kellermedia.com

140

✓ **TIPS**
*Please have expertise
in your subject area
before you write.
We can help you
with everything else.*

Agents: Wendy Keller (sr. agent), Deborah Charles (assoc. agent), Vince Garcia (assoc. agent)

Background: Ms. Keller has been an agent for over 15 years and represents 30–40 projects per year. Sold approximately 9 titles in the last year. More than 450 deals sold since 1989. "We also own a speaker's bureau. Our focus is 90 percent on marketing, 10 percent content." Ms. Keller has a background in journalism.

Represents: Nonfiction: business (sales, marketing, management, finance), self-help (all categories), popular psychology, consumer reference, inspirational and metaphysical, history, health and alternative health

Does not represent: Fiction, first-person medical sagas, bios by non-celebrities, children's, screenplays

Workshop topics: Becoming an author who speaks; marketing your book; preparing a killer marketing plan; how to get on radio and TV even before you sell your book

Conferences: National Speakers Association, U.S. Women's Chamber of Commerce, assorted writers conferences

Recent sales: *Forever in Your Debt,* by Harvey Warren (Wiley); *Connecting with Your Teen,* by Dr. D. Ciavola (New Harbinger); *Emotional Attachment: Parenting with Love,* by Dr. Zeynep Biringen (Penguin/Perigee)

HOW TO SUBMIT | **Send 1-page query letter by e-mail (no attachments) stating your subject and credentials, plus your contact information and Web site URL (if applicable). Responds within 10 business days if interested.**

LYNN C. FRANKLIN ASSOCIATES, LTD.

1350 BROADWAY, SUITE 2015
NEW YORK NY 10018

PHONE	FAX
212.868.6311	212.868.6312

Agent: Lynn Franklin

Background: Currently handles approximately 50 clients. Member of PEN America. This agency has a strong reputation for follow-through in pre- and post-publication. Ms. Franklin is also a partner in Franklin & Siegal Associates, Inc., an international scouting agency.

Represents: Nonfiction: self-help, memoirs, spirituality, alternative medicine, biography; Fiction: commercial, literary

Does not represent: Poetry, romance, mysteries, sci-fi/fantasy

Conferences: Associated Writing Program, panel on memoir

Clients: Archbishop Desmond Tutu, Edvard Radzinsky, Faith Adiele, Richard Mollica, Frank Lipman, Philip Goldberg, Jim Kokoris

Recent sales: *Meeting Faith,* by Faith Adiele (Norton); *Healing Invisible Wounds,* by Richard Mollica (Harcourt); *God Has a Dream,* by Desmond Tutu (Doubleday)

✓ **TIPS**
Keep query letters straightforward.

141

HOW TO SUBMIT	**Send query letter and outline or synopsis by mail. Also accepts submissions by referral.**

SAMUEL FRENCH, INC.

45 W. 25TH ST.
NEW YORK NY 10010-2751

PHONE / FAX	E-MAIL	WEB SITE
212.206.8990	samuelfrench	www.samuelfrench.
212.206.1429	@earthlink.net	com

Agent: Lawrence Harbison (editor)

Background: The company has been in business for 173 years and handles hundreds of clients including Neil Simon, David Mamet, August Wilson

Represents: Stage plays only

✓ **TIPS**
Be 100 percent professional.

THE GAGE GROUP

14724 VENTURA BLVD., SUITE 505
SHERMAN OAKS CA 91403

PHONE	FAX	E-MAIL
818.905.3800	818.905.3322	gagegroupla@yahoo.com

Agents:	Jonathan Westover (head of department/feature), Sharon Moist (TV)
Background:	This agency has been in operation since 1976 and handles 34 clients. Member of DGA, WGA.
Represents:	Movie scripts, feature film, TV scripts, plays

HOW TO SUBMIT **Send query letter by mail with SASE or e-mail.**

MAX GARTENBERG, LITERARY AGENT

12 WESTMINSTER DR.
LIVINGSTON NJ 07039

PHONE	FAX	E-MAIL
973.994.4457	973.535.5033	gartenbook@att.net

Represents:	Primarily nonfiction, established writers, very few new writers
Does not represent:	Category fiction

HOW TO SUBMIT **Send query letter by mail with SASE.**

THE LAYA GELFF LITERARY AND TALENT AGENCY

16133 VENTURA BLVD., SUITE 700
ENCINO CA 91436

PHONE
818.996.3100

Agent:	Laya Gelff
Background:	Ms. Gelff has been an agent since 1985. Member of WGA, SAG, AFTRA, AEA, DGA. Prior to this, she was an entertainment business executive. Her agency is known for its good reputation, industry contacts, and hard-working office.
Represents:	Mainly scripts for feature film; occasionally manuscripts to publishers
Does not represent:	Coming-of-age-stories, self-help, children's, romantic comedy, TV
Workshop topics:	Business of show biz; how to write a query; how to focus yourself in writing.

✓ **TIPS**
Please do not start your letter by stating your name. Business is like a roller coaster —get ready for the ride!

HOW TO SUBMIT

Send 1-page query letter by mail with SASE. Indicate if work is a screenplay or book. Must include SASE for reply. Address query to ATTENTION: LITERARY DEPT.

THE GISLASON AGENCY

219 MAIN ST. S.E., SUITE 506
MINNEAPOLIS MN 55414-2160

PHONE
612.331.8033

E-MAIL
gislasonbj@aol.com

Agent:	Barbara J. Gislason
Background:	Ms. Gislason has been an agent for 11 years and handles approximately 20 clients. Member of MWA, RWA. Prior to working at this agency, she was an attorney (family law and art and entertainment law).
Represents:	Nonfiction: animals, alternative spirituality, health; Fiction: mainstream, literary, sci-fi/fantasy, romance, mysteries, historical
Does not represent:	Poetry, short stories/collections, memoirs, children's/young adult, screenplays
Workshop topics:	Insider's view on the publishing industry; writing about animals
Conferences:	Willamette Writers' Conference, Southwestern Writers' Conference, Shuswap International Writers' Festival, Society of Southwest Authors Conference, Surrey International Writers' Conference
Clients:	Deborah Woodworth, Linda Cook, Einar Mar Gudmundsson, Terence Faherty

HOW TO SUBMIT

For fiction, send query letter, synopsis, cover letter, and first 3 chapters (50 pages maximum) by mail with SASE. For nonfiction, send query letter, full proposal (including chapter-by-chapter outline), and the book's introduction by mail with SASE.

GOODMAN ASSOCIATES

500 WEST END AVE.
NEW YORK NY 10024-4317

PHONE
212.873.4806

Agent:	Elise Simon Goodman
Background:	Member of AAR.
Represents:	Fiction, nonfiction
Does not represent:	Poetry, articles, individual stories, children's, young adult

HOW TO SUBMIT

Accepting new clients through professional recommendations only.

IRENE GOODMAN LITERARY AGENCY

521 FIFTH AVE., 17TH FLOOR
NEW YORK NY 10175

Agent:	Irene Goodman, Danny Baror, Irene Webb
Background:	Ms. Goodman has been an agent for 25 years handles approximately 35 clients. Member of AAR. Prior to working at this agency, she was an editorial assistant for a publisher.
Represents:	Commercial fiction
Does not represent:	Sci-fi/fantasy, horror, children's, literary fiction

HOW TO SUBMIT	**Send query letter, 1 chapter, and a synopsis by mail. No e-mail submissions.**

THE THOMAS GRADY AGENCY

209 BASSETT ST.
PETALUMA CA 94952-2668

PHONE / FAX	E-MAIL	WEB SITE
707.765.6229	tom@tgrady.com	www.tgrady.com
707.765.6810		

Agent:	Tom Grady
Background:	Mr. Grady has been an agent for 7 years and handles approximately 40 clients. Member of AAR. Prior to opening his agency, he was editorial director and publishers, Harper San Francisco.
Represents:	Nonfiction: religion, spirituality, personal growth
Does not represent:	Fiction, poetry, children's, illustrated books
Clients:	Huston Smith, Sylvia Boorstein, Andrew Harvey, Daniel Ladinsky

HOW TO SUBMIT	**Send proposal by mail with SASE or e-mail (send proposal as 1 attachment and type "query" in the e-mail's subject line). The proposal should include a 1–2 page description of your book, a 1-sentence statement of the book's purpose and promise, a competition analysis that notes how your book differs from others, a brief biography that includes your qualifications and publishing history, a table of contents with chapter descriptions and estimate of final page count, a sample chapter (10–15 pages), the anticipated completion date for your manuscript, and information about any publishers and/or agents who have reviewed or are currently reviewing your proposal.**

GRAHAM AGENCY

311 W. 43RD ST.
NEW YORK NY 10036

PHONE
212.489.7730

Agent: Earl Graham
Background: Mr. Graham has been an agent since 1971 and handles approximately 35 clients. Prior to opening his agency, he worked at Ashley Famous Agency (now ICM). Member of WGA.
Represents: Full-length stage plays and musicals for adults only

HOW TO SUBMIT **Send query letter by mail. Include a brief description of the play or musical indicating what it's about, NOT what happens; also indicate style of music.**

GRAYBILL & ENGLISH

1875 CONNECTICUT AVE. N.W., SUITE 712
WASHINGTON DC 20009

PHONE **FAX**
202.588.9798 202.457.0662

✓ TIPS
Ms. English: *Know the target market and have a well-written, solid manuscript with an inventive plot, good pacing, strong dialogue, and realistic, strong characters.*

Ms. Auclair: *Do the research, know what goes into a good book proposal, understand that it takes a lot of work and that going the extra mile can make all the difference.*

Ms. Whittaker: *Most of all, be good writers. Also, have books on topics I love. Teach me about something new.*

Agents: Nina Graybill, Elaine English, Jeff Kleinman, Kristen Auclair, Lynn Whittaker
Background: Member of AAR.
Represents: **MS. GRAYBILL:** Serious nonfiction: race and ethnicity, politics, history, current events, biography and memoir, health and science, sociology, psychology; Fiction: literary, literary/commercial
MS. ENGLISH: Women's fiction, including romance and mysteries
MR. KLEINMAN: Nonfiction: narrative with a historical bent, health, parenting, aging, pets, how-to, nature, ecology, politics, military, espionage, equestrian, memoir, biography; Fiction: character-driven novels, some sci-fi/fantasy, suspense, thrillers, mainstream commercial, literary
MS. AUCLAIR: Nonfiction: narrative (women's stories), practical (self-help, parenting, health); Fiction: well-written commercial, literary
MS. WHITTAKER: Nonfiction: memoir, sports, history, biography, nature/science, celebrity, women's self-help; Fiction: literary, mysteries,
Does not represent: **MS. GRAYBILL:** How-to, children's, genre fiction (except some mysteries and suspense), poetry, New Age, spirituality, screenplays, stage plays
MS. ENGLISH: Westerns, time travel, paranormal romances, nonfiction

MR. KLEINMAN: Mysteries, romance, westerns, children's or young adult, poetry, plays, screenplays

MS. AUCLAIR: Children's, young adults, genre fiction, screenplays

MS. WHITTAKER: Children's/young adult, scripts, romance, westerns, sci-fi/fantasy, screenplays

Conferences: Oklahoma Writer's Federation, Washington Independent Writer's, Arizona Writer's Conference, Algonkian Workshop, Associated Writing Programs, Creative Nonfiction, Romance Writers of America, Novelist's Ink, Washington Romance Writers

Recent sales: *A Telling of Stars,* by Caitlin Sweet (Penguin Putnam); *I May be Wrong But I Doubt It,* by Charles Barkley and Michael Wilbon (Random House); *The C-Section Survival Guide,* by Maureen Connolly and Dana Sullivan (Broadway); *Gullible's Travels,* by Cash Peters (Globe Pequot); *On Thin Ice,* by Deirdre Martin (Berkley); *Never Say Never,* by Phyllis George (McGraw-Hill); *The Mind-Body Diabetes Revolution,* by Dr. Richard Surwit with Alisa Bauman (Free Press); *Married to the Military,* by Meredith Leyva (Fireside); *One Hell of a Candidate,* by William F. Gavin (St. Martin's Press); *The Case for Staying Married,* by Dr. Linda Waite & Maggie Gallagher (Oxford); *The People Next Door,* by Bettye Griffin (Dafina); *The Sand and the Rose,* by Diane Whiteside (Brava/Kensington); *Secret Soldiers,* by Philip Gerard (Dutton); *Gentleman's Blood,* by Barbara Holland (Bloomsbury USA); *The Man Who Changed How Boys & Toys Were Made,* by Bruce Watson (Viking/ Penguin); *Learning to Speak Alzheimer's,* by Joanne Koenig-Coste (Houghton-Mifflin); *Trim Kids in Twelve Weeks,* by Melinda Sothern, Kris von Almen, & Heidi Schumacher (HarperCollins)

HOW TO SUBMIT

MS. GRAYBILL: Send query letter with a 1-page synopsis and sample chapters (for fiction) or a proposal and a bio (for nonfiction) by mail with SASE.

MS. ENGLISH: Send query letter and 1-page synopsis by mail or e-mail (no attachments).

MR. KLEINMAN: Send query letter with a proposal that includes bio, sample chapter and/or outline (for nonfiction) or the first few pages of the novel (for fiction) by mail or e-mail (no attachments).

MS. AUCLAIR: Send query letter with a proposal, sample chapter and/or outline (for nonfiction) or the first few chapters of the novel (for fiction) by mail or e-mail (no attachments).

MS. WHITTAKER: Send query letter, outline, sample chapter (up to 30 pages), and author credentials by mail or e-mail (no attachments, no sample).

Mr. Kleinman: ENHANCE YOUR CREDENTIALS. Get published, or have some kind of platform or fresh perspective that really stands out above the crowd. Show me (so I can show a publisher) that you're a good risk for publication.

Ms. Graybill: If writers are referred by someone I know, I will look at their project a little more closely than I might a stranger's. But mostly I am interested in a query letter offering a fresh treatment of an intriguing topic by someone with the appropriate credentials to write such a book. In the case of fiction, I look for writers who, their natural talent aside, have read many, many good books in their area of interest, such as literary fiction or mysteries, and who have studied fiction writing enough— through reading, courses, workshops, writing groups— to understand the demands of their chosen type of fiction.

147

ASHLEY GRAYSON LITERARY AGENCY

1342 18TH ST.
SAN PEDRO CA 90732

FAX
310.514.1148

✓ **TIPS**
Avoid hype; stick to describing the book.

Agents: Dan Hooker, Ashley Grayson, Carolyn Grayson

Background: Mr. Hooker has been an agent for 12 years and handles 20 clients. The agency sold approximately 30 titles in the last year. Member of SCBWI. Prior to working at this agency, he worked in the hotel industry. The agency is known for strong editorial, outstanding reputation, and the ability to recognize new talent; known by publishers as handling high-quality books.

Represents: Nonfiction: a wide variety by authors with national reputations and proven ability to proactively market their books; Fiction: mainstream, mystery, thrillers, sci-fi, dark/contemporary fantasy, literary, adults and young adults

Does not represent: Epic or high fantasy, religion, poetry, short stories, screenplays, memoirs (unless the authors are celebrity figures)

Recent sales: *Fat White Vampire Blues,* by Andrew Fox (Ballantine); *Dhampir,* by Barb and J.C. Hendee (Roc/Penguin); *Dreaming Pachinko,* by Isaac Adamson (HarperCollins)

HOW TO SUBMIT

Send query letter with a brief proposal (for nonfiction) or a brief description of the manuscript and the author's writing background (for fiction) by mail. Do not include an SASE; instead supply an e-mail address and phone number. Responds only if interested in seeing more material.

JILL GROSJEAN LITERARY AGENCY

1390 MILLSTONE RD.
SAG HARBOR NY 11963-2214

PHONE / FAX	E-MAIL	WEB SITE
631.725.8632	Jill6981@aol.com	www.hometown.aol.
631.725.8632		com/JILL6981/my
		homepage/index.html

Agent:	Jill Grosjean	
Background:	Ms. Grosjean has been an agent for 8 years and handles 26 clients. Prior to agenting, she managed an independent bookstore and worked in publishing and advertising. The agency is known for strong editorial skills and dedication to clients.	
Represents:	Literary fiction, mysteries	
Does not represent:	Sci-fi, horror, children's, nonfiction	
Workshop topics:	Relationship between agent & author; query letters	
Conferences:	Texas Writers & Agents Conference, Book Passage Mystery Writers Conference	
Success story:	2-book deal for a client after 47 submissions.	
Clients:	Greg Garrett, Marie Giordano, Tony Broad Bent, David Fickett	
Recent sales:	*Sanctuary,* by Greg Garrett (Kensington); *Spectres in the Smoke,* by Tony Broad Bent (Thomas Dunne/SMP); *I Love You Like a Tomato,* by Marie Giordano (Forge Books)	

HOW TO SUBMIT	**Send query letter and synopsis by mail or e-mail (no attachments).**

THE GROSVENOR LITERARY AGENCY

5510 GROSVENOR LN.
BETHESDA MD 20814

PHONE
301.564.6231

FAX
301.581.9401

E-MAIL
dcgrosveno@aol.com

Agent:	Deborah C. Grosvenor
Background:	Ms. Grosvenor has been an agent for 7 years and represents about 36 clients. Sold approximately 12 titles in the last year. Prior to work as an agent, she worked in book publishing as an acquisitions editor and in foreign and subsidiary rights sales. "Still actively building client list. Have purposely kept agency to a certain size so that I can have strong, 1-on-1 relationships with my clients. Offer strong editorial support and personal hands-on attention. Am always accessible to my clients."
Represents:	Nonfiction: history, biography, current affairs, science, adventure, military, psychology, politics; Fiction: literary and commercial
Does not represent:	Children's
Workshop topics:	Author/agent relationship; how to write a nonfiction book proposal
Clients:	Curtis Wilkie, Henry Allen, Eleanor Clift, Susan McDougal, Steve Neal, Morton Kondracke, Tom Oliphant, Diane Freund, Alston Chase, Jason Berry
Recent sales:	*Nam-a-rama,* by Phillip Jennings (Forge Books); *Food to Die For,* by Gayden Metcalfe (Miramax Books); *Radical Innocent: Upton Sinclair, A Biography,* by Anthony Arthur (Random House)

HOW TO SUBMIT   **Send query letter and the first 10 pages (for fiction) by mail. Also accepts submissions at conferences by referral.**

THE SUSAN GURMAN AGENCY

865 WEST END AVE., #15A
NEW YORK NY 10025-8403

PHONE	FAX	E-MAIL
212.749.4618	212.861.5055	gurmanagency@earth link.net

Agent: Susan Gurman

Background: Ms. Gurman has been an agent for 9 years and represents 30 clients. Sold 1 script in the last year—doing only theater except for recent screenplay sale. Member of WGA, Dramatists Guild, Directors Guild. Prior to opening her agency, she was a professor of finance. Her agency is known for marketing, reputation, and building a talented client list.

Represents: Playwrights, composers, lyricists, theater directors

Does not represent: Books, screenplays

HOW TO SUBMIT	Send query letter and author bio.

✓ TIPS
Go out and get credentials, then look for an agent.

151

REECE HALSEY NORTH

98 MAIN ST., #714
TIBURON CA 94920

PHONE	E-MAIL	WEB SITE
415.789.9191	info@reecehalsey north.com	www.kimberley cameron.com

Agent: Kimberley Cameron, Adam Marsh (assistant)

Background: Ms. Cameron has been an agent for 10 years and handles 20-25 clients. Member of AAR. Prior to agenting, she was a publisher. She is looking for new voices, offers editorial assistance to her clients, and is serious about the writers she represents.

Represents: Nonfiction, literary and mainstream fiction

Does not represent: Screenplays, children's

Workshop topics: Writing from the heart; how to succeed in the publishing industry; right action for writers

Conferences: Whidbey Island Writers Conference

Success story: Lots of those. I believe in the talent of every writer I represent and will go as far as I can to get them published, often with Herculean efforts!

HOW TO SUBMIT	Send a polite query letter with synopsis and first 10 pages by mail with SASE.

✓ TIPS
Treat this as a serious business and don't waste anyone's time . . .

★ RECOMMENDATION
Use the AAR Web site.

THE MITCHELL J. HAMILBURG AGENCY

11718 BARRINGTON CT., #732
LOS ANGELES CA 90049-2930

PHONE
310.471.4024

FAX
310.471.9588

Agents:	Michael Hamilburg, Joan Kern
Background:	Mr. Hamilburg has been an agent since 1963. Member of WGA. The agency has been in business since the 1930s and currently handles approximately 50 clients.
Represents:	Fiction, nonfiction, MOW

HOW TO SUBMIT
Send query letter by mail, including synopsis, first chapter, first 10 pages, or proposal.

RICHARD HENSHAW GROUP

127 W. 24TH ST., 4TH FLOOR
NEW YORK NY 10011

PHONE / FAX
212.414.1172
212.414.1182

E-MAIL
submissions@
henshaw.com *or*
rhgagents@aol.com

WEB SITE
www.richh.addr.
com

153

Agents: Richard Henshaw (agent), Susannah Taylor (associate agent)

Background: Mr. Henshaw has been an agent for 15 years and Ms. Taylor has been an agent for 3 years. Members of HWA, MWA, RWA, SFWA. The agency handles 18 clients and sold 19 titles in the last year. "We are a deliberately small agency. We enjoy working closely with our clients to build their careers." Prior to starting his own agency, Mr. Henshaw was an agent and director of foreign rights at Richard Curtis Associates.

Represents: Nonfiction: business, celebrity biography, computers, current events, health, history, how-to, movies, popular culture, popular reference, popular science, psychology, self-help, cooking, sports; Mainstream and genre fiction: mysteries, thrillers, sci-fi/fantasy, horror, historical, literary, women's fiction, romance

Does not represent: Nonfiction: coffee table books, cookbooks, scholarly books; Fiction: children's, juvenile, young adults, westerns, poetry, short stories

Clients: Dana Stabenow, Margaret Coel, James D. Doss, Susan Wise Bauer, Jessie Wise, Karen Taylor, Peter van Dijk

Recent sales: *A Grave Denied,* by Dana Stabenow (St. Martin's Press); *The Well-Educated Mind,* by Susan Wise Bauer (W.W. Norton); *Killing Raven,* by Margaret Coel (Berkley Prime Crime); *Dead Soul,* by James D. Doss (St. Martin's/Minotaur); *The Clueless Groom's Guide,* by Peter van Dijk (Contemporary/McGraw-Hill)

✓ **TIPS**
Always include a SASE, do not bind material, and let your writing voice come through in your query letter.

HOW TO SUBMIT

Nonfiction: send query letter by mail with SASE. E-mail submissions should be 250 words or less (no attachments). Fiction: send query letter, short synopsis, and first 3 chapters by mail with SASE.

SUSAN HERNER RIGHTS AGENCY

P.O. BOX 57
POUND RIDGE NY 10576

PHONE
914.234.2864

FAX
914.234.2866

Agent:	Susan Herner
Background:	Ms. Herner has been an agent since 1987 and handles 75 clients. Prior to agenting, she worked for publishers in editorial and subsidiary rights fields. The agency offers strong editorial help and active subsidiary rights representation for clients.
Represents:	Nonfiction: women's issues, spirituality, popular science; Fiction: women's, thrillers; also represents rights for publishers, packagers, and authors.
Does not represent:	Genre romance, sci-fi/fantasy, children's, poetry
Conferences:	Frankfurt Book Fair, London Book Fair
Author clients:	Raphael Simons, Himilce Novas, Michael Mallary
Rights clients:	Various "Beginner Books," Rebus Books, publishers of John Hopkins Medical Guides, Berkeley University Wellness Guides
Recent sales:	*The Feng Shui of Love,* by Raphael Simons (Crown/3 Rivers Press); *Our Improbable Universe,* by Michael Mallary (4 Walls, 8 Windows); *Everything You Need to Know About Latino History,* by Himilce Novas (Dutton/Plume); *Princess Papaya,* by Himilce Novas (Arte Publico Press)

HOW TO SUBMIT · **Send query letter, 3 sample chapters, and author bio by mail.**

HUDSON AGENCY

3 TRAVIS LN.
MONTROSE NY 10548

PHONE / FAX	E-MAIL	WEB SITE
914.737.1475	hudagency@	www.hudsonagency.
914.736.3064	optonline.net	net

Agents:	Susan Giordano, Cheri Santone, Sunny Bik
Background:	The agency has been in operation for 10 years and handles 10 clients. They are not looking for new clients unless they have credits already. The agency remains selective in order to focus on its existing clients.
Represents:	Family features scripts
Does not represent:	Fiction or nonfiction books, anything R-rated or associated with the occult
Clients:	Rick Gitelson, Christine Nee, Michael G. Stern, Tara Tandlich, Eric Snyder
Recent sales:	Most of this agency's writers have worked in animation on existing shows. The agency has also had a few features optioned.

✓ TIPS
Learn how to develop characters. The agency recommends all of Syd Field's books.

155

HOW TO SUBMIT	Send query letter by e-mail to Kelly Olenik at hudflicks@juno.com.

INKWELL MANAGEMENT

521 FIFTH AVE., SUITE 2600
NEW YORK NY 10175

PHONE	FAX
212.922.3500	212.922.0535

Agents:	Michael Carlisle, Richard Pine, Matthew Guma, Catherine Drayton, George Lucas
Background:	Carlisle & Company, Arthur Pine Associates, and Witherspoon Associates merged in 2004 to create InkWell Management. The agency is known for its international scope and its expertise in publishing, intellectual property licensing, brand-building, and lectures.
Represents:	Nonfiction: business/investing/finance, religious, mind/body/spirit, health, children's; Fiction: commercial, literary, juvenile
Does not represent:	Science fiction, romance
Clients:	Rebecca Wells, Susan Orlean, Simon Schama, Robert Harris, Andrew Weil, Sophie Kinsella, Arianna Huffington, Dava Sobel, Wayne Dyer, Colleen McCullough, Antonio Damasio, James Gleick, Gary Kinder, Susan Cheever, Rian Malan, David M. Kennedy, Christopher Reich

HOW TO SUBMIT	By referral only.

JABBERWOCKY LITERARY AGENCY

P.O. BOX 4558
SUNNYSIDE NY 11104-0558

PHONE
718.392.5985

156

Agent:	Joshua Bilmes
Background:	Mr. Bilmes has been an agent for 17 years. Currently handles approximately 40 clients. In the last year, this agency made over 50 deals in all markets (U.S., translation, film, etc.), covering over 100 books. Member of SFFWA. "Where it is wanted, I am willing to provide (if appropriate) strong editorial guidance that has helped many a published book. We are very strong in foreign rights and in providing attention to detail for the life of your book. Our service only begins with selling the book."
Represents:	Fiction and nonfiction; current specialties in sci-fi/fantasy, mystery/thriller and horror, but looking at a broad range
Does not represent:	Children's, romance
Conferences:	London Book Fair, I-CON, Malice Domestic, World SF Convention, Bouchercon
Clients:	Elizabeth Moon, Charlaine Harris, Tanya Huff, Simon Green
Recent sales:	*Dead to the World,* by Charlaine Harris (ACE); *Speed of Dark* and *Trading in Danger,* by Elizabeth Moon (Ballantine/Del Rey); *Vampire Thrall,* by Michael Schiefelbein (Alyson); *Blood Road,* by Edo Van Belkon (Pinnacle); *Hot Blood* series, edited by Gelf & Garrett (Kensington)

HOW TO SUBMIT	**Send query letter only by mail with SASE. No manuscript material unless requested. However, "of course, if I am at a conference or convention or the like, I am there to meet people."**

MELANIE JACKSON

41 W. 72 ST., #3F
NEW YORK NY 10023

PHONE
212.873.3373

FAX
212.799.5063

Agent:	Melanie Jackson
Background:	Member of AAR.

HOW TO SUBMIT	**Send query letter by mail.**

JCA LITERARY AGENCY

27 W. 20TH ST., SUITE 1103
NEW YORK NY 10011

PHONE / FAX	E-MAIL	WEB SITE
212.807.0888	jeff@jcalit.com	www.jcalit.com
212.807.0461		

Agents:	Jeff Gerecke, Peter Steinberg
Background:	This agency has been in operation since 1978. Currently handles 50–75 clients. Member of AAR, MWA, Authors Guild. Has a strong focus on writers' needs and careers.
Represents:	Well-written work by writers not afraid to improve their work through revision.
	MR. GERECKE: Nonfiction: business, history, military, narrative, pop culture; Fiction: commercial, crime, literary
	MR. STEINBERG: Nonfiction: memoir, narrative, true crime; Fiction: literary, short stories
Does not represent:	Sci-fi, juvenile; cheap concept or one-of-a-kind books
Clients:	Ernest J. Gaines, Brad Watson, Karl Iagnemma, David Ellis, Gwen Hunter, Kenneth Ackerman
Recent sales:	*Jury of One,* by David Ellis (Putnam); *Eating Mammals,* by John Barlow (Harper/Fourth Estate); *The Dark Horse,* by Kenneth Ackerman (Caroll & Graf); *The Rope Eater,* by Ben Jones (Doubleday)

✓ TIPS
Don't hype the agent—be clear and straightforward in providing detailed information on your writing.

HOW TO SUBMIT	**Send query letter and sample chapters by mail with SASE or e-mail.**

THE JENKS AGENCY

24 CONCORD AVE., SUITE 412
CAMBRIDGE MA 02138

PHONE
617.354.5099

E-MAIL
cbjenks@att.net

✓ **TIPS**
No cold calls.
No sending sample
chapters or full
manuscripts with-
out request. Do
not bind manu-
scripts. Exclusive
submission only.

Agent:	Carolyn Jenks
Background:	Ms. Jenks has been an agent for more than 15 years and handles 15–20 clients. Member of WGA. Prior to opening this agency, Ms. Jenks was a managing editor at Ballantine Books. She has also worked in theater producing and artists' management, and as a rights agent. Her agency is known for strong editorial and strategic marketing.
Represents:	Commercial nonfiction, literary and commercial fiction
Does not represent:	Romance novels, sci-fi
Workshop topics:	Story structure; the writing life; the writer and media
Conferences:	Writing & Yoga in Florence, Italy
Success story:	The success of *The Red Tent* by Anita Diamant continues with aggressive marketing. Listed Number 3 in Top 50 classic best-sellers in 2002.
Clients:	Anita Diamant, Tom Foley, Jane Ward, Dan Montague, Dick Wolf

HOW TO SUBMIT

Send brief query letter and bio by e-mail. No sample chapters, please.

NATASHA KERN LITERARY AGENCY

P.O. BOX 2908
PORTLAND OR 97208-2908

PHONE
503.297.6190

E-MAIL
www.natashakern.com

Agent:	Natasha Kern
Background:	Ms. Kern has been an agent for 17 years and handles 40 clients. Sold 45 titles in the last year. Member of RWA, MWA. Prior to working at this agency, Ms. Kern worked with other agents in publishing in New York. The agency is responsible for the sale of over 500 books and is known for its commitment to building successful careers for clients and supporting them throughout the publishing process.
Represents:	Nonfiction: narrative, body/mind/spirit, health/alternative medicine, science/environment, investigative journalism, inspiration and religion, popular psychology, sociology, anthropology, self-help, parenting and relationships, garden-ing, animals and shamanism, business, biogra-phy, controversial, multicultural, women's issues, any trade nonfiction by prominent authorities in their fields; Fiction: popular; main-stream women's, romantic suspense, romantic comedies, chick lit, contemporary and historical romances; medical, legal, spiritual, and interna-tional thrillers; psychological suspense and mys-teries; ethnic; historical and adventure
Does not represent:	Pervasive themes of physical, sexual, or sub-stance abuse, gratuitous violence, or an extreme-ly negative or dark tone; science fiction, fantasy, horror, children's or young adult, sports, scholar-ly subjects, poetry, cookbooks, gift books, coffee table books, short stories, war memoirs, stage plays, screenplays
Workshop topics:	How to get published; how to work with agents and editors; what's hot in publishing; how to earn a living as a writer; how to make career changes successfully; how to write a book proposal
Conferences:	RWA, Mystery Writers Conference, BEA, CBA
Success story:	Eliot Pattison won an Edgar and worldwide acclaim for *The Skull Mantra* after being turned down by a dozen publishers and being repre-sented by a previous agent who could not sell this novel. Connie Mason became a *USA Today* best-selling author when she turned to writing later in life after raising a family as a military wife. Jim Gardner's book *Biocosm* was turned down by every New York publisher, and before it was published by Inner Ocean, received blurbs and accolades from several Nobel Laureates. It was featured in a story in *US News and World Report.* Cindy Champnella's book *The Waiting*

159

★ RECOMMENDATIONS
The Sell Your Novel Toolkit, by Elizabeth Lyon; *Nonfiction Proposals Anybody Can Write,* by Elizabeth Lyon; *How to Write a Damn Good Novel,* by James Frey

Success story *cont.*: *Child* relates the tremendous faith and commitment of her 6-year-old daughter Jaclyn in saving a younger child. It was excerpted in *Ladies' Home Journal* and Jaclyn was nominated for the National Angel in Adoption Award by a U.S. Senator.

Clients: Eliot Pattison, Connie Mason, Lewis Perdue, Robin Lee Hatcher, Kimberly Raye, Leigh Greenwood, Mitchell Cheftiz, Nina Bangs, Nicolas Kublicki, Kathleen Morgan, Maureen McCade

Recent sales: *Biocosm,* by James N. Gardner (Inner Ocean); *Running the Spiritual Path,* by Roger Joslin (St. Martin's Press); *Slatewiper,* by Lewis Perdue (Forge); *Kiss Me Once, Kiss Me Twice,* by Kimberly Raye (Warner Books); *Bone Mountain,* by Eliot Pattison (St. Martin's); *Silver Linings,* by Melissa West (Fair Winds Press); *American Nightmare: The History of Jim Crow,* by Jerrold Packard (St. Martin's Griffin); *Song of the Seals,* by Christy Yorke (Penguin USA); *Spirit Babies,* by Walter Makichen (Bantam Books); *Beyond the Shadows,* by Robin Lee Hatcher (Tyndale); *Meteors,* by Chris Cokinos (Tarcher/Penguin)

HOW TO SUBMIT **Send query letter with overview and author bio (for nonfiction) or synopsis and first 3 pages (for fiction) by mail or e-mail. Also accepts submissions at conferences and by referral.**

HARVEY KLINGER, INC.

301 W. 53RD ST., SUITE 21-A
NEW YORK NY 10019

PHONE / FAX	E-MAIL	WEB SITE
212.581.7068	queries@harvey	www.HarveyKlinger.
212.315.3823	klinger.com *or*	com *or*
	JenLBent@aol.com	www.jennybent.com

Agents: Harvey Klinger, Jenny Bent, David Dunton, Wendy Silbert

Background: The agency handles about 100 clients and sells between 50 and 100 titles per year.
MR. KLINGER: Agent since 1975. Member of AAR. Prior to opening his agency Mr. Klinger "worked for an agent who taught me how *not* to be an agent. Prior to that, I did a brief stint at Doubleday right after I received my M.A. in The Writing Seminars at Johns Hopkins. We're a great 'boutique' agency and every client gets the editorial and creative attention to make his/her book as good as it can possibly be."
MS. BENT: Agent for 11 years. Member of AAR, Women's Media Group. "In 1992, I sold 45 books. (What is really important is how much money you make by selling the books. You can sell 10 books a year and make more money for your clients than someone who sells 100 books a year. You'll also have a lot more time to devote to those clients. So remember to consider quality over quantity when it comes to this kind of thing.)" Prior to working at this agency, she worked at 2 other agencies. "I think we have a strong reputation for being ethical and easy to work with. We're all laid-back, friendly and approachable."

Represents: **MR. KLINGER:** Great fiction and nonfiction in a variety of areas
MS. BENT: Preferably any kind of book (literary, self-help, etc.) dealing with women; I like funny books, and I love dark literary fiction. I also seem to sell a lot of short story collections, oddly enough. I would love to see very high-quality thrillers or just plain scary books with strong female protagonists. Oh, and I love animals, so any kind of books about animals.

Does not represent: **MR. KLINGER:** Children's, sci-fi/fantasy, poetry, short stories
MS. BENT: Children's, medical thrillers, political thrillers, scifi/fantasy, psychology (although I used to rep a lot of it), spiritual fiction

Conferences: Washington Romance Writers Retreat, Suncoast Writers Conference

✓ **TIPS**
Ms.Bent: *Find books that are genuinely similar to your book. Look in the acknowledgments and try to find the name of the agent. Then send them a submission letter that says: Dear Agent X, I know you represented one of my favorite books, Y, and I really think that my book Z has some similarities. I hope you will be interested in taking a look. This really does work. Also, keep the query letter short: One paragraph summing up the book, and one paragraph about you. If you can, try to figure out a hook or a catchy way to pitch your book in the letter. ("It's JAWS meets PRIDE AND PREJUDICE!" OK, maybe not that one. But you get the idea.)*

Mr. Klinger: *Don't try to sell yourself, just tell us what your book is. If it's nonfiction, your platform is vitally important.*

161

Success story: Laurie Notaro tried unsuccessfully to sell her book for 7 years. When it finally got published, it spent 2 months on the *New York Times* bestseller list. I've also sent books out to everyone in town, been rejected by everyone, waited 6 months, and then sold the book to the 1 editor who didn't see it the first time around for good money (i.e., 6-figure deals).

Clients: MR. KLINGER: Jill Conner Browne, Barbara De Angelis, Terry Kay, Augusta Trobaugh, Brian Morton, Barbara Wood

MS. BENT: Jill Conner Browne, Laurie Notaro, Michael Farquhar, Pamela Raphael Berkman, Ann Cummins, Janelle Denison

Recent sales: *Perfect Evil,* by E.C. Sheedy (Kensington Books); *The Book of Ralph,* by John McNally (Free Press); *You Are a Dog,* by Terry Bain (Harmony Books); *Grosse Pointe Girl,* by Sarah Grace McCandless (Simon and Schuster); *Rules of Engagement,* by Kathy Caskie (Warner Books)

| HOW TO SUBMIT |

MR. KLINGER: **Send query letter by mail or e-mail. No faxes or phone calls—*ever!***
MS. BENT: **Send query letter, outline or synopsis if you have it, the first 50 pages, and a bio or resume by mail with SASE or e-mail (no attachments unless specifically requested). Please do not call or fax. See my Web site for more details.**

LINDA KONNER LITERARY AGENCY

10 W. 15TH ST., SUITE 1918
NEW YORK NY 10011-6829

PHONE	FAX	E-MAIL
212.691.3419	212.691.0935	ldkonner@cs.com

Agent: Linda Konner

Background: Ms. Konner has been an agent since February 1996 and handles approximately 65 clients. She is the author of 8 books. Prior to opening her agency, she was a magazine editor (editor-in-chief, *Weight Watchers Magazine,* also features editor at *Redbook* and *Seventeen).* Her agency is "very hands-on, with strong editorial and marketing input, accessibility, and fast turn-around. I often bring ideas/projects to my clients."

Represents: Adult nonfiction only: self-help, how-to, pop psychology, women's issues, personal finance, entertainment written by experts in their field

Does not represent: Fiction, children's, nonfiction by authors without a suitable platform

Workshop topics: 18 ways to make an agent love you

Conferences: ASJA

Clients: Congresswomen Linda and Loretta Sanchez, Comedienne Phyllis Diller, Restaurateur Walter Staib (City Tavern, Philadelphia)

Success story: I contacted chess grandmaster Maurice Ashley after seeing his picture on a McDonald's poster in an airport. I sold his book to Doubleday within a few months.

Recent sales: *Sister to Sister: Congresswomen Loretta & Linda Sanchez' Guide to Making History,* by Loretta and Linda Sanchez (Regan); *Build It, Sell It and Make a Mint,* by Joe John Duran (Wiley); *Molly Fox's Yoga Weight Loss Program,* by Molly Fox and Jonny Bowden (Adams Media)

HOW TO SUBMIT **Send query letter only by mail with SASE or by e-mail.**

✓ **TIPS**
Have the right platform or team with someone who does; just being smart about your topic (or having a Ph.D) isn't enough anymore.

★ **RECOMMENDATIONS**
Publishers Marketplace (Web site); Publishers Weekly Rights Alert (Web site); *Publishers Weekly* magazine

ELAINE KOSTER LITERARY AGENCY, LLC

55 CENTRAL PARK W., SUITE 6
NEW YORK NY 10023

PHONE	FAX
212.362.9488	212.712.0164

Agents:	Elaine Koster, Stephanie Lehmann
Background:	Ms. Koster has been an agent since 1998. Handles 35 clients. Sold 27 titles in the last year. Member of AAR, Women's Media Group, MWA. Prior to opening her agency, she was President and Publisher of Dutton NAL for over 20 years. "Having had a long career on the other side of the table, I have a very high profile in the publishing community. I have the editorial ex-pertise to help shape submissions to interest editors, have strong negotiating skills and can guide the author through every step of the publishing process, once the initial sale has been made."
Represents:	Nonfiction: how-to, health, cooking, memoir, narrative; Quality fiction: literary, ethnic, suspense/thriller, anything really interesting and well done
Does not represent:	Sci-fi/fantasy
Recent sales:	*The Kite Runner,* by Khaled Hosseini (Riverhead); *The Last Victim in Glen Ross,* by M.G. Kinkaid (Pocket Books); *Instant Persuasion,* by Laurie Puhn (Tarcher Books); *Truth be Told,* by Victoria Christopher Murray (Touchstone)
HOW TO SUBMIT	**Send query letter by mail with SASE.**

OTTO R. KOZAK LITERARY & MOTION PICTURE AGENCY

P.O. BOX 152
LONG BEACH NY 11561-0152

Agent:	Yitka Kozak
Background:	Mr. Kozak has been an agent for 24 years and handles 18 clients. Sold 6 scripts in the last year. Member of WGA. Prior to opening his agency, he was a film importer and a script editor. This agency handles and guides novice scriptwriters.
Represents:	Film/TV screenplays only
Does not represent:	Novels
Workshop topics:	Breaking into script market and sales; quality vs. commerciality
Conferences:	Cannes Film Festival
Success story:	I discovered an illustrator with a writing talent and she is now working on a book with her own illustrations.
Recent sales:	3 to European producers—children/family animated stories.

✓ **TIPS**
*Market more than
one script.*

★ **RECOMMENDATION**
The Agency Manual
that guides novice
scriptwriters through
theoretical and practi-
cal steps. Designed
as a scriptwriting
college course.
Query with the
agency.

HOW TO SUBMIT	**Send query letter and outline by mail with SASE.**

KRAAS LITERARY AGENCY

IRENE KRAAS
256 RANCHO ALEGRE RD.
SANTE FE NM 87508

ASHLEY KRAAS
507 N.W. 22ND AVE., SUITE 104
PORTLAND OR 97210

WEB SITE
www.kraasliteraryagency.com

Agents:	Irene Kraas (principal), Ashley Kraas (associate)
Background:	The Kraas Literary Agency (previously the Irene Kraas Agency) has been in business since 1990. During that time it has launched many new authors in both young adult and adult fiction. Member of AAR. After several years in the corporate sales and marketing arena, Ms. Ashley Kraas became an associate at the Kraas Literary Agency in 2002 to expand the agency's representations. Previous experience includes working as an associate at the Anita Diamant Agency. She was also an editorial assistant in the Warner Books romance and women's fiction department, where she worked with authors such as Helen Mittermeyer, Millie Criswell, Sherryl Woods, and Renaldo Fischer. Ashley also works as a freelance editor.
Represents:	MS. IRENE KRAAS: Seeks "big books," thrillers of all types—psychological, medical, and biological—and good, quirky, well-written mysteries, either series ideas or stand-alones. The voice must be fresh and bring something new to the genre; also looking for outstanding new voices in the area of literary fiction. I will still look at an occasional science fiction work (no fantasy), and very special young adult fiction, but only by previously published authors. Please look at some of the agency's young adult authors before you submit.
	MS. ASHLEY KRAAS: Nonfiction: including, but not limited to, biographies, business, self-help, spiritual, memoirs; Fiction: looking for authors with powerful, passionate voices in the areas of romance (historical, contemporary, Regency, paranormal, suspense); women's, historical
Conferences:	MS. IRENE KRAAS: Wrangling with Writing, The Society of Southwestern Authors, The Durango Writers Conference
	MS. ASHLEY KRAAS: Rocky Mountain Writers Conference, Willamette Writers Conference, The Shuswap Lake International Writers' Festival, Wrangling with Writing, The Society of Southwestern Authors, The Surrey International Writers Conference
Success story:	Recently, Ms. Irene Kraas made a couple of 6-figure sales for a first-time author, as well as a major movie deal for one of the agency's well-established authors.

Recent sales: *The Sword of the Land,* by Noel-Anne Brennan (Ace Books); *Night Terror,* by Chandler McGrew (Dell Publishing Co.); *Night Blooming: The Chronicles of Saint-Germain,* by Chelsea Quinn Yarbro (Warner Books)

| HOW TO SUBMIT |

Send the first 50 pages (or first 3 chapters, if the break is better) of a completed manuscript by mail with SASE. No e-mail submissions. Please note that nonfiction submissions, except for narrative nonfiction, should follow Jeff Herman's format in *Write the Perfect Book Proposal: 10 That Sold and Why.* It also doesn't hurt to include your e-mail address if you have one. Please make sure you send submissions to the appropriate address.

BERT P. KRAGES ATTORNEY AT LAW

6665 S.W. HAMPTON ST. SUITE 200
PORTLAND OR 97223-8354

PHONE	E-MAIL	WEB SITE
503.597.2525	krages@onemain.com	www.krages.com

Agent: Bert Krages

Background: Mr. Krages has been an agent for 2 years and handles 25 clients. Sold 4 titles in the last year. Prior to agenting, he was an attorney. He is known for being responsive to clients and is still building his client list.

Represents: Mostly nonfiction with particular interests in science, health, psychology

Does not represent: New Age, poetry, picture books

Clients: Leonard DuBoff, Greg Mannarino, Matthew Bauer, Max Elliott

Recent sales: *Spreadsheet Sorcery,* by Orrin White (Apress); *Guide to Acupressure and Acupuncture,* by Matthew Bauer (Avery/Penguin); *Antique and Art Collector's Legal Guide,* by Leonard DuBoff (Sphinx/Sourcebooks); *Gregorian Strategy for Multiple Deck Blackjack,* by Greg Mannarino (Citadel/Kensington)

168

HOW TO SUBMIT | **Send query letter by mail or e-mail.**

PETER LAMPACK AGENCY, INC.

551 FIFTH AVE., SUITE 1613
NEW YORK NY 10176-0187

PHONE
212.687.9106

FAX
212.687.9109

Agents:	Peter Lampack, Sandra Blanton (handles foreign territories, no U.S. sales), Loren Soeiro (all query letters)
Background:	Mr. Soeiro has been an agent for 8 years and handles approximately 15 clients. Sold 10–20 titles last year. Prior to agenting, he wrote free-lance book reviews. "I am the only agent at the Peter Lampack Agency who is currently accepting new clients. We have solid contacts at all the major publishers due to our strong list of commercial clients."
Represents:	Small novels, written with wit (but not comic novels); suspense fiction high on verisimilitude; commercial and literary fiction; nonfiction from recognized experts in a given field; prescriptive nonfiction
Does not represent:	Genre work such as westerns, romance, sci-fi/fantasy
Workshop topics:	What agents are looking for in a submission package; how to present one's work in a professional manner
Clients:	Stephen Horn, Miles Keaton Andrew, Nicole Stansbury, Patrick Foss; the agency at large represents Clive Cussler, Martha Grimes, Judith Kelman, Gerry Spence, J.M. Coetzee
Recent sales:	*The Husband's Dilemma,* by Nicole Stansbury (Avalon); *The Bang Devils,* by Patrick Foss (Perennial Dark Alley); *A Trojan Odyssey,* by Clive Cussler (Putnam); *How to Argue and Win Every Time,* by Gerry Spence (St. Martin's Press)

✓ **TIPS**
Take care to send only your best work; do not submit partially completed fiction. Edit and proofread everything before sending it to an agent. Also, do not refer to your work as a "fiction novel."

169

HOW TO SUBMIT	**Send query letter and no more than 10 introductory pages of your work by mail with SASE or e-mail.**

MICHAEL LARSEN/ELIZABETH POMADA LITERARY AGENTS

1029 JONES ST.
SAN FRANCISCO CA 94L09-5023

PHONE
415.673.0939

E-MAIL
larsenpoma@aol.com

WEB SITE
www.larsenpomada.com

✓ **TIPS**
We see too many writers seeking representation for projects before they are ready to be submitted. Unfinished, unpolished work that has not been vetted or edited—or even read! Craft counts. Writers should use their networks to make their work 100 percent. We think everyone should read Publishers Lunch regularly to keep up with what's happening in the publishing world.

170

Agents: Michael Larsen, Elizabeth Pomada

Background: Mr. Larsen and Ms. Pomada have been agents since they started the company in 1972. Members of AAR, ASJA, WNBA (Calif.), Writer's Club, National Writers Union, PEN, and Authors Guild. They handle approximately 100 clients and sell about 25–30 books a year. Prior to opening this agency, Mr. Larsen worked at Bantam, Morrow, and Pyramid; Ms. Pomada worked at Holt, David McKay, and The Dial Press. "Our openness to new writers, our experience as authors as well as agents, our reputation all make the agency attractive to new clients. As we say in our brochure, we have been launching careers since 1972."

Represents: Adult fiction: literary, commercial, genre; Adult nonfiction: narrative, self-help, business

Does not represent: Westerns, science fiction, anything on or about abuse of any kind, children's, poetry, plays, screenplays

Workshop topics: How to make yourself irresistible to any agent or publisher; get paid to write your book—how to write a book proposal; guerrilla marketing for writers, test market your book; publishing from A to Z

Conferences: San Francisco Writers Conference, Maui Writers Conference, Santa Barbara Writers Conference

Recent sales: *The Only Negotiating Guide You'll Ever Need,* by Peter Stark (Broadway Books); *Permission to Party,* by Jill Murphy Long (Sourcebooks); *Freedom,* by Leonard Frank (Random House); *The Runaway Duke,* by Julie Anne Long (Warner Books); *Guerilla Marketing for Free,* by Jay Conrad Levinson (Houghton Mifflin)

HOW TO SUBMIT

Authors may contact us by e-mail, briefly, to see if there's interest. For nonfiction, send a title and promotion plan first by mail with SASE or e-mail. For fiction, send the first 10 pages and a 2-page synopsis by mail with SASE and phone number.

LESCHER & LESCHER LTD.

47 E. 19TH ST.
NEW YORK NY 10003

PHONE	FAX	E-MAIL
212.529.1790	212.529.2716	rl@lescherltd.com *or* mc@lescherltd.com

Agents: Robert Lescher, Susan Lescher, Michael Choate

Background: The agency was founded in 1964 and handles approximately 100 clients. Sold approximately 30 titles in the last year. Member of AAR. Has agents in all countries.

Represents: Nonfiction: psychology, biography, contemporary issues and current affairs, memoir, law, travel, cookbooks, popular culture, narrative history; Fiction: literary and commercial, including mystery and suspense; Handles film and TV rights for clients only

Does not represent: Sci-fi/fantasy, romance, self-help, spiritual

Clients: Steven Bach, T. Berry Brazelton, M.D., Anne Fadiman, Frances FitzGerald, Paula Fox, Madeleine L'Engle, Robert M. Parker, Jr., Thomas Perry, Neil Sheehan, Calvin Trillin, Judith Viorst

171

HOW TO SUBMIT

Send query letter, double-spaced synopsis describing the project at length, and author bio by mail with SASE. No unsolicited manuscripts.

LEVINE GREENBERG LITERARY AGENCY, INC.

EAST COAST OFFICE:
307 SEVENTH AVE., SUITE 1906
NEW YORK NY 10001

WEST COAST OFFICE:
112 AUBURN ST.
SAN RAPHAEL CA 94901

PHONE
212.337.9034 (East)

PHONE
415.785.1582 (West)

WEB SITE
www.levine
greenberg.com

✓ **TIPS**
Pet peeves include writers who send an unsolicited manuscript with no SASE and then keep calling.

Agents: James A. Levine, Daniel Greenberg, Stephanie Kip Rostan, Arielle Eckstut (West Coast)

Background: The agency sold 70–80 titles last year. "We feel passionately about feeling passionately about the projects we take on."

Represents: MR. LEVINE: Any work that's smart and original
MR. GREENBERG: Any genre fiction except romance
MS. ROSTAN: Commercial and literary fiction, including mystery/suspense and women's fiction, plus self-help and psychology

Does not represent: MS. ROSTAN: Business, cookbooks, science fiction, children's, academic

Clients: Amanda Brown, Anders Henriksson, Peggy Klaus, Patricia Seybold

Recent sales: *Raising Fences,* by Michael Datcher (Riverhead); *Crossing the Chasm,* by Geoffrey Moore (HarperBusiness); *Our Dumb Century,* by The Onion (Crown); *Queen Bees and Wannabes,* by Rosalind Wiseman (Three Rivers Press)

172

HOW TO SUBMIT	**Fill out the submission form on the agency Web site. Responds in 2 weeks if interested.**

PAUL S. LEVINE LITERARY AGENCY

1054 SUPERBA AVE.
VENICE CA 90291-3940

PHONE / FAX
310.450.6711
310.450.0181

E-MAIL
pslevine@ix.netcom.
com

WEB SITE
www.netcom.com/~ps
levine/lawliterary.html

✓ **TIPS**
Do your homework. Don't try to get an agent until your work is completely finished and ready to be published.

Agent: Paul S. Levine

Background: Mr. Levine has represented writers for 22 years. Handles 40 clients and sold 30 titles in the last year. Prior to agenting, he practiced law and is both a literary agent and entertainment law attorney. Member, State Bar of California.

Represents: Adult, young adult, and children's fiction and nonfiction

Does not represent: Sci-fi/fantasy, horror

Workshop topics: The legal and business aspects of the book publishing business

HOW TO SUBMIT	**Send query letter only by mail or e-mail. Also accepts submissions at writer's conferences or by referral.**

ROBERT H. LIEBERMAN, AUTHOR'S REPRESENTATIVE

400 NELSON RD.
ITHACA NEW YORK 14850

PHONE / FAX	E-MAIL	WEB SITE
607.273.8801	rhl10@cornell.edu	www.people.cornell.
801.749.9682		edu/pages/RHL10/

Agent: Robert H. Lieberman

Background: The agency was established 1993. Mr. Lieberman represents 30 clients; many are highly recognized in their fields of expertise. For a look at my novel *The Last Boy* (just released in paperback) go to the publisher's Web page at www.sourcebooks.com/publicity/orderlastboy.html.

Represents: College-level text books; CD-ROM software; popular tradebooks in science, math, engineering, economics

Does not represent: Fiction, self-help, screenplays

HOW TO SUBMIT **Send query letter by mail with SASE or by e-mail (preferred). Exclusive submissions preferred; simultaneous queries okay. Finds most new clients by referral.**

173

WENDY LIPKIND AGENCY

120 EAST 81 ST.
NEW YORK NY 10028

PHONE	FAX	E-MAIL
212.628.9653	212.585.1306	lipkindag@aol.com

Agent: Wendy Lipkind

Background: Ms. Lipkind has been an agent for 26 years and currently handles 30 clients. Sold 10 titles in the last year. Member of AAR. Her agency has a small client list, gives personal attention, and has a strong editorial reputation.

✓ **TIPS**
Write an intelligent query letter, a comprehensive proposal.

Represents: Adult nonfiction: popular health, psychology, social history, memoir, women's issues

Does not represent: Fiction, children's

Workshop topics: The role of the literary agent

Clients: Dr. Ross Greene, Jennifer Kries

Recent sales: *In the Land of Lyme,* by Pamela Weinhaut (Random House); *The Prostate Health Program,* by Daniel Nixon and Max Gomez (Free Press)

HOW TO SUBMIT **Send query letter by e-mail only. No attachments.**

THE LITERARY GROUP

270 LAFAYETTE ST., #1505
NEW YORK NY 10012

PHONE / FAX	E-MAIL	WEB SITE
212.274.1616	JS@theliterarygroup.	www.theliterarygroup.
212.274.9876	com	com

✓ **TIPS**
*Manuscripts that are
worn and tattered or
single-spaced get
returned immediately.*

★ **WEB SITE
RECOMMENDATION**
www.firstfiction.org

Agents: Frank Weimann, Steve Laube, Ian Kleinert

Background: This agency has had 30 best-sellers in 40 months and represents 200 authors in general trade, 100 authors in the Christian market. Sold approximately 100 titles in the last year.

Represents: Fiction and nonfiction—everything but poetry

Workshop topics: How to write a book proposal; how to find a literary agent

Conferences: None yet scheduled, but we do a dozen a year.

Success story: *Flags of Our Fathers* was rejected by 27 houses and has now gone on to sell more than a million copies.

Clients: Bill Bonanno, Homer Hickam, James Bradley, Kareem Abdul Jabbar, Terry Bradshaw, Judith Landsdowne, H.W. Brands, Mike Medavoy, Laura Corn, Mary Monroe, Robert Ellis, Bill Russell, Sam Giancana, Susan Schindehette, Victoria Gotti, Britney Spears

Recent sales: *The Last of the Tin Can Sailors,* by James Hornfischer (Bantam); *Meditations on Good & Evil,* by Roger DePue (Warner Books); *The Million Dollar Mystery* series, by Mindy Starns Clark (Harvest House)

HOW TO SUBMIT

Send query letter by mail or e-mail with proposal and overview (for nonfiction) or synopsis and first 3 chapters (for fiction).

174

LITWEST GROUP, LLC

379 BURNING TREE CT.
HALF MOON BAY CA 94019

PHONE / FAX
212.980.3499
212.308.6405

WEB SITE
www.LitWest.com
www.Preskilllaw.com

Nancy Ellis
P.O. Box 1564
Willits CA 95490
nellis@mcn.org

Katherine Boyle
1157 Valencia St., #4
San Francisco CA 94110
kboyle1@mindspring.com

Linda Mead
P.O. Box 3063
Half Moon Bay
CA 94019
linda@litwest.com

Robert Preskill
LitWest Group
2130 Fillmore St., #313
San Francisco CA 94115-2224
literaryagent.geo@yahoo.com

Agents:	Katherine Boyle, Nancy Ellis, Linda Mead, Robert Preskill
Background:	Please see Web site for further details about each agent.
Represents:	**MS. BOYLE:** Nonfiction: narrative/memoir, social issues/current affairs, women's issues, pop culture, music, natural science and history, serious religion and spirituality, psychology, biography (especially art and music related); Literary fiction only (especially Southern, dark, some avant garde)
	MS. ELLIS: Nonfiction: health, sexuality, psychology, pop culture, narrative, military, parenting, business, politics, women's issues, spirituality, Asiana; Fiction: women's, male adventure and military, mystery, thrillers, life-in-transition fiction, literary, historical
	MS. MEAD: Nonfiction: business/personal finance, credentialed prescriptive self-help in parenting/health/psychology, narrative/memoir; Fiction: historical (steeped in research), ethnic/cultural, mysteries (especially cozies)
	MR. PRESKILL: Nonfiction: sports, travel, leisure, lifestyle, fitness, men's health, business, men's interest, design/architecture/art, politics, subculture, graphic novels, narrative; Literary fiction: some thrillers and mysteries, literary quality sci-fi
Conferences:	Mendocino Coast Writers Conference, Willamette Writers Conference, Austin Writers' League, Southwest Writers Conference, Southern Oregon Writers Conference, Maui Writers Conference, San Diego State University Writers' Conference, Jack London Writers Conference, American Society of Journalists and Authors, Pacific Northwest Writers Conference

175

Recent sales:	*Sometimes the Soul,* by Gioia Timpanelli (W.W. Norton, Vintage) American Book Award winner; *Every Day a Blessing,* by Aaron Zerah (Warner); *A Tax-Deductible Death,* by Malinda Terrieri (Berkley/Putnam); *Dancing Naked at the Edge of Dawn,* by Kris Radish (Bantam); *Zen and the Art of Persuasion,* by Kitta Reeds (Crown)

HOW TO SUBMIT	**Send query letter that describes the project and author (including a list of prior publications) by mail with SASE or e-mail (no attachments) to the agent whose areas of interest best fit your project. Please note each agent has his or her own address.**

STERLING LORD LITERISTIC, INC.

65 BLEECKER ST.
NEW YORK NY 10012

Agents:	Sterling Lord, Philippa Brophy, Peter Matson, Claudia Cross, Jim Putman, Neeti Madan, Laurie Liss, Chris Calhoun, George Nicholson, Charlotte Sheedy
Represents:	Fiction, nonfiction
Does not represent:	Science fiction, westerns
Clients:	James McBride, John McCain, Bob Kerrey

HOW TO SUBMIT	**Send a proposal that includes the first 3 chapters (no more than 50 pages) and a synopsis by mail.**

NANCY LOVE LITERARY AGENCY

250 E. 65TH ST.
NEW YORK NY 10021-6614

PHONE
212.980.3499

FAX
212.308.6405

E-MAIL
nloveag@aol.com

Agents:	Nancy Love, Miriam Tager
Background:	Ms. Love has been an agent for 18 years and handles 60 clients. Sold approximately 15 titles in the last year. Member of AAR, ASJA, Authors Guild. Prior to agenting, Ms. Love was a staff writer and editor at magazines, managing editor of a regional book publishing company, and a freelance writer of books and articles for major magazines. She has a strong reputation and knowledge of the business, many contacts, strong editorial input, and a solid author list.
Represents:	Nonfiction: current affairs, history, health, parenting, crime, inspirational, biography; Fiction: mysteries and thrillers only
Does not represent:	Memoir, poetry, children's, fiction (except mysteries and thrillers)
Workshop topics:	Platform building; how to sell a mystery; how to impress an agent
Clients:	Stephen Kenzer, Ben Render, The Children's Hospital of Philadelphia
Recent sales:	*7 Tools People Use to Quit Addiction,* by Stanton Peele (Random House); 2-book contract for untitled mysteries by Ben Rehder (St. Martin's Press); *Back Pain,* by Emile Hiesiger, MD (Pocket Books); *Searching for Irma,* by June Erlick (Seal Press)

✓ **TIPS**
State clearly what your book is about. Be sure you are sending it to the right agent. Don't send anything that hasn't been polished.

177

HOW TO SUBMIT | **For nonfiction, send proposal and first chapter by mail with SASE. For mysteries, send query letter and first chapter by mail with SASE. Nothing will be returned without an SASE.**

ANDREW LOWNIE LITERARY AGENCY LTD.

17 SUTHERLAND ST.
LONDON SW1V4JU
ENGLAND

PHONE / FAX
(0) 20 7828 1274
(0) 20 7828 7608

E-MAIL
lownie@globalnet.
co.uk

WEB SITE
www.andrewlownie.
co.uk

Agent: Andrew Lownie

Background: Mr. Lownie has been an agent since 1985 and currently handles 130 clients. Sold approximately 50 titles in the last year. Member of Association of Authors' Agents, PEN (Executive Committee), Society of Authors. Prior to opening his agency, he was publisher at Hodder, a journalist and author, and director at John Farquharson/Curtis Brown. "I concentrate on an area I know—history and biography—and in which I write myself. I have good connections throughout the media as a former journalist and use them to help promote my authors. I see my relationship with authors as a long-term pastoral one."

Represents: History, biography, current affairs; anything that is original and well-written

Does not represent: Poetry, short stories, fiction, mind/body/spirit

Workshop topics: Biography; how to place nonfiction

HOW TO SUBMIT **Send synopsis of about 20 pages and a sample chapter by mail or e-mail. Prefer approaches in writing.**

DONALD MAASS LITERARY AGENCY

160 WEST 95TH ST., SUITE 1B
NEW YORK NY 10025

PHONE	E-MAIL	WEB SITE
212.866.8200	info@maassagency.com	www.maassagency.com

Agents:	Donald Maass, Jennifer Jackson, Rachel Vater, Cameron McClure
Background:	Mr. Maass has been an agent for 24 years, member of AAR, MWA, SFFWA; Ms. Jackson for 10 years, member of AAR; Ms. Somberg for 2 years, member of AAR; and Ms. Vater for 1 year, member of AAR. Represents more than 100 authors, many of them full-time novelists. Sold approximately 100 titles in the last year. Prior to opening his agency, Mr. Maass was an agent with the Scott Meredith Literary Agency and an editor at Dell Publishing. He is a pioneer in the development of fiction careers and an innovator in editorial work with novelists.
Represents:	Fiction, all kinds
Does not represent:	Children's illustrated books, nonfiction, poetry
Workshop topics:	Mr. Maass teaches *Writing the Breakout Novel* workshops in cities around the country; see the following Web site for dates and locations: www.free-expressions.com
Conferences:	Multiple RWA chapter conferences, Pennwriters Conference, Dark & Stormy (MWA, Chicago), Malice Domestic, WorldCon, World Fantasy Con, Bouchercon, RWA National, Willamette Writers' Conference, Surrey (B.C.) Writers Conference
Success story:	Oregon journalist Gregg Keizer sent me a query letter about his first novel, a WWII thriller called *Save One.* We had never met, he was referred by no one—he just picked my name out of a directory. I worked with him for several months on revisions to the novel and subsequently sold it to G.P. Putnam's Sons for 6 figures.
Clients:	Mystery/thrillers: Anne Perry, Stuart Kaminsky, Parnell Hall, Gregg Keizer; Sci-fi/fantasy: Diane Duane, Nalo Hopkinson, Anne Bishop, Jim Butcher; Romance/women's: Lauren Baratz-Logsted, Lori Herter, Patricia Rosemoor Historical: Jack Whyte
Recent sales:	*No Graves As Yet,* by Anne Perry (Ballantine); *Save One,* by Gregg Keizer (G.P. Putnam's Sons); *Dragon's Kin,* by Anne & Todd McCaffrey (Del Rey); *Eastern Standard Tribe,* by Cory Doctorow (TOR)

✓ **TIPS**
Keep your query letter short and businesslike—not that anybody listens to that advice!

★ **BOOK RECOMMENDATIONS**
The Career Novelist and *Writing the Breakout Novel,* by Donald Maass.

HOW TO SUBMIT	**Send query letter and the first 5 pages of the manuscript, if desired, by mail with SASE.**

THE ROBERT MADSEN LITERARY AGENCY

1331 EAST 34TH ST., #1
OAKLAND CA 94602-1032

PHONE
510.223.2090

Agents:	Robert Madsen, Liz Madsen
Background:	The agency handles approximately 8 clients and is actively building a client list. It sold 4 books last year. Mr. Madsen has been an agent for 11 years. Prior to opening his agency, he worked in printing and publishing.
Represents:	General nonfiction, genre and mainstream fiction
Clients:	Paul Suter, Marita Golden, Tim Egan, Elizabeth Mehren, Fox Butterfield, Shelby Steele, Dr. William Julius Wilson, Thomas Sowell, Tufts University's Eilliot Pearson School of Education America 24/7 creators, Dr. Judith Wallerstein

HOW TO SUBMIT | **Send query letter, a brief (1- or 2-page) synopsis, and the first 50 pages by mail with SASE.**

MANUS & ASSOCIATES LITERARY AGENCY, INC.

425 SHERMAN AVE., SUITE 200
PALO ALTO CA 94306

PHONE / FAX	E-MAIL	WEB SITE
650.470.5151	ManusLit@ManusLit.	www.manuslit.com
650.470.5159	com	

Agents: Jillian Manus, Jandy Nelson, Stephanie Lee

Background: The agency currently handles approximately 75 clients. Ms. Manus lends her time to professional, artistic, and practical endeavors. She serves on several local and national boards including the Board of Trustees for New York University, WISH List (Women in the Senate and House), and College Track. She also remains very active in the efforts of numerous literacy and mentoring programs across the country. Reflecting her standing in the community, she was a participant in the Women's Business Leaders Forum at the White House in March 2001. Hosted by the First Lady, the event brought together some of the nation's most respected female executives for a discussion of critical issues. Ms. Manus has been a television agent at International Creative Management, director of development at Warner Brothers and Universal Studios, vice president of media acquisitions at Trender AG, and an associate publisher of 2 national magazines, *Upside* and *Premiere,* covering entertainment and technology. Because of this remarkably comprehensive background, she is a much sought after speaker on writing, women in business, politics, and the media industry. Known for paying special attention to books that empower women physically, psychologically, and spiritually, Ms. Manus brings to her work extensive knowledge of the marketplace and editorial sensitivity that has been acquired in the course of a distinguished and multi-faceted career.

Represents: Fiction, nonfiction

Does not represent: Children's, poetry, romance, westerns, science fiction, fantasy, screenplays

Workshop topics: How to write a nonfiction book proposal; the perfect pitch

Conferences: BEA, Mega Book Marketing University, Maui Writer's Conference

Clients: Newt Gingrich; Dr. Laraine Zappert, Ph.D; Mother Theresa (with Dr. Richard Bergland); Mark Victor Hansen; Robert G. Allen; Jim Karas; Dr. Fred Luskin, Ph.D.; Alexander Sanger; Kenneth T. Walsh; Doug Wead; Molly Davis; Kristine Van Raden; Lalita Tademy;

✓ **TIPS**
Before you query, make sure that your work is 100 percent polished. Give your book or proposal to 10 people whose opinions you trust (local booksellers, librarians, your writers group, old professors) and get objective feedback. Write an outstanding query letter (read "The Perfect Pitch" at www.manuslit.com to get started). We get over 1,000 submissions a month, so get us excited about your work. Research the agents you are submitting to, either in writer's guides, agency Web sites, or by browsing the "Acknowledgments" section in your favorite books. Be familiar with our client lists and the types of material we handle, as this will help you better focus your submission process as well as help convince us that we could be the right match.

181

Clients *cont.*: Glenn Kleier; Frank Baldwin; Alan Jacobson; Derek Hansen; Dini Petty; Ann Brandt

HOW TO SUBMIT

For nonfiction, send a query letter, which pitches your project and includes any pertinent biographical information, and a complete proposal (see "How To Write a Nonfiction Proposal" in the Info for Writers section of our Web site); include sample chapters that are double-spaced, single-sided, and unbound by mail with SASE. For fiction, send a query letter, which pitches your project and includes any pertinent biographical information, and the first 30 pages of your manuscript (double-spaced, single-sided, and unbound) by mail with SASE. Always include an SASE for our reply, or a larger SASE if you need your materials returned. For e-mail or fax queries, please send only your query letter without attachments. Query only one of our agents with your project. If it is not right for one agent's list, but we feel that it might be right for another, we will pass it on for you to the correct person. Our agency cannot accept checks, cash, or money orders for postage. Please send stamps or postal vouchers only (vouchers can be purchased at post offices everywhere). Our offices receive a tremendous amount of material daily, all of which requires personal attention from at least three readers before a final decision is made. We do reply to every submission, and we appreciate your patience while we evaluate your material. If we haven't contacted you within 8 weeks, feel free to e-mail or call us.

MARCH TENTH, INC.

4 MYRTLE ST.
HAWORTH NJ 07641-1740

PHONE	FAX	E-MAIL
201.387.6551	201.387.6552	hchoron@aol.com

Agents:	Sandra Choron, Harry Choron
Background:	Mr. Choron has been an agent for 21 years and handles 50 clients. Sold 14 titles in the last year. Prior to agenting, he was an editor at Hawthorn Books from 1974–1980 and an editor at Dell Publishing from 1980–1982. "We're constantly looking at new areas and "staying fresh." We have a strong editorial background and excellent contacts at publishers both large and small."
Represents:	General nonfiction, with a special emphasis on popular culture; Mainstream and literary fiction
Workshop topics:	Author-publisher relations; preparing book proposals
Conferences:	BEA
Clients:	Dave Marsh, Rabbi Arthur Hertzberg, John Waters, David Niven, James Saywell and Evelyn McFarlane, Kathi Goldmark
Recent sales:	*The 100 Simple Secrets of Happy Families,* by David Niven (Harper San Francisco); *The Case for Zionism,* by Arthur Hertzberg (HarperCollins); *The Appalachians,* by Mari-Lynn Evans (Random House); *The Uncollected Stories of Henry James,* by Floyd Horowitz (Carrol and Graf)

183

HOW TO SUBMIT	**Send query letter that includes a concise description of the project, all background details, and contact information by mail or e-mail.**

EVAN MARSHALL LITERARY AGENCY

SIX TRISTAM PL.
PINE BROOK NJ 07058-9445

PHONE
973.882.1122

FAX
973.882.3099

Agent: Evan Marshall

Background: Mr. Marshall has been an agent for 21 years, currently handles 60 clients, and has sold about 150 titles in the past year. Prior to opening his own agency, he was an agent at The Sterling Lord Agency (now Sterling Lord Literistic). Prior to that he was a book editor at Houghton Mifflin, NAL, Everest House, and Dodd, Mead. His agency's strengths are managing the careers of fiction writers and helping them achieve their goals.

Represents: General fiction, mystery, romance, fantasy/sci-fi, suspense, romantic suspense, thrillers, young adult, mainstream women's fiction, literary fiction, chick lit, romantic comedy, mainstream fiction, romantic fiction, literary thrillers

Does not represent: Nonfiction, children's

Conferences: SleuthFest, Heartland Writers Guild

Clients: Erica Spindler, Elaine Barbieri, Barbara Colley, Isis Crawford, Jerrilyn Farmer, Judith E. French, Hannah Howell, Bobby Hutchinson, Laura Levine, Constance O'Banyon, Charles O'Brien, Candace Robb, Evelyn Rogers, Lynsay Sands, David Schulman, Bobbi Smith

HOW TO SUBMIT **Send query letter by mail with SASE.**

MCHUGH LITERARY AGENCY

1033 LYON RD.
MOSCOW ID 83843-9167

PHONE	FAX	E-MAIL
208.882.0107	847.628.0146	elisabetmch@ turbonet.com

Agent: Elisabet McHugh

Background: McHugh has been an agent since 1995 and handles 42 clients. Prior to opening her agency, she was a full-time writer/book author for 14 years. She has also been a newspaper editor and a technical translator.

Represents: Nonfiction: open to most subjects except business; Fiction: romance, historical, mystery/suspense, mainstream

Does not represent: Sci-fi/fantasy, horror, young adult, juvenile

Conferences: Willamette Writer's Conference, Pacific Northwest Writers Association Conference

Clients: Chrystopher Spicer, Anne Peterson, Cynthia York

★ **WEB SITE RECOMMENDATION**
www.authorlink.com

HOW TO SUBMIT | **Send query letter by e-mail (no attachments). Be brief and professional.**

185

MARTHA MILLARD LITERARY AGENCY

145 WEST 71 ST., #8A
NEW YORK NY 10023

PHONE	FAX
212.787.7769	212.787.7867

HOW TO SUBMIT | **By referral only.**

THE STUART M. MILLER CO.

11684 VENTURA BLVD., #225
STUDIO CITY CA 91604-2699

PHONE	FAX	E-MAIL
818.506.6067	818.506.4079	smmco@aol.com

Agent:	Stuart M. Miller
Background:	Mr. Miller has been an agent since 1967 and currently handles 10–12 clients. Prior to opening his agency, he was Executive Vice President, Agency For The Performing Arts, Los Angeles and New York 1982–1995 Head of Literary, Packaging and New Media.
Represents:	Motion picture screenplays, television packages, fiction and nonfiction books, new media content, technology
Does not represent:	PPEC series television scripts, poetry

HOW TO SUBMIT

Send a 2–3 page narrative outline (for screenplays) or a 5–10 page, double-spaced narrative outline (for manuscripts) with all of the major story beats, leaving nothing for me to guess at, by e-mail. If sent as an attachment, be sure to include your name and e-mail address on any attached documents.

MOCKNICK PRODUCTIONS LITERARY AGENCY

237 BROOKS ST.
WILLOW GROVE PA 19090

PHONE / FAX	E-MAIL	WEB SITE
215.659.1344	davemocknick@yahoo.	www.mocknick.com
215.659.1344	com	

Agent:	David L. Mocknick
Background:	Mr. Mocknick has been an agent for 2 years and handles approximately 50 clients. Prior to opening his agency, he was a writer, producer, director, and actor. He is open to taking on new writers.
Represents:	Fiction, nonfiction of all genres
Does not represent:	Erotica, pornography

HOW TO SUBMIT

Send 1-page synopsis and first 3 chapters by mail or e-mail.

DEE MURA LITERARY

269 WEST SHORE DR.
MASSAPEQUA NY 11758-8225

PHONE
516.795.1616

FAX
516.795.8797

Agents:	Dee Mura, Frank Nakamura, Karen Roberts, Brian Hertler
Background:	This agency has been in operation since 1987. Member of WGA. Prior to opening the agency, Ms. Mura was a public relations executive with a roster of film and entertainment clients, and she also worked in editorial for major weekly news magazines.
Represents:	A wide range of nonfiction books, novels, and scripts. Especially interested in literary and commercial fiction and nonfiction, thrillers and espionage, self-help, inspirational, medical, scholarly, true-life stories, true crime, and women's stories and issues

HOW TO SUBMIT | **Send query letter that includes a brief paragraph on yourself and a short synopsis by mail with SASE or e-mail (no attachments). No fax queries. Responds within 2 weeks.**

JEAN V. NAGGAR LITERARY AGENCY

216 EAST 75TH ST., SUITE 1E
NEW YORK NY 10021

✓ TIPS

Pet peeve: Writers who compare themselves and/or their work to someone or something already published and obviously very successful.

Agents:	Jean Naggar, Alice Tasman, Jennifer Weltz (children's books only), Anne Engel (serious nonfiction only)
Background:	Ms. Naggar has been an agent for 28 years. Sold approximately 35 titles in the last year. Member of AAR, WMG, WF. Before becoming an agent, Ms. Naggar worked as a book reviewer, translator, and editor. She notes that "clients are drawn to our strong reputation and our emphasis on marketing and strategy."
Represents:	Mainstream fiction, nonfiction
Does not represent:	Formula fiction
Success story:	Elizabeth Crane—a short-story writer whose first collection, *When the Messenger Is Hot,* was very well received. Her second collection will be published in spring 2005. She came to me over the transom with an excellent query letter and sample materials.
Clients:	Jean Auel, Maud Casey, Elizabeth Crane, Phillip Margolin, Mary McGarry Morris, Ellen Potter, Lily Prior, Carl Safina, Nancy Willard
Recent sales:	*Olivia Kidney Stops for No One,* by Ellen Potter (Philomel/Penguin); *The Snow Fox,* by Susan Fromberg Schaaffer (Norton); *Ardor,* by Lily Prior (Ecco); *Trust Me,* by Judy Markey (Mira); *A Hole in the Universe,* by Mary McGarry Morris (Viking)

HOW TO SUBMIT

Send an outline and the first 10 pages by mail with SASE. Query letters should be concise (1 page with a clear description of the book and an author bio). It is always very helpful to include a list of previous publications.

HAROLD OBER ASSOCIATE INC.

425 MADISON AVE.
NEW YORK NY 10017

PHONE
212.759.8600

FAX
212.759.9428

Agents: Phyllis Westberg, president (member of AAR)—literary; Emma Sweeney (member of AAR)—literary; Alexander C. Smithline—literary, film, TV; Craig Tenney (member of AAR)—literary, permissions; Pamela Malpas (member of AAR)—literary and translation rights; Don Laventhall, director of film rights

Background: This agency was founded in 1929. The Knox Burger agency merged with Harold Ober Associates in 2000.

Represents: General fiction, nonfiction

Does not represent: Plays, film scripts

HOW TO SUBMIT | **Send query letter by mail with SASE. No unsolicited manuscripts; no fax or e-mail queries. Obtains most clients through recommendations.**

OMNIQUEST ENTERTAINMENT

1416 N. LA BREA AVE.
HOLLYWOOD CA 90028

FAX
323.802.1633

E-MAIL
info@omniquestmedia.com

WEB SITE
www.omniquestmedia.com

Agent: Michael Kaliski

Represents: Novels, short story collections, novellas, movie scripts, feature film, TV scripts, TV movie of the week, episodic drama, sitcom, miniseries, syndicated material, stage plays

HOW TO SUBMIT | **By referral only.**

BARRY PERELMAN AGENCY

1155 N. LACENIGA, #412
W. HOLLYWOOD CA 90069

PHONE
310.659.1122

Background:	Member of DGA, WGA.
Represents:	Movie scripts: action, biography, contemporary issues, crime, historical, horror, mystery, thriller, science fiction, romantic comedy, romantic drama
Does not represent:	Fiction or nonfiction books

HOW TO SUBMIT **Send query letter and synopsis by mail with SASE.**

ALISON J. PICARD, LITERARY AGENT

P.O. BOX 2000
COTUIT MA 02635

PHONE   **E-MAIL**
508.477.7192   ajpicard@aol.com

Agent:	Alison Picard
Background:	Picard has been an agent since 1982 and currently handles 50 clients. Sold 20 titles in the last year. The agency is known for strong editorial and marketing reputation; it is still actively building a client list.
Represents:	Nonfiction; Fiction: mainstream and literary, contemporary and historical romances, mysteries and thrillers, juvenile and young adult books. Especially interested in commercial nonfiction, romances, and mystery/suspense/thrillers.
Does not represent:	Short stories, articles, poetry, plays
Clients:	Osha Gray Davidson, David Ely, Rachel Swift

HOW TO SUBMIT **Send query letter by mail or e-mail (no attachments). No phone or fax queries.**

A PICTURE OF YOU LITERARY AGENCY

1176 ELIZABETH DR.
HAMILTON OH 45013-3507

PHONE
513.863.1108

FAX
513.863.1108

Agents:	Lenny Minelli, Michelle Chang
Background:	Mr. Minelli has been an agent for 9 years and currently handles approximately 25 clients. Sold 4 titles in the last year. Member of WGA. Prior to working at this agency, he was an actor, talent agent, and producer.
Represents:	Screenplays of all genres
Recent sales:	*I am Pretty Sure I Have a Fear of Commitment,* by Terry Cosgrove (Alex Rose Productions); *Heir,* by Chera Federle (Popcorn Productions); *I Should Have Married Joe,* by Chera Federle (Accent Pictures)

✓ **TIPS**
Please make sure your material is the best it can be before seeking out an agent.

HOW TO SUBMIT

Send a query letter and 1-page synopsis only by mail with SASE or e-mail.

SUSAN RABINER LITERARY AGENCY

240 W. 35TH ST.
NEW YORK NY 10001

PHONE	PHONE	E-MAIL
212.279.0316	646.733.9137	susan@rabiner.net
(Ms. Rabiner)	(Ms. Arellano)	

★ **BOOK RECOMMENDATION**
Thinking Like Your Editor: How to Write Great Serious Nonfiction and Get it Published, by Susan Rabiner and Alfred Fortinato (Norton)

Agents: Susan Rabiner, Susan Arellano

Background: Ms. Rabiner has been an agent for 6 years and represents approximately 50 clients. Sold 10–15 titles in the last year. "We specialize in serious nonfiction and are ex-editors ourselves." Ms. Rabiner was editorial director at Basic Books, then at the serious nonfiction division of HarperCollins Publishers.

Represents: Serious nonfiction: history, science, psychology, education, law, politics, business (by academics), economics, books about the lives of women

Does not represent: Personal memoir, self-help

Workshop topics: How to write a selling proposal

Clients: Iris Chang, Elizabeth Warren, Stephanie Coontz

Recent sales: *The Equation that Couldn't be Solved,* by Mario Livio (Simon & Schuster); *The Bombs of June,* by Constantine Pleshakov (Houghton Mifflin); *Searching for Satisfaction,* by Gregory Burns (Holt); *Extradimensions,* by Lawrence Krauss (Viking Penguin)

HOW TO SUBMIT	**Send a query letter by e-mail.**

JODIE RHODES LITERARY AGENCY

8840 VILLA LA JOLLA DR., SUITE 315
LA JOLLA CA 92037-1957

PHONE / FAX	E-MAIL	WEB SITES
858.625.0544	jrhodes1@san.rr.com	writers.net
858.625.0544		literaryagent.com

Agents: Jodie Rhodes, Clark McCutcheon (fiction agent-at-large), Bob McCarter (nonfiction agent-at-large)

Background: Ms. Rhodes has been an agent for 5 years and handles 60 authors. Sold 30 titles in the last year, including some series; almost all were written by previously unpublished authors. Member of AAR. Prior to opening her agency, she served as vice president, media director for N.W. Ayer's West Coast office for many years. Wrote 2 novels in the early 1980s: *American Beauties* (Bantam), and *Winners and Losers* (Putnam), which made the best-seller list its first week in print. Also wrote scripts for various TV series and conducted writing workshops. Ms. Rhodes has a strong editorial background, provides editorial guidance to her clients, and has very fast turn-around time with her projects.

Represents: Nonfiction: women's issues, multicultural, memoirs and biographies, history, politics, world issues, law, military, medicine and science, health, fitness, parenting; Fiction: literary, multicultural, women's issues, sophisticated classy thrillers and suspense novels, mysteries with fresh plot ideas and charismatic protagonists, mainstream contemporary novels notable for their wit and intelligence. Considers literary young adult and teen novels.

Does not represent: Religion, spiritual, inspirational, children's, sci-fi/fantasy, horror, erotica, romance novels, westerns

Workshop topics: How to find the right agent for your particular book; how to approach an agent; how to write a query letter that will get their attention; how to do a synopsis; the importance of the first page of your book; how to do a book proposal; the importance of research; the importance of "voice"

Success story: The most exciting story is that of brand-new author Kavita Daswani (see page 18 in this directory for the full story).

Recent sales: *Infidelity* (MacAdam/Cage and Broadway) and *Living in a Black and White World* (Wiley), by Ann Pearlman, co-author of *Inside the Crips* (St. Martins); *For Matrimonial Purposes,* by Kavita Daswani (Putnam, U.S., HarperCollins UK, translation rights sold in France, Germany, Italy, Spain, Greece, Holland, Israel, and

193

Recent sales *cont.*: Japan); *Like Sound Through Water* (Simon & Schuster) and *Post Adoption Blues* (Rodale), by Karen Foli; *Sapphire's Grave,* by Hilda Gurley Highgate (Doubleday); *When the Brain Can't Hear,* by Teri Bellis (Simon & Schuster); *Ghostly Encounters* (Warner) and *The Myrtles* (Warner), by Frances Kermeen; *Inside Wall Street,* by Susan Scherbel (HarperCollins); *The Anorexia Diaries,* by Linda and Tara Rio (Rodale); *The Dwarf in Louis XIV's Court,* by Paul Weidner (Univ of Wisconsin Press, U.S., and Kinneret-Zmora, Israel)

HOW TO SUBMIT **Send query letter, brief (less than 3 full pages) synopsis, and the opening 30–50 pages of the book by mail with SASE. E-mail and fax queries will not be considered. We are open to queries from all writers who are writing books that fit our list. Submissions must be computer generated; no handwritten or typewriter-produced material.**

ANGELA RINALDI LITERARY AGENCY

P.O. BOX 7877
BEVERLY HILLS CA 90212-7877

PHONE	FAX	E-MAIL
310.842.7665	310.837.8143	info@rinaldiliterary.com

Agent:	Angela Rinaldi
Background:	Ms. Rinaldi has been an agent for 10 years and handles 50 clients. Member of AAR. Prior to opening her agency, she was executive editor at Bantam Books; executive editor, NAL; senior editor, Pocket Books; and manager, book publishing, *Los Angeles Times.* The agency is distinguished by knowledge of the industry and editors. Ms. Rinaldi has been in the publishing business since 1969, acquiring, editing, and managing. The agency is known for its excellent reputation and sales to major houses. Experience in shaping nonfiction proposals and giving editorial feedback on novels.
Represents:	Nonfiction, literary and commercial fiction. Very interested in women's fiction—commercial and literary
Does not represent:	Genre/category—romances, historical romance, science fiction, fantasy, cookbooks, poetry, children's, young adult, technothrillers
Clients:	Dr. Spencer Johnson, Dr. Joseph Parent, Louise Oxhorn, Lynne Oxhorn-Ringwood, Dr. Marjorie Krausz, Dr. Ridha Arem, Stephanie Kane, Marjorie Reynolds, Peter Goodman, Eben Paul Perison, Bonnie Shimko, Drusilla Campbell

195

HOW TO SUBMIT

For nonfiction, send a query letter that contains the concept and a brief outline if a proposal is not available by mail with SASE. For fiction, send first 3 chapters with cover letter (no query letter needed). Fast response given if the SASE is standard envelope and material does not have to be returned. Very brief e-mails accepted. Because of the volume and virus scares, I do not open attachments nor can I go to author Web sites.

ANN RITTENBERG LITERARY AGENCY, INC.

1201 BROADWAY, SUITE 708
NEW YORK NY 10001

WEB SITE
www.rittlit.com

Agents:	Ann Rittenberg, Ted Gideonse
Background:	Ms. Rittenberg began working as an agent for the Julian Bach Agency. She formed her own agency in 1992. Mr. Gideonse joined the agency in 2002.
Represents:	General nonfiction, mainstream and literary fiction
Does not represent:	Genre fiction, screenplays
Clients:	Mark Caldwell, Melody Chavis, Kathleen George, Dennis Lehane, Brad Smith

HOW TO SUBMIT	**Send a query letter by mail with SASE. Do not send queries by fax or e-mail.**

B.J. ROBBINS LITERARY AGENCY

5130 BELLAIRE AVE.
NORTH HOLLYWOOD CA 91607-2908

PHONE   **FAX**
818.760.6602   818.760.6616

Agents:	B.J. Robbins, Regina Su Mangum
Background:	The agency has been in operation since 1992 and represents approximately 40 clients. Members of AAR.
Represents:	Nonfiction, literary and mainstream fiction. Especially interested in representing narrative nonfiction.
Recent sales:	*The Sex Lives of Cannibals,* by J. Maarten Troost (Broadway); *Coffee and Kung Fu,* by Karen Brichoux (NAL); *The Last Summer,* by John Hough, Jr. (Simon & Schuster, NAL)

HOW TO SUBMIT	**Send query letter with 3 sample chapters, and outline/proposal by mail with SASE. Do not send queries by fax or e-mail.**

THE ROSENBERG GROUP

23 LINCOLN AVE.
MARBLEHEAD CA 01945

PHONE
781.990.1341

FAX
781.990.1344

WEB SITE
www.rosenberg
group.com

Agent:	Barbara Collins Rosenberg
Background:	The agency represents approximately 35 clients. Member of AAR, RWA, Authors Guild. Ms. Rosenberg founded the agency in 1998 with her husband; she now runs the agency alone.
Represents:	Nonfiction: current affairs, autobiography, memoirs, pop culture, psychology, women's issues, women's health, textbooks; Fiction: literary, romance, women's
Does not represent:	Inspirational, time travel, futuristic, paranormal
Clients:	Jeff Guinn, Marilyn Kentz, Shawn Messonnier, Donald M. Murray

HOW TO SUBMIT | **Send a query letter by mail with SASE. Do not query by fax or e-mail. For specific guidelines for submission, please visit the Web site. For fiction, please query before sending a synopsis and sample chapters.**

RITA ROSENKRANZ LITERARY AGENCY

440 WEST END AVE., SUITE 15D
NEW YORK NY 10024

PHONE
212.873.6333

Agent:	Rita Rosenkranz
Background:	Ms. Rosenkranz has been an agent for 13 years and currently handles 30 clients. Sold 25 titles in the last year. Prior to opening her agency, she was an editor at major New York houses. She offers her clients strong editorial refinements.
Represents:	Most nonfiction categories
Does not represent:	Fiction, poetry

HOW TO SUBMIT | **Send query letter by mail with SASE.**

CAROL SUSAN ROTH LITERARY

P.O. BOX 620337
WOODSIDE CA 94062

PHONE
650.323.3795

E-MAIL
carol@authorsbest.com

198

Agent:	Carol Susan Roth
Background:	Roth has been an agent for 8 years and handles 50 clients. Sold 16 titles in the last year. Prior to opening her agency, Roth was a producer of events featuring best-selling authors in health, personal growth, spirituality, and business. Trained as a psychotherapist (M.A., California Institute of East West Studies). Her agency is known for her strong promotional and market-ing experience; it has represented 3 national best-sellers with several first-time authors.
Represents:	Nonfiction: health, personal growth, spirituality, business
Does not represent:	Fiction, poetry, children's, "channeled" writings
Workshop topics:	How to create a national best-selling book (Learning Annex)
Conferences:	BEA
Success story:	Testimonial letter from Jennifer Lawler, author of *Dojo Wisdom: 100 Simple Ways to Become a Stronger, Calmer, More Courageous Person:* "Prior to Carol becoming my agent, I had had four other agents, none of whom sold any of my books. I got 16 books published myself with modest advances. Carol has gotten ad-vances for me as much as 10 times higher than any I negotiated for myself! Although I have always thought of myself as a niche writer, Carol showed me how I could successful-ly bring my message to a broader, more main-stream audience, thus earning substantially larger advances and reaching more readers … In the less than 2 years we've worked together, she has sold 7 book projects for me to major publishers. We're working on the 8th sale now. Carol always has my career goals in mind and will discourage me from taking on projects that don't fit with those goals, while at the same time hunting for editors and projects who will take me closer to my dreams."
Clients:	Georg Feurstein, Jennifer Lawler, Jeff Strong
Recent sales:	*How Great Decisions Get Made,* by Don Maruska (AMACOM); *Dojo Wisdom for Writers,* by Jennifer Lawler (Viking); *Protols Guide,* by Jeff Strong (John Wiley); *Pilates Fusion,* by Shirley Archer (Chronicle Books)

HOW TO SUBMIT **Send query letter by e-mail (please no files or attachments).**

VICTORIA SANDERS LITERARY AGENCY

241 AVENUE OF THE AMERICAS
NEW YORK NY 10014-4822

E-MAIL
queriesvsa@hotmail.
com

WEB SITE
www.victoriasanders.
com

✓ TITS
ite a great pitch
r. No typos, etc.

Agents: Victoria Sanders, Diane Dickensheid

Background: Ms. Sanders has been an agent for over 10 years and represents 75 clients. Sold approximately 10 titles in the last year. Prior to opening her agency, she was director of contracts at Simon & Schuster, Inc.

Represents: Nonfiction: memoir, biography; Fiction: literary and commercial

Does not represent: Children's, science fiction

Clients: Karin Slaughter, Connie Briscoe, Yolanda Joe, Kim Creen, Estate of Zora Neale Hurston, Carol Bolt

Recent sales: *Indelible and Faithless,* by Karin Slaughter (William Morrow); *Angry Black Women's Guide to Life,* by Denene Millner, Angela Burt-Murray, Mitzi Miller (Dutton); *My Jim,* by Nancy Rawles (Crown); *Mom's Book of Answers,* by Carol Bolt (Abrams)

HOW TO SUBMIT | Send query letter by mail or e-mail.

SANDUM & ASSOCIATES

144 E. 84TH ST.
NEW YORK NY 10028-2035

PHONE
212.737.2011

E-MAIL
h.sandum@verizon.net

Agent: Howard E. Sandum

Background: Sandum has been an agent since 1987. Prior to opening his agency, he worked 25 years as editor-in-chief of trade books at 4 major publishers.

Represents: Mainstream nonfiction, literary fiction

Does not represent: Genre fiction, how-to, self-help

HOW TO SUBMIT | Send query letter with brief writing sample by mail only, preferably with referral.

PETER RUBIE LITERARY AGENCY

240 W. 35TH ST., SUITE 500
NEW YORK NY 10001

PHONE / FAX
212.279.1776
212.279.0927

E-MAIL
peterrubie@prlit.com

WEB SITE
www.prlit.com

Agents: Peter Rubie, June Clark, Hanna Rubin

Background: MR. RUBIE: Peter Rubie is a former BBC Radio and Fleet Street journalist and has been the director of the New York University Summer Publishing Institute. He is a member of the NYU faculty and teaches the only university-level course in the country on how to become a literary agent. Member of AAR.

Prior to becoming an agent, he was a publishing house editor for nearly 6 years, during which time his authors won prizes and critical acclaim. He has also been the editor-in-chief of a Manhattan local newspaper, a freelance editor and book doctor for major publishers, a regular reviewer for the international trade magazine *Publishers Weekly,* and a professional jazz musician. He is a published author of fiction and nonfiction and regularly lectures and writes on publishing and the craft of writing.

MS. CLARK: Ms. Clark has been with the agency for 5 years. She has an MA in writing and publishing from Emerson College and, under the name June Rifkin, is the author of *The Everything Mother Goose Book* and co-author of *The Complete Book of Astrology* (with Ada Aubin), and *Signature For Success* (with Arlyn Imberman). Her play, *Separation Anxiety,* ran in Boston. Prior to being an agent, Ms. Clark worked in marketing and promotion for several major cable operators and program networks. She is the recipient of a Cable ACE award, among other industry merits.

MS. RUBIN: Ms. Rubin is a former magazine editor who has held deputy-editor positions on Hachette's *Travel Holiday* and *Boating.* Her editorial credits include award-winning stories on the environment, travel, adventure, and American cultural history. As well as being an agent, she writes on books for the San Diego *Union-Tribune* and on ballet for *Dance Magazine* and *Playbill.* Other writing credits include *Martha Stewart Living, The New York Times Book Review,* and *Time Out: New York.* She is the author of Rizzoli-Universe's *The Ballet Book.*

Represents: MR. RUBIE: A broad range of high-quality fiction and nonfiction. Nonfiction: narrative, popular science, spirituality, history, biography, pop culture, business/technology, parenting,

Represents cont.: health, self-help, music, food; Fiction: literate thrillers, crime, sci-fi/fantasy, literary

MS. CLARK: Nonfiction: TV/film/theater, pop culture, women's issues, parenting, commercial New Age, prescriptive self-help, trendy or off-beat business and reference

MS. RUBIN: Nonfiction: American history and biography, travel narrative, business, environmental reporting; Fiction. Looking for distinct voices and literate writers who have a passionate investment in their work.

Does not represent: **MR. RUBIE:** Romance, children's, plays, screenplays, illustrated coffee table books

MS. CLARK: Fiction

MS. RUBIN: Romance, children's, plays, screenplays, illustrated coffee table books

Clients: The Friars Club, Soupy Sales, Jose Torres, Pilot Pen CEO Ron Shaw, Wrestling legend Missy Hyatt

Recent sales: *Seven Steps to Heaven: How to Communicate With Your Dearly Departed Loved Ones in Seven Easy Steps,* by Joyce Keller (Fireside); *Into the Bermuda Triangle,* by Gian Quasar (International Marine/Ragged Mountain Press); *The Saucy Sisters' Guide to Wine,* by Barbara Nowak and Beverly Wichman (New American Library); *An Askew View: The Films of Kevin Smith,* by John Kenneth Muir (Applause Theatre & Cinema Book Publishers); *How to Adapt Anything Into a Screenplay,* by Richard Krevolin (Wiley); *Mean Chicks, Cliques, and Dirty Tricks,* by Erika Shearin Karres (Adams Media Corporation)

HOW TO SUBMIT

MR. RUBIE: Send a query letter by mail or e-mail to peterrubie@prlit.com. For fiction, include a short synopsis detailing the beginning, middle, and end of your story and the first 30–40 pages; for nonfiction, include a half-page or 1-page overview of the book (an in-a-nutshell description); a table of contents listing each chapter, chapter title, and subtitle; a 1-page or so expansion of each chapter, describing the contents of each chapter in more detail; and 1 or 2 sample chapters. Bear in mind that an editor who cannot see a completed manuscript wants at least to have a clear idea of the book he or she is buying and the style it will be written in. The more you can make their life easier, the better. (See Web site for more submission tips.)

MS. CLARK: Send query letter by mail with SASE or e-mail to pralit@aol.com. (See Web site for more details.)

MS. RUBIN: Send query letter by mail with SASE or e-mail to hanna.rubin@prlit.com. (See Web site for more details.)

REGINA RYAN PUBLISHING ENTERPRISES INC.

251 CENTRAL PARK W., 7D
NEW YORK NY 10024

E-MAIL
reginaryanbooks@rcn.com

Agent: Regina Ryan

Background: Ms. Ryan has been an agent for 27 years. Member of Authors Guild, Women's Media Group. Prior to opening her agency, Ms. Ryan was editor-in-chief of adult trade books at Macmillan Publishing. She offers strong editorial guidance and is well-known in the industry for doing first-rate books.

Represents: Adult nonfiction of first-rate quality

Does not represent: Fiction, juvenile (whether fiction or nonfiction)

Clients: Andrea Warren; Walter Keady; Miriam Chaikin; Paul Holinger, M.D.; Richard Moskovitz, M.D.; Wayne Craven

Recent sales: *Anatomy of a Suicide,* by Edwin Shneidman (Oxford); *What Babies Say Before They Can Talk,* by Paul Holinger, M.D. (Fireside Books); *Harlem Renaissance,* by Lionel Bascom (Source Books Media Fusion)

HOW TO SUBMIT

Send query letter, proposal, and sample chapter by mail or e-mail.

SCHIAVONE LITERARY AGENCY, INC.

236 TRAILS END
WEST PALM BEACH FL 33413-2135

PHONE / FAX
561.966.9294
561.966.9294

E-MAIL
profschia@aol.com

WEB SITE
www.publishersmarket
place.com/members/
profschia

Agent:	James Schiavone, Ed.D.
Background:	Mr. Schiavone has been an agent for 8 years and handles approximately 65 clients. Member of National Education Association. Prior to becoming an agent, Schiavone was a professor of developmental skills at City University of New York.
Represents:	Nonfiction, fiction, celebrity biography
Does not represent:	Poetry
Workshop topics:	How to get a literary agent
Conferences:	Key West Literary Seminar, South Florida Writer's Conference

✓ **TIPS**
Write a concise 1-page query letter. Include a list of published books by title, publisher, date of publication.

HOW TO SUBMIT	**Send 1-page query letter only by mail with SASE or e-mail. Absolutely no attachments.**

SUSAN SCHULMAN, A LITERARY AGENCY

454 W. 44TH ST.
NEW YORK NY 10036-5205

PHONE / FAX
212.713.1633/4/5
212.581.8830

E-MAIL
schulman@aol.com

WEB SITE
www.susanschulman
agency.com

Agents:	Susan Schulman, Eleanora Tevis, Sandra Gannon
Background:	Ms. Schulman has been an agent for 22 years. Member of AAR, WGA, Dramatists Guild, New York Women in Film. Prior to becoming an agent, she was Assistant Professor of English teaching history of the English language and linguistics courses. "We are interested in new trends, fresh ideas, original voices."
Represents:	Books for, by, and about women and women's issues and interests (including men, children, careers, health, professions); also, books about health, finances, trends, biographies, psychology
Does not represent:	New Age, romance, inspiration

HOW TO SUBMIT	**Send query letter by mail with SASE.**

LAURENS R. SCHWARTZ AGENCY

5 E. 22ND ST., SUITE 15 D
NEW YORK NY 10010-5325

✓ TIPS
Do not send out a mass mailing to all agents. Do not send everything you've ever written. Choose one work and promote that. Always include an SASE, but never send your only copy. Always include a background sheet on yourself and a 1-page synopsis of the work. Too many summaries end up being as long as the work.

Agent: Laurens R. Schwartz

Background: This agency has been in operation since 1984 and represents 100 clients. Member of WGA. Extremely selective, this agency only takes on 1–3 new clients per year and is known for working with authors on long-term career goals and promotion.

Represents: Nonfiction, fiction. Also handles movie and TV tie-ins, licensing, merchandising.

HOW TO SUBMIT

Send query letter by mail with SASE. No unsolicited manuscripts.

SCOVIL CHICHAK GALEN LITERARY AGENCY

381 PARK AVE. S., SUITE 1020
NEW YORK NY 10016

PHONE / FAX	E-MAIL	WEB SITE
212.679.8686	mailroom@scglit.com	www.scglit.com
212.679.6710		

Agents: Russell Galen, Anna Ghosh, Jack Scovil

Background: The agency sells approximately 100 titles per year. Members of AAR.

Recent sales: *Can't Find My Way Home: The Drug Experience from the Be-Bop Era to the Present,* by Martin Torgoff (Simon & Schuster); *Ambitious Brew: The Story of the Immigrants and Entrepreneurs who Invented American Beer,* by Maureen Ogle (Harcourt Brace); *Metro Stop Dostoevsky,* by Ingrid Bengis (Farrar Straus & Giroux); *Lord John and the Private Matter,* by Diana Gabaldon (Delacorte); *Naked Empire,* by Terry Goodkind (Tor Books)

HOW TO SUBMIT

Send proposal that includes the first 3 chapters (no more than 50 pages) and a synopsis by mail. Accepts e-mail queries.

SEBASTIAN LITERARY AGENCY

557 W. 7TH ST., SUITE 2
ST. PAUL MN 55102

PHONE
651.224.6670

E-MAIL
laurie@sebastian
agency.com or
dawn@sebastian
agency.com

WEB SITE
www.sebastian
agency.com

Agents:	Laurie Harper, Dawn Frederick (assoc. agent)
Background:	Ms. Harper has been an agent for 18 years, and Frederick is in her first year. The agency represents, on average, 40 active clients maximum at any given time. Sells an average of 15–20 titles per year. Members of AAR, Authors Guild. The agency has a reputation for integrity and professionalism, knowledge, and established relationships with editors at both the major publishers and select independent publishers. "Our focus is longer-term with each author, not single book sales. We respect authors and all people working in publishing."
Represents:	Adult nonfiction: anthropology/sociology for lay audience, popular history, popular science, parenting, health/medical/ psychology, business (management), investment, current affairs; Limited fiction: commercial women's, mainstream, literary, suspense/mystery
Does not represent:	Children's, poetry, scholarly/academic/textbooks, cookbooks, gift books, screenplays, spirituality, sci-fi/fantasy/horror novels, romance (genre)
Workshop topics:	Proposal writing—approaches that make more sense for a writer; the author-agent relationship; de-coding the publishing process itself
Clients:	Robert Hagstrom, Suzanne Caplan, Darryl Brock, Nancy Steinbeck, Mitch Anthony, Lisa McLeod, Tina Tessina, Kelly James-Enger
Recent sales:	*Building Big Profits in Real Estate,* by Wade Timmerson and Suzanne Caplan (John Wiley); *Swimming with Maya,* by Eleanor Vincent (Capital Books Inc.); *Did You Get the Vibe?,* by Kelly James-Enger (Kensington Pub./Strapless); *Doctor's Guide to Weight Loss Surgery,* by Dr. Louis Flancbaum and Erica Manfred (Bantam/Dell)

✓ **TIPS**
*Tell me enough to
understand "Why
this book?" and
"Why you?" and
"Who cares?"*

*Understand that each
agency must choose
clients/books for the
marketplace, publishers, and to "balance"
their own overall
client list. It is not
just about your book.
Some of it is timing,
and at different times
we will choose differently. Keep going and
don't be discouraged!*

HOW TO SUBMIT	**Send query letter by mail with SASE or e-mail (no attachments). By mail, include an outline or sample material, if you like, or overview from proposal—enough to give an accurate sense of the book.**

LYNN SELIGMAN, LITERARY AGENT

400 HIGHLAND AVE.
UPPER MONTCLAIR NJ 07043

PHONE
973.783.3631

Agent:	Lynn Seligman
Background:	Ms. Seligman has been an agent for 23 years and handles 35 clients. Member of WMG. Prior to opening her agency, Ms. Seligman worked at the Julian Bach Literary Agency for 4 years. Before that, she handled subsidiary rights at Simon & Schuster, Doubleday. She is known for strong, long-term relationships with her clients, not just handling one book alone.
Represents:	Adult fiction and nonfiction, especially parenting, psychology, health, business, entertainment, literary fiction, romance, science fiction
Does not represent:	Children's
Workshop topics:	Finding the right agent for you; the client/agent relationship; query letters
Clients:	Roberta Israeloff, Carol McD Wallace, Dr. Myrna Shure, Dr. Glenn Gaesser
Recent sales:	*Your Thinking Child,* by Dr. Myrna Shure with Roberta Israeloff (Contemporary); *20,001 Names for Baby* (revised), by Carol McD Wallace (Harper/Avon); *All Dressed in White,* by Carol McD Wallace (Penguin)

HOW TO SUBMIT

Send first chapter and synopsis (for fiction) or query letter and author's credentials (for nonfiction) by mail with SASE.

SEVENTH AVENUE LITERARY AGENCY

1663 W. 7TH AVE.
VANCOUVER, BC
V6J 1S4 CANADA

PHONE / FAX	E-MAIL	WEB SITE
604.734.3663	info@seventh	www.seventhavenue
604.734.8906	avenuelit.com	lit.com

Agents: Robert Mackwood, Perry Goldsmith, Sally Harding

Background: Mr. Mackwood has been an agent for 8 years and currently handles 40–50 clients. Sold approximately 15 titles in the last year. Prior to working at this agency, Mr. Mackwood was vice president, director of marketing at Bantam/Doubleday Canada in Toronto. This agency is known for strong editorial, marketing, and reputation and is still actively building a client list.

Represents: Nonfiction, fiction

Does not represent: Poetry, children's, young adult, sci-fi/fantasy, horror, erotica

Workshop topics: So you think you need an agent? Developing a game plan for marketing your book

Conferences: London Book Fair, BEA, Book Expo Canada

Clients: Vanessa Grant, Ian Mulgrew, Michael Clarkson

Recent sales: *Nanocosm,* by William Atkinson (Amacom); *sMothering,* by Wendy French (Forge); *How Hard Can it Be? Adventures of Tool Girl,* by Mag Ruffman (McClelland & Stewart)

★ RECOMMENDATION
Subscribe to
Publisher's Lunch
(www.publishers
marketplace.com)

HOW TO SUBMIT

Send query letter and first chapter (for fiction) or chapter outline (for nonfiction) by mail with SASE.

THE SEYMOUR AGENCY

475 MINER ST.
CANTON NY 13617

PHONE / FAX	E-MAIL	WEB SITE
315.386.1831	marysue@slic.com	www.theseymour
315.386.1076		agency.com

Agents:	Mary Sue Seymour
Background:	Member of AAR, RWA, Authors Guild
Represents:	Nonfiction; Fiction: romance, literary, Christian, some westerns
Does not represent:	New Age, screenplays, poetry, children's
Conferences:	RWA, BEA, CBA, Desert Rose RWA
Clients:	Tori Phillips, Gail Sattler, Terry Powell, Ph.D.
Recent sales:	Gail Sattler's 4-book deal (Steeple Hill); *Barbara Cameron's Everything Book,* by Barbara Cameron (Adam's Media Corp.); *Dealing with Aging Parents,* by Dr. Fran Praver (Greenwood Pub.)

HOW TO SUBMIT	**Send query letter by e-mail. No e-mail submissions or faxed queries.**

KEN SHERMAN & ASSOCIATES

9507 SANTA MONICA BLVD.
BEVERLY HILLS CA 90210

PHONE	FAX	E-MAIL
310.273.8840	310.271.2875	ksassociates@ earthlink.net

Agent:	Ken Sherman
Background:	Mr. Sherman has been an agent for over 20 years and handles over 25 clients. Sold over 20 titles in the last year. The agency is known for being hands-on, personal, almost managerial in approach. Prior to opening this agency, Mr. Sherman was a reader at Columbia Pictures, spent over 4 years with the William Morris Agency, 4 years at the Lantz Office, and 2 years at Paul Kohner, Inc.
Represents:	Screenplays, teleplays, books (fiction and nonfiction), film and TV rights to books, life rights, video games
Workshop:	The business of writing for screen, TV, and books
Conferences:	University of Hawaii
Success story:	*Back Roads,* by Tawni O'Dell, was an Oprah Book Club pick and is being developed into a feature film.
Clients:	David Cauterson, Joan Updike, Star Hawk, Tawni O'Dell, Anne Perry, Jordan Mechner

HOW TO SUBMIT	**Send query letter by e-mail. Also accepts submissions at conferences by referral only.**

ROSALIE SIEGEL, INTERNATIONAL LITERARY AGENCY INC.

1 ABEY DR.
PENNINGTON NJ 08534

PHONE
609.737.1001

FAX
609.737.3708

Agents:	Rosalie Siegel, Denise Lager
Background:	Ms. Siegel has been an agent since 1967. She handles approximately 30 clients and sold more than a dozen books in the last year. Member of AAR. She worked as an editor before becoming an agent.
Represents:	Nonfiction, adult and young adult fiction
Does not represent:	Genre fiction
Conferences:	BEA, London Book Fair
Clients:	Jonathan Ames, Dennis Covington, Meredith Broussard, William Wharton
Recent sales:	*Mistress of Dorchester,* by Ann Rinaldi (Harcourt); *Hex and Gargantuan,* by Maggie Estep (Three Rivers); *Wake Up, Sir!,* by Jonathan Ames (Scribner)

HOW TO SUBMIT   **Accepts submissions by referral only.**

SILVER SCREEN PLACEMENTS

602 65TH ST.
DOWNERS GROVE IL 60516-3020

PHONE
630.963.2124

FAX
630.963.1998

E-MAIL
silverscreen11@
yahoo.com

Agents:	William Levin, Bernadette LaHaie
Background:	This agency has been in operation since 1987 and handles 12 clients. Sold 3 titles in the last year. Prior to agenting, Mr. Levin did product placement in motion pictures. The agency is known for numerous contacts in industries.
Represents:	Novels, screenplays
Does not represent:	Horror, religious, X-rated
Workshop topics:	Engaging an agent; how to write good queries

✓ **TIPS**
Common mistakes writers should avoid: calling agents by their given names without prior permission; writing long or cute queries; printing their work in too-small fonts.

HOW TO SUBMIT   **Send query letter and 1–2 page synopsis by mail with SASE.**

JEFFREY SIMMONS LITERARY AGENCY

15 PENN HOUSE, MALLORY ST.
LONDON NW8 8SX ENGLAND

PHONE	FAX	E-MAIL
(0) 20 7226 8917	(0) 70 7224 8918	jas@london-inc.com

Agent:	Jeffrey Simmons
Background:	Mr. Simmons has been an agent for 25 years and handles 25 clients. Sold 15 titles in the last year. He is known for his long publishing and editing experience plus his successful record.
Represents:	Fiction, biography, autobiography, show business, personality books, law, crime, politics, world affairs, history
Does not represent:	Science fiction, horror, fantasy, children's, specialist subjects
Recent sales:	Town Without Pity, by Don Hale (Random House); War of the Windsors, by Lynn Picknett, Stephen Prior, and Clive Prince

HOW TO SUBMIT | **Send brief plot outline and author bio by mail or e-mail.**

BEVERLEY SLOPEN LITERARY AGENCY

131 BLOOR ST. W., SUITE 711
TORONTO ONTARIO
M5S 1S3 CANADA

PHONE /FAX	E-MAIL	WEB SITE
416.964.9598	slopen@ca.inter.net	www.slopenagency.
416.921.7726		on.ca

Agent:	Beverley Slopen
Background:	Ms. Slopen has been an agent for 30 years and represents 75 clients.
Represents:	Nonfiction, fiction (mostly by Canadian authors)
Does not represent:	Children's, poetry
Conferences:	Frankfurt, London Book Fair, Book Expo Canada
Clients:	Donna Morrissey, Ken McGoogan, Don Gutteridge, Howard Engel, Morley Torgov, Modris Eksteins

HOW TO SUBMIT | **Send submissions by mail and e-mail. Referrals are welcome.**

MICHAEL SNELL LITERARY AGENCY

P.O. BOX 1206
TRURO MA 02666-1206

PHONE
508.349.3718

Agents:	Michael Snell, Patricia Snell
Background:	This agency has been in operation for 25 years and represents 120 clients. Sold 40 titles in the last year. Prior to working at this agency, Mr. Snell was a publisher and editor. The agency is known for idea and project development, adding value to good proposals, expert coaching, developmental editing, and career support. Extensive contacts with all major publishers.
Represents:	Adult nonfiction: self-help and how-to in all subjects, particularly business, psychology, relationships, parenting, pets, health, fitness
Does not represent:	Fiction, memoirs
Success story:	Persistence pays. We sold 1 book this year after 12 months of marketing and 17 rejections. We also sold another book the day it landed on publishers' desks.
Clients:	David James Duncan, Roger Lonnors, Tom Smith, Craig Hickman, Richard Shell, Myrna Milani, Paul Coleman, Richard Heyman, Janine Adams, Deborah Swiss
Recent sales:	*Out for Your Competitors,* by Gene Marks (Adams); *Done Deal: The Art of Negotiating,* by Michael Benoliel (Adams); *Complete Idiot's Guide to Classic Cars*, by Tom Benford (Macmillan); *What Your Horse Wants You to Know,* by Gincy Bucklin (Wiley); *Business, Law, and Strategy,* by Richard Shell (Random House); *Penny Pincher's Passport to Luxury Travel,* by Joel Widzer (Traveler's Tales)

HOW TO SUBMIT	**Send 1-page query letter by mail with SASE. Brochure "How to Write a Book Proposal" available upon request.**

✓ **TIPS**
Try to be a good student when working with an agent who has many years of experience. Listen and learn to take directions. Practice a little strategic humility.

★ **BOOK RECOMMENDATIONS**
Tom Gorman's *How to Write the Breakthrough Business Book;* Mike Snell's *From Book Idea to Best-seller.*

CAMILLE SORICE AGENCY

13412 MOORPARK ST., #C
SHERMAN OAKS CA 91423

PHONE
818.995.1775

E-MAIL
Camille@dock.net

✓ TIPS
*Check spelling prior
to submitting.*

Agent: Camille Sorice
Background: Ms. Sorice has been an agent since 1988 and handles 6 clients. Member of WGA. Prior to working at this agency, Ms. Sorice was a manager. The agency is known for having a select client list and strong client/agent relationships.
Represents: Screenplays, a few novels.

HOW TO SUBMIT | **Send query letter and synopsis by mail with SASE. No phone calls.**

SPECTRUM LITERARY AGENCY

320 CENTRAL PARK W., SUITE 1-D
NEW YORK NY 10025

WEB SITE
www.spectrumliteraryagency.com

Agents: Eleanor Wood, Lucienne Diver
Background: Ms. Wood has been an agent for 25 years, and Ms. Diver has been an agent for 10 years. The agency handles approximately 90 clients and sold approximately 100 titles last year. Both Ms. Wood and Ms. Diver are members of AAR, RWA, MWA, SFWA. Ms. Wood is the agent for SFWA. She started the agency in 1976.
Represents: Commercial fiction especially—science fiction/fantasy, mystery, suspense, romance
Does not represent: New Age, self-help, religious fiction and nonfiction, children's, poetry, short-story collections, screenplays, gift books
Clients: David Eddings, Larry Niven, Jerry Pournelle, Lois McMaster Bujold, Susan Krinard

HOW TO SUBMIT | **Send a query letter with a synopsis (first chapter optional) by mail with SASE. Do not send a query by fax or e-mail. Do not send a disk.**

THE SPIELER AGENCY

154 W. 57TH ST., 13TH FLOOR, ROOM 135
NEW YORK NY 10019

E-MAIL
spieleragency@spieleragency.com

Agents:	F. Joseph Spieler, John F. Thornton, Deirdre Mullane, Eric Myers, Lisa Ross, Victoria Shoemaker
Represents:	Serious nonfiction: biography, history, religion, business; literary fiction
Does not represent:	Humor, how-to, genre science fiction, memoirs
Clients:	Richard Connitt, Julian Keenan, R.A. Scotti
Recent sales:	*Strangers & Kin,* by Saidiya Hartman (FSG); *A Sudden Sea,* by R.A. Scotti (Little Brown); *Face in the Mirror,* by Julian Keenan (Ecco)

HOW TO SUBMIT	**Send query letter by e-mail (no attachments).**

STARS, THE AGENCY

23 GRANT AVE., 4TH FLOOR
SAN FRANCISCO CA 94108

PHONE	**FAX**
415.421.6272	415.421.7620

Agent:	Roger C. Meier
Background:	Mr. Meier has been an agent for 12 years and handles 7 clients. Member of WGA. Prior to working at this agency, he was a talent and literary agent. The agency is known for building a new client list and having a dynamic young agent.
Represents:	Movie scripts, feature film, TV movie of the week, nonfiction novels
Does not represent:	Comic books

HOW TO SUBMIT	**Send query letter by mail or e-mail that includes synopsis of material, genre, and length.**

THE SUSIJN AGENCY

64 GREAT TITCHFIELD ST., 3RD FLOOR
LONDON W1W 7QH ENGLAND

PHONE / FAX	E-MAIL	WEB SITE
(0) 20 7580 6341	info@thesusijn	www.thesusijn
(0) 20 7580 8626	agency.com	agency.com

Agent: Laura Susijn

Background: Ms. Susijn established her agency in 1998 and currently handles 50 clients. Prior to opening her agency, she was foreign rights director at Sheil Land, and, prior to that, at Fourth Estate. "Our focus is on authors with international appeal, selling rights worldwide. We are one of the few agencies to represent writers writing in various different languages, with a particular interest in literature with a cross-cultural theme."

Represents: Literary fiction

Does not represent: Self-help, sci-fi/fantasy, romance, sagas, computer, illustrated, children's, business, military

Clients: Peter Ackroyd (translation rights only), Uzma Aslam Khan, Gilad Atzmon, Robin Baker, Robert Craig, Helena Echlin, Eugenio Fuentes, Paul Gogarty, Radhika Jha, Tessa De Loo, Karel Van Loon, Jeffrey Moore, Anita Nair, Tor Norretranders, Mineke Schipper, Paul Sussman, Shimon Tzabar, Dubravka Ugresic, Alex Wheatle, Henk Van Woerden, Adam Zameenzad

HOW TO SUBMIT

Send synopsis and 2 sample chapters by mail; include SASE if material needs to be returned. Allow 1 month for a reply.

PATRICIA TEAL LITERARY AGENCY

2036 VISTA DEL ROSA
FULLERTON CA 92831-1336

PHONE
714.738.8333

FAX
714.738.8333

Agent:	Patricia Teal
Background:	Ms. Teal has been an agent for 25 years and handles 25 clients. Sold 22 titles in the last year. Member of AAR. Prior to opening her agency, Ms. Teal earned her M.A. in English literature from Cal State Fullerton. Her agency is known for its reputation and marketing.
Represents:	Commercial nonfiction, women's fiction
Does not represent:	Short works: articles, poetry, short stories, novellas
Workshop topics:	I love speaking to novice groups. I cover a litany of topics.
Conferences:	BEA
Success story:	I just sold book number 168 for a romance author I've represented for 22 years.
Clients:	Marie Ferrarella, Sterling Johnson

215

HOW TO SUBMIT	**Send 1- or 2-page query letter by mail with SASE.**

✓ **TIPS**
Not enough thought and care goes into query letters.

★ **RECOMMENDATIONS**
Publishers Weekly, a must to be alert to news of the industry. Join writer's organizations.

THREE JACKETS LITERARY AGENCY, INC.

2160 NE 56TH ST., #3
FT. LAUDERDALE FL 33308

PHONE
954.772.5634

Agent:	H. Allen Etling
Background:	Mr. Etling has been an agent for 8 years. Prior to working at this agency, he worked in the publishing field and the newspaper business.
Represents:	Three areas: Innocent Expressions—children's stories; Lawyer's Literary Agency—true crime stories; American Reflections—American history stories

HOW TO SUBMIT	**Send first 3 chapters by mail.**

SⒸOTT TREIMEL NY

434 LAFAYETTE ST.
NEW YORK NY 10003

PHONE	FAX	E-MAIL
212.505.8353	212.505.0664	st.ny@verizon.net

216

✓ **TIPS**
Do NOT pitch your work or its marketability. Write professional, brief cover letters. Do NOT call before submitting.

★ **RECOMMENDATIONS**
Read issues of *Publishers Weekly;* browse the children's/ teen section in bookstores.

Agent: Scott Treimel

Background: SⒸott Treimel NY opened in 1995 and represents 35 clients. Sold 15 titles in the last year. Member of AAR, Authors Guild, SCBWI. Prior to opening his agency, Mr. Treimel worked at Curtis Brown, Ltd.; Scholastic, Inc.; United Features Syndicate; and Warner Bros. International Publishing (founding director).

Represents: Children's only—board books through teen novels

Does not represent: Adult, religion, didactic/moralistic, previously published, plays, film scripts. Does not consider picture book authors, only picture book author/ artists.

Workshop topics: Author/agent relationship; contracts; editorial development; craft; career development

Conferences: SCBWI Miami, Kindling Words

Clients: Barbara Joosse, Gail Gailes, Arthur Slade, Pat Hughes

Recent sales: *Open Ice,* by Pat Hughes (R-H/Wendy Lamb Books); *Maple Syrup Spring,* by Ann Purmell (Holiday House); *Theories of Relativity,* by Barbara Haworth-Attard (HarperCanada); *Papa, Do You Love Me?,* by Barbara Joosse (Chronicle Books); *Dodgeball,* by Janice Repka (Dutton)

HOW TO SUBMIT

Send complete chapter book (if manuscript is 60 or fewer pages) or query letter, story synopsis with attention to character development, and 2 sample chapters (if manuscript is more than 60 pages) by mail with SASE. Text submissions must be in standard manuscript form: double-spaced type in a standard size font. No multiple submissions or queries. Our period of exclusivity is 90 days from our receipt. Submissions received without an SASE are recycled upon receipt. Picture book dummies and/or thumbnail storyboards may be submitted only if the author is also the illustrator. Always include the manuscript separately as well. No film scripts are considered. No toy projects are considered. Do not telephone before submitting work.

2M COMMUNICATIONS LTD.

121 W. 27 ST., #601
NEW YORK NY 10001

PHONE / FAX	E-MAIL	WEB
212.741.1509	morel@bookhaven.	www.2m
212.505.0664	com	communications.com

Agent:	Madeleine Morel
Background:	Ms. Morel has been an agent for 20 years and handles 40 clients. Sold 15 titles in the last year. Prior to working at this agency, she worked in various publishing companies. She is known for her energy, personal treatment, always looking for new clients, speedy responses, and experience in the business.
Represents:	Adult nonfiction: health and beauty, parenting, multi-cultural, cookbooks, pop culture, history
Does not represent:	Fiction, children's

HOW TO SUBMIT	**Send query letter and author's bio by mail or e-mail (use submission form on the Web site).**

UNITED TRIBES MEDIA

240 W. 35TH ST., SUITE 500
NEW YORK NY 10001

PHONE	FAX	E-MAIL
212.534.7646	212.279.0927	janguerth@aol.com

Agent:	Jan-Erik Guerth
Background:	Mr. Guerth has been an agent since 1998. He represents approximately 30 clients. Prior to founding his agency, he worked as a comedian, print journalist, radio producer, film distributor, and editor. Mr. Guerth has taught at New York University's Center for Publishing.
Represents:	Serious and narrative nonfiction: ethnic, social, gender, and cultural issues; spirituality/inspiration; self-help/wellness; science; arts; history; politics; biography; travel; nature; business; economics
Does not represent:	Fiction
Conferences:	London Book Fair, Bologna Book Fair, Frankfurt Book Fair, BEA
Recent sales:	*Squatting in the City of Tomorrow,* by Robert Neuwirth (Routledge); *Into the Melting Pot,* by James McWilliams (Columbia University); *Tolkien and C.S. Lewis,* by Colin Duriez (Paulist Press)

HOW TO SUBMIT	**Send query letter by mail with SASE or by e-mail (no attachments).**

THE RICHARD R. VALCOURT AGENCY

177 E. 77TH ST. PHC
NEW YORK NY 10021-1934

PHONE
212.570.2340

FAX
212.570.2340

Agent: Richard R. Valcourt

Background: Mr. Valcourt has been an agent since 1995. Prior to working at this agency, he was an academic and an editor. The agency has a strong reputation in the national security sector.

Represents: Only scholarly and professional works on intelligence and related national security topics.

HOW TO SUBMIT **Send proposal, outline, and synopsis by mail with SASE. Also accepts submissions by personal referral.**

VENTURE LITERARY

8895 TOWNE CENTRE DR., SUITE 105, #141
SAN DIEGO CA 92122

PHONE / FAX	E-MAIL	WEBSITE
619.807.1887	agents@venture	www.ventureliterary.
772.365.8321	literary.com	com

Agents:	Frank R. Scatoni, Greg Dinkin
Background:	The agency was founded in October 2000 and handles 20 clients. Sold 20 titles in the last year. Prior to opening the agency, Mr. Scatoni was an associate editor at Simon & Schuster and the author of 2 pop culture books; Mr. Dinkin was a former business consultant and the author of a book on personal finance. Venture Literary specializes in developing first-time nonfiction authors.
Represents:	**MR. SCATONI:** Nonfiction: narrative, sports, history, biography, memoir; Fiction: mainstream, mystery **MR. DINKIN:** General nonfiction: narrative, sports, gambling, business, finance, how-to, African-American studies
Does not represent:	Children's, young adult, genre-based fiction other than mysteries and thrillers
Workshop topics:	How to get your nonfiction published
Conferences:	SDSU Writers Conference, Southern California Writers Conference
Clients:	Alan Grant, "Amarillo Slim" Preston, Gary Stevens, Brad Stone, Art Chansky, Caroline Waxler, Marianne Jennings
Recent sales:	*50 Things Every Guy Should Know How To Do,* by Daniel Kline and Jason Tomaszewski (Plume); *The Book of Bluffs,* by Matt Lessinger (Warner Books); *Brave Old World,* by Rockwell Schnabel with Francis X. Rocca (Rowan & Littlefield Publishers)

HOW TO SUBMIT	**Send query letter by e-mail only (no attachments). If we're interested in your query, we will contact you directly, asking you to send us a hard copy of your work.**

RALPH VICIANANZA, LTD.

111 EIGHTH AVE., SUITE 1501
NEW YORK NY 10011

PHONE
212.924.7090

FAX
212.691.9644

Agents: Ralph M. Viciananza, Chris Lotts, Chris Schelling
Represents: Nonfiction: biography, autobiography, business, economics, history, pop culture, religious, inspirational, science/technology; Fiction: literary, mainstream, multicultural, sci-fi/fantasy, thriller, women's

| HOW TO SUBMIT | **Accepts clients by referral only.** |

THE VINES AGENCY, INC.

648 BROADWAY, SUITE 901
NEW YORK NY 10012

PHONE / FAX	E-MAIL	WEBSITE
212.777.5522	jv@vinesagency.com	www.vinesagency.com
212.777.5978		

Agents: James C. Vines, Alexis B. Caldwell

Background: Mr. Vines has been an agent for 14 years. The agency handles 35 clients. Sold 50 titles in the last year. Members of Authors Guild, WGA. Prior to working at this agency, Mr. Vines worked at Raines & Raines Literary Agency and Virginia Barber Literary Agency. "We are actively looking for new clients."

Represents: Nonfiction: how-to, prescriptive, narrative, investigative journalism, history; Fiction: women's, thrillers, African-American, romance, sci-fi, mystery

Does not represent: Children's, young adult, picture books, coffee table books

Conferences: BEA

Clients: Bernice L. McFadden, Shannon Holmes, Don Winslow, Joe R. Lansdale, Estate of Terry Southern, Koji Suzuki, Laura Doyle, Cindy Holby, Marcia Talley, Darren Coleman, Julia Spencer-Fleming, John Mannock, Chris Moriarty, Stephen Woodworth, Keith Miller, David Gibson, Beth Saulnier

Recent sales: *Sunset and Sawdust,* by Joe R. Lansdale (Knopf); *The Ring,* by Koji Suzuki (Vertical); *The Power of the Dog,* by Don Winslow (Knopf); *The Surrendered Single,* by Laura Doyle (Simon & Schuster); *Before I Let Go,* by Darren Coleman (HarperCollins); *Bad Girlz,* by Shannon Holmes (Simon & Schuster); *Camilla's Roses,* by Ber-nice L. McFadden (Dutton/Plume); *A Fountain Filled with Blood,* by Julia Spencer-Fleming (St. Martin's Press); *The Coming Catholic Church,* by David Gibson (Harper-SanFrancisco); *Spin State,* by Chris Moriarty (Bantam Dell); *Through Violet Eyes,* by Stephen Woodworth (Bantam Dell); *Iron Coffin,* by John Mannock (New American Library)

221

✓ **TIPS**
Please don't follow up on your query letter by calling the agency to make sure we got it. We will only reply if you include an SASE. Never send your original or only copy of anything. For information on the publishing business, read Publishers Weekly *or any number of commercially available books on the subject, rather than calling agencies and asking for advice or help.*

★ **RECOMMENDATION**
Publishers Weekly *is a great resource for any serious author.*

HOW TO SUBMIT

Send 1-page query letter by mail with SASE or send 2-paragraph query letter by e-mail (no attachments).

WALES LITERARY AGENCY, INC.

P.O. BOX 9428
SEATTLE WA 98109-0428

PHONE	FAX	E-MAIL
206.284.7114	206.322.1033	waleslit@waleslit.com

222

✓ **TIPS**
Research your agents; know their specialties and interests. Create an engaging query letter and always include an SASE. Put your best foot forward by submitting polished final drafts of your work and proposal.

Agents: Elizabeth Wales, Adrienne Reed (foreign rights)

Background: Ms. Wales has been an agent for 14 years and handles 60 clients. Sold 14 titles in the last year. Member of AAR. Prior to opening her agency, Ms. Wales worked at Oxford University Press and Viking Penguin. Founded in 1990, the agency offers a wealth of experience in the book trade, excellent contacts in the publishing industry, a firm commitment to its authors, and success in sales and reviews. The agency is looking for talented storytellers, with a special interest in writers from the Northwest, Alaska, and the West Coast.

Represents: Narrative nonfiction, mainstream and literary fiction

Does not represent: Children's books, celebrity, romance, mysteries, thrillers, science fiction, historicals, true crime, horror, action adventure, how-to, self-help

Conferences: Pacific Northwest Writer's Conference

Clients: Bruce Barcott, Julia Boyd, Karen Brennan, Rebecca Brown, Natalie Fobes, Kenny Fries, John Haines, Lyanda Lynn Haupt, Jean Hegland, Kate Lake, Nancy Lord, David Mas Masumoto, Farnoosh Moshiri, Dan Savage, Migael Scherer, Eric Scigliano, Duff Wilson, and a dozen independent presses

Recent sales: *Michelangelo's Mountain,* by Eric Scigliano (Free Press/Simon & Schuster); *In Praise of Small Things: Darwin, Birds, and the Evolution of Insight,* by Lyanda Lynn Haupt (Little, Brown); *The Bathhouse,* by Farnoosh Moshiri (Beacon Press)

HOW TO SUBMIT	**Send query letter, information about the book and writer, and sample pages by mail with SASE or e-mail (no attachments).**

JOHN A. WARE LITERARY AGENCY

392 CENTRAL PARK W.
NEW YORK NY 10025

PHONE
212.866.4733

FAX
212.866.4734

Agent:	John Ware
Background:	This agency has been in operation since 1978 and represents 60 clients.
Represents:	Nonfiction, novels
Does not represent:	Personal memoirs, how-to, science fiction
Recent sales:	*Under the Banner of Heaven: A Story of Violent Faith,* by Jon Krakauer (Doubleday); *Ada Blackjack: A Biography,* by Jennifer Niven (Hyperion); *Seven Sundays: A History of Sunday,* by Craig Harline (Doubleday); *The Traveler: A Biography of John Ledyard,* by Bill Gifford (St. Martin's); *The Family Business: Portrait of the McIlhenny [Tabasco] Family,* by Jeffrey Rothfeder (HarperCollins)

✓ **TIPS**
Writers must have appropriate credentials for authorship of proposal (nonfiction) or manuscript (fiction); no publishing track record required. Open to good writing and interesting ideas by new or veteran writers.

HOW TO SUBMIT	Send query letter only by mail with SASE. No e-mail or fax queries.

WATERSIDE PRODUCTIONS, INC.

2187 NEWCASTLE AVE., #204
CARDIFF-BY-THE-SEA CA 92007

PHONE / FAX
760.632.9190
760.632.9295

E-MAIL
admin@waterside.com

WEB SITE
www.waterside.com

Agents:	William Gladstone (president and founder), Matt Wagner, Carole McClendon, David Fugate, Margot Maley Hutchison, Christian Crumlish, Danielle Jatlow, Jawahara Saidullah, Kimberly Valentini, Neil Gudovitz (foreign rights)
Background:	Waterside Productions has been agenting since 1982
Represents:	General nonfiction: business, parenting, humor, body/mind/spirit, cookbooks, computer and technology

HOW TO SUBMIT	Complete the query form on the agency's Web site.

WATKINS LOOMIS AGENCY, INC.

133 E. 35TH ST., SUITE 1
NEW YORK NY 10016

PHONE
212.532.0080

FAX
212.889.0506

Agents:	Gloria Loomis, Katherine Fausset
Represents:	Narrative nonfiction, literary fiction
Does not represent:	Genre fiction, children's, self-help

HOW TO SUBMIT **Send query letter with synopsis and first chapter, if desired, by mail only.**

DONNA WAUHOB AGENCY

5280 S. EASTERN AVE., #A3
LAS VEGAS NV 89119

PHONE
702.795.1523

FAX
702.795.0696

E-MAIL
dwauhob@aol.com

✓ TIPS
Writers should have their work edited before presenting it to us. First-time writers try to tell us what to do and how their screenplay is OK. Many just don't want to listen.

Agents:	Donna Wauhob, Mel Wauhob (staff), Michael Madsen, Cal Maefield, Betty Mirich
Background:	Ms. Wauhob has been an agent for American Federation of Musicians since 1968. Member of SAG, WGA, AFTRA. Prior to becoming an agent, Ms. Wauhob was a model, secretary, executive receptionist, public relations professional, and animal activist. "New clients are attracted to us through our reputation, working hard for our clients, and our integrity."
Represents:	Actors, screenplay/novel writers, singers, dancers, acts of all kinds
Success story:	Steve Johnson's novel *Walk Don't Run* is now with a publishing company and being polished. It is the story of Steve "Rusty" Johnson growing up with Edward James Olmos, their trials and tribulations, and their striving for fame and fortune. This manuscript was submitted to more than 80 publishing companies until it was picked up. Steve, along with us, never gave up and kept submitting. We all kept a positive attitude!
Clients:	Evelyn Khelama, Irene Slater, Steve Johnson, Joey Giambra, Bruce McGowan

HOW TO SUBMIT **Send query letter by mail with SASE or e-mail. Phone queries accepted, but long-distance calls are not returned.**

CHERRY WEINER LITERARY AGENCY

28 KIPLING WAY
MANALAPAN NJ 07726-3711

PHONE	FAX	E-MAIL
732.446.2096	732.792.0506	Cherry8486@aol.com

Agent: Cherry Weiner

Background: Ms. Weiner has been an agent for 27 years and handles 40 clients. Sold at least 48 titles in the last year. Member of WWA (Western Writers of America). Prior to opening her agency, she worked for a big New York literary agent. She is known for reputation and strong 1-on-1 contact with her clients. "Although no longer a member, I do have contacts with RWA SFWA, HWA, NJHWA."

Represents: All genres, some nonfiction

Does not represent: Children's, young adult, poetry, short stories

Workshop topics: How to submit to an agent or editor; explaining the ins and outs of publishing.

Conferences: WWA

HOW TO SUBMIT

By referral only, with a letter stating what you have to submit and who referred. If I ask to see the work, I would like to see a complete manuscript.

✓ **TIPS**

Research who you should submit to. Do not send a mystery story to a V.P. because you heard his/her name being talked about; he/she might be a V.P. but he/she also might be head of a totally different genre. Make sure you submit correctly. You would be surprised at how many manuscripts I get single-spaced, sometimes both sides of the page, and bound.

Make sure you know the gender of the person you are submitting to. My name is CHERRY and yet I get a bulk of mail addressed to MR. Cherry Weiner!

TED WEINSTEIN LITERARY MANAGEMENT

287 DUNCAN ST.
SAN FRANCISCO CA 94131-2019

E-MAIL
query@twliterary.com

WEB SITE
www.twliterary.com

✓ **TIPS**
Common, avoidable mistakes: not researching a particular agency before submitting; unpolished, un-professional queries (typos, etc.); mass-mailed, unpersonalized submissions.

★ **BOOK RECOMMENDATIONS**
Thinking Like Your Editor, by Susan Rabiner and Alfred Fortunato

How to Write a Book Proposal, by Michael Larsen

Publicize Your Book: An Insider's Guide to Getting Your Book the Attention It Deserves, by Jacqueline Deval

★ **WEB SITE RECOMMENDATIONS**
www.mobylives.com
www.publishers marketplace.com
www.publishers weekly.com

Agent:	Ted Weinstein
Background:	Currently handles 35 clients. Member of AAR, Authors Guild, American Historical Association, Northern California Science Writers Association. Mr. Weinstein has broad experience on both the business and editorial sides of publishing. He has held several senior publishing positions in licensing, marketing, and business develop-ment. Also a widely published author, Mr. Weinstein has been the music critic for NPR's "All Things Considered" and a commentator for a wide variety of print publications. Focus is on building clients' careers; astute, insightful editorial guidance; scope of relationships with editors at every major publisher; disciplined, hard-working professionalism; and integrity.
Represents:	Serious nonfiction, with particular interest in narrative nonfiction, current affairs, politics, biography, history, business, science, tech-nology, environment, health, medicine
Does not represent:	Fiction, stage plays, screenplays, poetry, children's, young adults
Success story:	A client had tried unsuccessfully to sell his book directly to publishers several years ago. We worked with him to refine his proposal and then sold it to an editor at a major publish-ing house who had rejected the author the first time.
Recent sales:	*The Math Instinct,* by Kevin Devlin, Ph.D. (Thunder's Mouth Press/Avalon Publishing); *Fresh: How Local Food Can Save the American Meal,* by Terry Harrison and Laird Harrison (Algonquin Books/Workman Publishing); *50 Simple Ways to Live a Longer Life,* by Suzanne Bohan Thompson and Glen Thompson (Sourcebooks)

HOW TO SUBMIT

Send query letter or complete proposal by e-mail (preferred) or mail with SASE. Use the words "Author Submission" in the e-mail's subject line and include all materials in the body of the message (no attachments).

PEREGRINE WHITTLESEY AGENCY

345 E. 80TH ST.
NEW YORK NY 10021

Agent:	Peregrine Whittlesey
Background:	This agency has been in operation since 1986 and handles 22 clients. Sold 10 plays in the last year. Prior to opening this agency, Whittlesey was in literary management. The agency is known for strong editorial work and reputation.
Represents:	Extraordinary plays by exceptionally talented playwrights
Does not represent:	Screenplays
Workshop topics:	Play development
Success story:	Nilo Cruz won the 2003 Pulitzer Prize in Drama.
Clients:	Nilo Cruz, Heather McDonald
Recent sales:	*Anna in the Tropics,* by Nilo Cruz (Theatre Communications Group); *When Grace Comes In,* by Heather McDonald

HOW TO SUBMIT	**This agency is taking on almost no new clients but can be contacted by mail.**

WIESER & ELWELL

80 FIFTH AVE., SUITE 1101
NEW YORK NY 10011

PHONE
212.260.0860

Agent:	Jake Elwell
Background:	Currently handles 35 clients. Member of AAR, Authors Guild.
Represents:	Nonfiction, fiction

HOW TO SUBMIT	**Send outline and opening 20 pages (for fiction) or proposal (for nonfiction) with SASE.**

ANN WRIGHT REPRESENTATIVES

165 W. 46TH ST., #1105
NEW YORK NY 10036-2501

PHONE	FAX	E-MAIL
212.764.6770	212.764.5125	danwrightlit@aol.com

✓ TIPS
Know to whom you are writing. Be concise with query.

Agents: Dan Wright, Ann Wright

Background: The agency has been in operation for 41 years. The agency currently represents 13 clients but can handle 20. Sold 4 titles in the last year. Prior to agenting, the agents gained experience as a television executive, writer, and film production manager.

Represents: Screenplays, novels that have strong film potential

Does not represent: Nonfiction, short stories

Workshop: Writing for film

Clients: Tom Dempsey, Inderjit Bhaduar, Amanda Paluch

HOW TO SUBMIT

Send information about the author and the work by mail with SASE.

228

WRITERS HOUSE

21 W. 26TH ST.
NEW YORK NY 10010

PHONE
212.685.2400

Agents: Al Zuckerman, Susan Ginsburg, Merilee Heifetz, Michele Rubin, Simon Lipskar, Jennifer Lyons

Background: Members of AAR.

MS. GINSBURG: Ms. Ginsburg has been an agent for 15 years and currently handles 50 clients. Sold 30 titles in the last year. Prior to working at this agency, she was executive editor at Pocket Books, executive editor at St. Martin's Press, and editor-in-chief at Atheneum/Macmillan. She is known for her great reputation, strong editorial, personal attention, and significant publishing house experience.

MR. ZUCKERMAN: Mr. Zuckerman has been an agent for 30 years and currently has 50–70 clients. Sold 50 titles in the last year. Prior to working at this agency, he was in the U.S. Navy and U.S. Foreign Service, was a writer of stage plays and TV series, had two novels published, and was a professor of playwriting at Yale. He has a reputation for strong editorial, major clients, and much success.

MR. LIPSKAR: Mr. Lipskar has been an agent for 5 years and actively handles about 40 clients. Sold 25 titles in the last year. "Writer's House attracts new clients because we have an established and respected reputation in the industry, and are always eager to work with and build new writers that excite us."

Represents: **MS. GINSBURG:** Nonfiction: narrative (science, business, history, popular culture), women's, parenting, self-help, cookbooks/food writing; Fiction: literary, commercial

MR. ZUCKERMAN: Nonfiction: biography, history, business, narrative, popular science, health; Fiction: literary, commercial

MR. LIPSKAR: Narrative nonfiction, literary and commercial adult and young adult fiction

Does not represent: **MS. GINSBURG:** Science fiction, category/genre fiction, academic, technical fiction

MR. ZUCKERMAN: Category romances, science fiction, juvenile books, screenplays

MR. LIPSKAR: Poetry, academic press works, how-to, cookbooks, parenting books, romance

Conferences: **MS. GINSBURG:** International Association of Culinary Professionals (IACP); Romance Writers of America (RWA); Bouchercon

✓ **TIPS**
New writers seeking representation should simply send me a polished, fantastic book, and they should approach the business of writing with a professional attitude and realistic expectations.

★ **BOOK RECOMMENDATION**
Writing the Blockbuster Novel, by Albert Zuckerman

Success story:	**MR. LIPSKAR:** *Eragon,* originally self-published by 19-year-old Christopher Paolini, sold to Knopf in a 3-book deal. My assistant reads a wide variety of literary journals, both in print and on-line, and discovered Stephanie Kallos via her published short story. He requested and read her novel, *Broken For You,* which I eventually sold at auction to Grove/Atlantic. Jennifer Donnelly's first novel, *The Tea Rose,* sold for a modest advance after dozens of submissions all over town. For her next 2 books, we sold U.S. and UK rights for a combined total just shy of 7 figures.
Clients:	**MS. GINSBURG:** David Berlinski, Lora Brody, Jane Seymour, Eileen Goudge, Edward Humes, Jane Feather, Rich Rodgers **MR. ZUCKERMAN:** Ken Follett, Stephen Hawking, Michael Lewis, Ridley Pearson, F. Paul Wilson, Bradley Trevor Greive, Robert Anton Wilson
Recent sales:	**MR. ZUCKERMAN:** *Hornet Flight,* by Ken Follett (Dutton); *The Universe in a Nutshell,* by Stephen Hawking (Bantam); *Moneyball,* by Michael Lewis (Norton); *The Art of Deception,* by Ridley Pearson (Hyperion); *Your Marketing Sucks,* by Mark Stevens (Crown); *The Blue Day Book,* by Bradley Trevor Greive (Andrews McMeel) **MR. LIPSKAR:** *The Immortal Life of Henrietta Lacks,* by Rebecca Skloot (Crown); 2 untitled novels by Michael Gruber (HarperCollins); *Broken For You,* by Stephanie Kallos (Grove/Atlantic)

HOW TO SUBMIT	**MS. GINSBURG: Send query letter with a synopsis and sample pages (for fiction) or an outline (for nonfiction) by mail.** **MR. ZUCKERMAN: Send a 1-page letter that explains what's wonderful about your book, what it's about, and why you are most qualified to write it by mail with SASE.** **MR. LIPSKAR: Send query letter by mail with SASE or e-mail.**

WYLIE-MERRICK LITERARY AGENCY

1138 S. WEBSTER ST.
KOKOMO IN 46902-6357

PHONE	PHONE	E-MAIL
765.459.8258	765.457.3783	www.wylie-merrick.com

Agents: Robert Brown, Sharene Martin

Background: Sharene Martin and Robert Brown have been agents for 4 years and handle 15 clients. Members of SCBWI, MWA. Prior to agenting, Mr. Brown was an engineer and dance instructor; he holds a B.S. in English. Ms. Martin was a language, science, and computer instructo; educational technologist; and curriculum specialist; she holds a M.S. in language education. The agency is known for strong editorial skills and client development. As a small agency, the agents can develop close relationships with clients. "We are currently reaching our maximum number of clients we can represent. Our list is getting full."

Represents: Adult and juvenile fiction and nonfiction; genre fiction such as mysteries (actively seeking), suspense/thriller, romance (actively seeking), gay/lesbian, chick-lit, pure science fiction; literary fiction; diet books; exercise books; cookbooks; contemporary young adult novels

MR. BROWN: Adult nonfiction, young adult and adult fiction

MS. MARTIN: Young adult fiction and nonfiction, adult fiction

Does not represent: Works in progress, works at 100,000-plus words (even if it is science fiction), historical of any kind, mainstream, memoirs, fantasy (adult or juvenile), poetry, erotica, experimental

Conferences: Pikes Peak Writers Conference

Workshop topics: Writing craft; contracts; publishing credits; picture books; category distinctions in juvenile literature

Success story: Each client we get published is a success story unto itself, and we are excited and thrilled when we can connect an editor with one of our authors, especially an editor who is enthusiastic about the writer's work. This is especially true of first-time writers whom we have gotten published—it is greatly satisfying to be in on the ground floor of a blossoming career.

Recent sales: *Death for Dessert,* by T. Dawn Richard (Five Star); *A Red Polka Dot in a World Full of Plaid,* by Varian Johnson (Genesis Press)

✓ **TIPS**
Some are listed on our Web site. Also, understand that publishing anything in today's climate is very difficult at best, so to catch an editor's eye your work must be better than what is already out there. We don't like to see "marketing pitches" in a query letter; just give us the basics of your project and let the sample of your writing speak for itself. Writers who are hostile toward the publishing industry should not let that show in their queries. And, finally, remember that there are several reasons for getting a rejection—do not take it personally or respond critically when given feedback designed to help. Use rejection and the feedback you get to improve your writing.

★ RECOMMENDATIONS *On Writing,* by Stephen King (great insight and writing craft tips, especially on tags, for writers). *Lessons from Lifetime of Writing,* by David Morrell; others listed on our Web site references and research tools page at www.wylie-merrick.com/tools.htm

HOW TO SUBMIT

Send query letter by mail or e-mail (no attachments) with brief synopsis of work (if not over 2 pages); author credentials; relevant publishing credits, if any; contact information, particularly an e-mail address if one is available; a 10-page writing sample; and an SASE—queries without an SASE are not reviewed. Also accepts submissions at conferences.

SCRIPT AGENTS SPECIALTIES INDEX

ACTION / ADVENTURE

Alpern Group, The
Baskow Agency
Bohrman Agency, The
Circle of Confusion Ltd.
Communications Management Associates
Gage Group, The
Miller Co., The Stuart M.
Omniquest Entertainment
Perelman Agency, Barry
Picture of You, A
Sherman & Associates, Ken
Silver Screen Placements
Wright Representatives, Ann

BIOGRAPHY / AUTOBIOGRAPHY

Alpern Group, The
Baskow Agency
Bohrman Agency, The
Circle of Confusion Ltd.
Communications Management Associates
Miller Co., The Stuart M.
Omniquest Entertainment
Perelman Agency, Barry
Picture of You, A
Sherman & Associates, Ken

CARTOON / ANIMATION

Alpern Group, The
Bohrman Agency, The
Circle of Confusion Ltd.
Communications Management Associates
Gage Group, The
Hudson Agency
Miller Co., The Stuart M.
Picture of You, A
Sherman & Associates, Ken

COMEDY

Alpern Group, The
Baskow Agency
Bohrman Agency, The
Circle of Confusion Ltd.
Communications Management Associates

Gage Group, The
Gurman Susan
Hudson Agency
Miller Co., The Stuart M.
Omniquest Entertainment
Picture of You, A
Sherman & Associates, Ken
Silver Screen Placements
Wright Representatives, Ann

CONTEMPORARY ISSUES

Alpern Group, The
Baskow Agency
Bohrman Agency, The
Circle of Confusion Ltd.
Communications Management Associates
Gage Group, The
Hudson Agency
Miller Co., The Stuart M.
Omniquest Entertainment
Perelman Agency, Barry
Picture of You, A
Sherman & Associates, Ken
Silver Screen Placements

DETECTIVE / POLICE / CRIME

Alpern Group, The
Bohrman Agency, The
Circle of Confusion Ltd.
Communications Management Associates
Gage Group, The
Gurman Susan
Hudson Agency
Miller Co., The Stuart M.
Omniquest Entertainment
Perelman Agency, Barry
Picture of You, A
Sherman & Associates, Ken
Silver Screen Placements
Wright Representatives, Ann

EROTICA

Alpern Group, The
Bohrman Agency, The
Circle of Confusion Ltd.

Communications Management Associates
Gage Group, The
Picture of You, A
Sherman & Associates, Ken

234

ETHNIC

Alpern Group, The
Bohrman Agency, The
Circle of Confusion Ltd.
Gage Group, The
Picture of You, A
Sherman & Associates, Ken

EXPERIMENTAL

Alpern Group, The
Bohrman Agency, The
Circle of Confusion Ltd.
Gage Group, The
Omniquest Entertainment
Picture of You, A
Sherman & Associates, Ken

FAMILY SAGA

Alpern Group, The
Baskow Agency
Bohrman Agency, The
Circle of Confusion Ltd.
Gage Group, The
Gurman Susan
Hudson Agency
Miller Co., The Stuart M.
Omniquest Entertainment
Picture of You, A
Sherman & Associates, Ken
Silver Screen Placements

FANTASY

Alpern Group, The
Bohrman Agency, The
Circle of Confusion Ltd.
Communications Management Associates
Gage Group, The
Hudson Agency
Omniquest Entertainment
Picture of You, A

Sherman & Associates, Ken
Silver Screen Placements

FEMINIST

Alpern Group, The
Bohrman Agency, The
Circle of Confusion Ltd.
Gage Group, The
Kozak Literary & Motion Picture Agency, Otto R.
Picture of You, A
Sherman & Associates, Ken

GAY/LESBIAN

Alpern Group, The
Bohrman Agency, The
Circle of Confusion Ltd.
Gage Group, The
Picture of You, A
Sherman & Associates, Ken
Wright Representatives, Ann

GLITZ

Alpern Group, The
Baskow Agency
Bohrman Agency, The
Circle of Confusion Ltd.
Gage Group, The
Picture of You, A
Sherman & Associates, Ken

HISTORICAL

Alpern Group, The
Bohrman Agency, The
Circle of Confusion Ltd.
Communications Management Associates
Gage Group, The
Miller Co., The Stuart M.
Omniquest Entertainment
Perelman Agency, Barry
Picture of You, A
Sherman & Associates, Ken
Silver Screen Placements
Wright Representatives, Ann

HORROR

Alpern Group, The
Bohrman Agency, The
Circle of Confusion Ltd.
Communications Management Associates
Gage Group, The
Gurman Susan
Perelman Agency, Barry
Picture of You, A
Sherman & Associates, Ken
Silver Screen Placements
Wright Representatives, Ann

JUVENILE

Alpern Group, The
Bohrman Agency, The
Circle of Confusion Ltd.
Communications Management Associates
Gage Group, The
Hudson Agency
Picture of You, A
Sherman & Associates, Ken
Silver Screen Placements

MAINSTREAM

Alpern Group, The
Bohrman Agency, The
Circle of Confusion Ltd.
Communications Management Associates
Gage Group, The
Gurman Susan
Miller Co., The Stuart M.
Omniquest Entertainment
Picture of You, A
Sherman & Associates, Ken
Silver Screen Placements
Wright Representatives, Ann

MULTIMEDIA

Alpern Group, The
Bohrman Agency, The
Circle of Confusion Ltd.
Gage Group, The
Miller Co., The Stuart M.
Omniquest Entertainment
Picture of You, A
Sherman & Associates, Ken

MYSTERY / SUSPENSE

Alpern Group, The
Baskow Agency
Bohrman Agency, The
Circle of Confusion Ltd.
Gage Group, The
Gurman Susan
Hudson Agency
Miller Co., The Stuart M.
Omniquest Entertainment
Perelman Agency, Barry
Picture of You, A
Sherman & Associates, Ken
Silver Screen Placements
Wright Representatives, Ann

PSYCHIC / SUPERNATURAL

Alpern Group, The
Bohrman Agency, The
Circle of Confusion Ltd.
Communications Management Associates
Gage Group, The
Omniquest Entertainment
Perelman Agency, Barry
Picture of You, A
Sherman & Associates, Ken
Wright Representatives, Ann

REGIONAL

Alpern Group, The
Bohrman Agency, The
Circle of Confusion Ltd.
Gage Group, The
Picture of You, A
Sherman & Associates, Ken

RELIGIOUS / INSPIRATIONAL

Alpern Group, The
Baskow Agency
Bohrman Agency, The
Circle of Confusion Ltd.
Communications Management Associates
Gage Group, The
Kozak Literary & Motion Picture Agency, Otto R.
Picture of You, A
Sherman & Associates, Ken

ROMANTIC COMEDY

Alpern Group, The
Baskow Agency
Bohrman Agency, The
Circle of Confusion Ltd.
Communications Management Associates
Gage Group, The
Gurman Susan
Hodges Agency, Carolyn
Hudson Agency
Miller Co., The Stuart M.
Omniquest Entertainment
Perelman Agency, Barry
Picture of You, A
Sherman & Associates, Ken
Wright Representatives, Ann

ROMANTIC DRAMA

Alpern Group, The
Baskow Agency
Bohrman Agency, The
Circle of Confusion Ltd.
Communications Management Associates
Gage Group, The
Gurman Susan
Hudson Agency
Miller Co., The Stuart M.
Omniquest Entertainment
Perelman Agency, Barry
Picture of You, A
Sherman & Associates, Ken
Wright Representatives, Ann

SCIENCE FICTION

Alpern Group, The
Baskow Agency
Bohrman Agency, The
Circle of Confusion Ltd.
Communications Management Associates
Gage Group, The
Miller Co., The Stuart M.
Omniquest Entertainment
Perelman Agency, Barry
Picture of You, A
Sherman & Associates, Ken

SPORTS

Alpern Group, The
Bohrman Agency, The
Circle of Confusion Ltd.
Gage Group, The
Hudson Agency
Miller Co., The Stuart M.
Picture of You, A
Sherman & Associates, Ken
Wright Representatives, Ann

TEEN

Alpern Group, The
Bohrman Agency, The
Circle of Confusion Ltd.
Communications Management Associates
Gage Group, The
Hudson Agency
Kozak Literary & Motion Picture Agency, Otto R.
Miller Co., The Stuart M.
Picture of You, A
Sherman & Associates, Ken

THRILLER / ESPIONAGE

Alpern Group, The
Baskow Agency
Bohrman Agency, The
Circle of Confusion Ltd.
Communications Management Associates
Gage Group, The
Gurman Susan
Miller Co., The Stuart M.
Omniquest Entertainment
Perelman Agency, Barry
Picture of You, A
Sherman & Associates, Ken
Silver Screen Placements
Wright Representatives, Ann

WESTERNS / FRONTIER

Alpern Group, The
Bohrman Agency, The
Circle of Confusion Ltd.
Communications Management Associates
Gage Group, The
Hudson Agency
Picture of You, A
Sherman & Associates, Ken
Wright Representatives, Ann

SCRIPT AGENTS FORMAT INDEX

ANIMATION

Communications Management Associates
Hudson Agency
Picture of You, A

DOCUMENTARY

Baskow Agency
Communications Management Associates
Hudson Agency
Picture of You, A

EPISODIC DRAMA

Alpern Group, The
Baskow Agency
Management Company, The
Omniquest Entertainment
Picture of You, A
Wright Representatives, Ann

FEATURE FILM

Alpern Group, The
Baskow Agency
Bohrman Agency, The
Circle of Confusion Ltd.
Communications Management Associates
Gage Group, The
Gelff Literary and Talent Agency, The Laya
Graham Agency
Gurman Susan
Hodges Agency, Carolyn
Hudson Agency
Kallen Agency, Leslie
Management Company, The
Miller Co., The Stuart M.
Omniquest Entertainment
Picture of You, A
Silver Screen Placements
Whittlesey Agency, Peregrine
Wright Representatives, Ann

MINI-SERIES

Alpern Group, The
Baskow Agency
Communications Management Associates
Hudson Agency
Management Company, The
Omniquest Entertainment
Picture of You, A

SIT-COM

Baskow Agency
Buchwald & Associates, Inc.,
Hudson Agency
Management Company, The
Omniquest Entertainment
Picture of You, A
Wright Representatives, Ann

THEATRICAL STAGE PLAY

Gage Group, The
Graham Agency
Gurman Susan

TV MOVIE OF THE WEEK

Alpern Group, The
Baskow Agency
Communications Management Associates
Gurman Susan
Hodges Agency, Carolyn
Hudson Agency
Kallen Agency, Leslie
Omniquest Entertainment
Perelman Agency, Barry
Picture of You, A
Wright Representatives, Ann

VARIETY SHOW

Baskow Agency

AGENTS INDEX

E

Eisenberg, Gail,
  (The Susan Gurman Agency)
Ellenberg, Ethan
  (Ethan Ellenberg Literary Agency)
Ellis, Nancy
  (LitWest Group, LLC)
Engel, Anne
  (Jean V. Nagger Literary Agency)
English, Elaine
  (Graybill & English, LLC)
Eth, Felicia
  (Felicia Eth Literary Representation)
Etling, H. Allen
  (Three Jackets Literary Agency)

F

Farber, Ann
  (Farber Literary Agency, Inc.)
Farber, Donald C.
  (Farber Literary Agency, Inc.)
Farber, Seth
  (Farber Literary Agency, Inc.)
Fausset, Katherine
  (Watkins Loomis Agency, Inc.)
Faust, Jessica
  (BookEnds, LLC)
Feldman, Leigh
  (Darhansoff, Verrill & Feldman Literary Agents)
Fleming, Peter
  (Peter Fleming Agency)
Fleury, Blanche
  (B.R. Fleury Agency)
Fleury, Margaret
  (B.R. Fleury Agency)
Foils, James S.
  (Appleseeds Management)
Franklin, Lynn
  (Lynn C. Franklin Associates, Ltd.)
Fugate, David
  (Waterside Productions, Inc.)

G

Galen, Russell
  (Scovil Chichak Galen Literary Agency)
Geiger, Elen
  (Curtis Brown, Ltd.)
Gelff, Laya
  (The Laya Gelff Literary and Talent Agency)

Gerecke, Jeff
  (JCA Literary Agency)
Ghosh, Anna
  (Scovil Chichak Galen Literary Agency)
Ginsberg, Peter
  (Curtis Brown, Ltd.)
Giordano, Sue
  (Hudson Agency)
Gislason, Barbara J.
  (The Gislason Agency)
Gladstone, William
  (Waterside Productions, Inc.)
Goodman, Arnold P.
  (Goodman Associates)
Goodman, Elise Simon
  (Goodman Associates)
Grady, Thomas
  (The Thomas Grady Agency)
Graybill, Nina
  (Graybill & English)
Grayson, Ashley
  (Ashley Grayson Literary Agency)
Grayson, Carolyn
  (Ashley Grayson Literary Agency)
Grosjean, Jill
  (Jill Grosjean Literary Agency)
Grosvenor, Deborah C.
  (The Grosvenor Literary Agency)
Gudovitz, Neil
  (Waterside Productions, Inc.)
Guerth, Jan-Erik
  (United Tribes Media)
Gurman, Susan
  (The Susan Gurman Agency)

H

Hackworth, Jennifer
  (Richard Curtis Associates, Inc.)
Halsey, Dorris
  (Reece Halsey Agency)
Hamilburg, Michael
  (The Mitchell J. Hamilburg Agency)
Harding, Elizabeth
  (Curtis Brown Ltd.)
Harper, Laurie
  (Sebastian Literary Agency)
Harriet, Sydney H.
  (Agents Incorporated for Medical
  and Mental Health Professionals)
Hendin, David
  (DH Literary, Inc.)
Henshaw, Rich
  (Richard Henshaw Group)

Higgs, Lisa
   (The Gislason Agency)
Hooker, Dan
   (Ashley Grayson Literary Agency)
Hruska, Michael
   (The Bohrman Agency)
Hultgren, Kellie
   (The Gislason Agency)
Hussung, Alleen
   (Samuel French, Inc.)
Hutchinson, Margot Maley
   (Waterside Productions, Inc.)

J

Jackson, Jennifer
   (Donald Maass Literary Agency)
Jacobson, Emilie
   (Curtis Brown, Ltd.)
Jatlow Danielle
   (Waterside Productions, Inc.)

K

Kaliski, Michael
   (Omniquest Entertainment)
Karsev, Vladimir P.
   (Fort Ross, Inc.)
Keller, Wendy
   (Forthwrite Literary Agency)
Kennedy, Frances
   (The Doe Coover Agency)
Kintopf, Adam
   (The Gislason Agency)
Kirlan, Linda
   (Samuel French, Inc.)
Kleinman, Jeffrey M.
   (Graybill & English LLC)
Knowlton, Perry
   (Curtis Brown Ltd.)
Knowlton, Timothy
   (Curtis Brown Ltd.)
Knowlton, Virginia
   (Curtis Brown, Ltd.)
Koster, Elaine
   (Koster Literary Agency, LLC)
Kouts, Barbara
   (Barbara S. Kouts, Literary Agent)
Kozak, Robert
   (Otto R. Kozak Literary & Motion
   Picture Agency)

Kozak, Yitka
   (Otto R. Kozak Literary & Motion
   Picture Agency)
Krages, Bert
   (Bert P. Krages, Attorney at Law)

L

Lampack, Peter
   (Peter Lampack Agency, Inc.)
Lee, Thomas R.
   (Communications Management Associates)
Lescher, Robert
   (Lescher & Lescher, Ltd.)
Lescher, Susan
   (Lescher & Lescher, Ltd.)
Levin, William
   (Silver Screen Placements)
Levine, Paul S.
   (Paul S. Levine Literary Agency)
Lipkind, Wendy
   (Wendy Lipkind Agency)
Liss, Laurie
   (Sterling Lord Literistic, Inc.)
Loomis, Gloria
   (Watkins Loomis Agency, Inc.)
Lord, Sterling
   (Sterling Lord Literistic, Inc.)
Lorenz, Brad
   (Samuel French, Inc.)
Lownie, Andrew
   (Andrew Lownie Literary Agency, Ltd.)

M

Maass, Donald
   (Donald Maass Literary Agency)
Madan, Neeti
   (Sterling Lord Literistic, Inc.)
Malpas, Pamela
   (Harold Ober Associates)
Manges, Kristen
   (Curtis Brown Ltd.)
Manus, Janet
   (Manus & Associates Literary Agency, Inc.)
Manus, Jillian
   (Manus & Associates Literary Agency, Inc.)
Marlow, Marilyn
   (Curtis Brown Lid.)
Martin, Paul
   (Silver Screen Placements)
Martin, S.A.
   (Wylie-Merrick Literary Agency)

Matson, Peter
　(Sterling Lord Literistic, Inc.)
Mattis, Lawrence
　(Circle of Confusion, Ltd.)
McAndrews, Rob
　(B.J. Robbins Literary Agency)
McCarter, Bob
　(Jodie Rhodes Literary Agency)
McClendon, Carole
　(Waterside Productions, Inc.)
McCutcheon, Clark
　(Jodie Rhodes Literary Agency)
Mead, Lind
　(LitWest Group, LLC)
Meier, Roger C.
　(Stars, The Agency)
Meo, Amy Victoria
　(Richard Curtis Associates, Inc.)
Miller, Stuart
　(The Stuart M. Miller Co.)
Minelli, Lenny
　(A Picture Of You)
Mohyde, Colleen
　(The Doe Coover Agency)
Moist, Sharon
　(The Gage Group)
Morel, Madeleine
　(2M Communcations, Ltd.)
Morris, Gary
　(David Black Literary Agency)
Mullane, Deidre
　(The Spieler Agency)
Mura, Dee
　(Dee Mura Enterprises, Inc.)
Myers, Eric
　(The Spieler Agency)

N

Nagger, Jena
　(Jean V. Nagger Literary Agency)
Nakamura, Frank
　(Dee Mura Enterprise, Inc.)
Narine, Shelly
　(Circle of Confusion Ltd.)
Nelson, Jandy
　(Manus & Associates, Literary Agency, Inc.)
Neuwirth, Gary
　(The Vines Agency, Inc.)
Nicholson, George
　(Sterling Lord Literistic, Inc.)
Nys, Claudia
　(Lynn C. Franklin Associates, Ltd.)

O

Ohlson, Ally
　(The Gislason Agency)
Olenik, Kelly
　(Hudson Agency)
Olson, Kristin
　(Fort Ross, Inc.)

P

Paltchikov, Konstantin
　(Fort Ross, Inc.)
Perelman, Barry
　(Barry Perelman Agency)
Peterson, Laura Blake
　(Curtis Brown, Ltd.)
Pomade, Elizabeth
　(Michael Larsen/Elizabeth Pomade
　Literary Agents)
Preskill, Rob
　(LitWest Group, LLC)

R

Raihofer, Susan
　(David Black Literary Agency)
Ramer, Susan
　(Don Congdon Associates, Inc.)
Ratneshwar, Priya
　(The Literary Group)
Ray, Roslyn
　(Communications and Entertainment, Inc.)
Rhodes, Jodie
　(Jodie Rhodes Literary Agency)
Robbins, B.J.
　(B.J. Robbins Literary Agency)
Roberts, Karen
　(Dee Mura Literary)
Robie, David A.
　(Bigscore Productions, Inc.)
Rosen, Janet
　(Sheree Bykofsky Associates, Inc.)
Rosenberg, Barbara Collins
　(The Rosenberg Group)
Rosenkranz, Rita
　(Rita Rosenkranz Literary Agency)
Ross, Lisa M.
　(The Spieler Agency)
Rowland, Laureen
　(David Black Literary Agency)
Rubie, Peter
　(The Peter Rubie Literary Agency)

Rutman, Jim
(Sterling Lord Literistic, Inc.)
Ryan, Ali,
(The Vines Agency, Inc.)

S

Sach, Jacky
(BookEnds, LLC)
Saidullah, Jawahara K.
(Waterside Productions, Inc.)
Sanders, Victoria
(Victoria Sanders & Associates)
Sandum, Howard E.
(Sandum & Associates)
Sansevieri, Penny C.
(Waterside Productions, Inc.)
Santone, Cheri
(Hudson Agency)
Sarulus, Crivolus
(Baskow Agency)
Scatoni, Frank R.
(Venture Literary)
Schelling Chris
(Ralph Viciananza, Ltd.)
Schiavone, James
(Schiavone Literary Agency, Inc.)
Schulman, Susan
(Susan Schulman, A Literary Agency)
Schwartz, Laurens R.
(Laurens R. Schwartz Agency)
Scovil, Jack Scovil
(Scovil Chichak Galen Literary Agency)
Seymour, Mary Sue
(The Seymour Agency)
Sheedy, Charlotte
(Sterling Lord Literistic, Inc.)
Sherman, Ken
(Ken Sherman & Associates)
Shoemaker, Victoria
(The Spieler Agency)
Siegel, Rosalie
(Rosalie Siegel, International Literary
Agency, Inc.)
Slopen, Beverley
(Beverley Slopen Literary Agency)
Smith, Trisha
(Circle of Confusion, Ltd.)
Smithline, Alexander C.
(Harold Ober Associates)
Soeiro, Loren G.
(Peter Lampack Agency, Inc.)
Sorice, Camille
(Camille Sorice Agency)
Spieler, F. Joseph

(The Spieler Agency)
Staffel, Rebecca
(The Doe Coover Agency)
Steinberg, Peter
(JCA Literary Agency)
Stewart, Douglas
(Curtis Brown Ltd.)
Stuart, Andrew
(The Literary Group)
Surdi, Paul
(The Vines Agency, Inc.)
Susijn, Laura
(The Susijn Agency)
Susman, Susannah
(Ann Rittenberg Literary Agency, Inc.)
Sweeney, Deborah
(The Gislason Agency)
Sweeney, Emma
(Harold Ober Associates)

T

Tasman, Alice
(Jean V. Naggar Literary Agency)
Teal, Patricia
(Patricia Teal Literary Agency)
Tenney, Craig
(Harold Ober Associates)
Thornton, John F.
(The Spieler Agency)
Treimel, Scott
(Treimel, S©ott, NY))
Tutela, Joy E.
(David Black Literary Agency)

V

Valcourt, Richard R.
(The Richard R. Valcourt Agency)
Valentini, Kimberly
(Waterside Productions, Inc.)
Van Buren, Christopher
(Waterside Productions, Inc.)
Van Nostrand, Charles R.
(Samuel French, Inc.)
Verrill, Charles
(Darhansoff, Verrill & Feldman Literary
Agents)
Viciananza, Ralph M.
(Ralph Viciananza, Ltd.)
Vines, James C.
(The Vines Agency, Inc.)

Wagner, Matt
  (Waterside Productions, Inc.)
Wales, Elizabeth
  (Wales, Literary Agency, Inc.)
Walters, Maureen
  (Curtis Brown Ltd.)
Ware, John
  (John A. Ware Literary Agency)
Waters, Mitchell
  (Curtis Brown Ltd.)
Wauhob, Donna
  (Donna Wauhob Agency)
Weidman, Frank
  (The Literary Group)
Weiner, Cherry
  (Cherry Weiner Literary Agency)
Weinstein, Ted
  (Ted Weinstein Literary Management)
Weiss, Marcia
  (The Agency)
Weltz, Jennifer
  (Jean V. Naggar Literary Agency)
Westberg, Phyllis
  (Harold Ober Associates)
Westover, Jonathan
  (The Gage Group)
Whittaker, Lynn
  (Graybill & English, LLC)
Whittlesey, Peregrine
  (Peregrine Whittlesey Agency)
Wilson, Imani
  (Victoria Sanders & Associates)
Wintle, Ed
  (Curtis Brown, Ltd.)
Wise, Liz
  (The Alpern Group)
Wright, Dan
  (Ann Wright Representatives)

LISTING INDEX

T

U

V

W